AF553453

Democratic Governance and Politics of the Left in South Asia

Edited by

Subhoranjan Dasgupta

DEMOCRATIC GOVERNANCE AND POLITICS OF THE LEFT IN SOUTH ASIA
Edited by Subhoranjan Dasgupta

First Published 2015

ISBN 978-93-5002-319-8

Published by
AAKAR BOOKS
28 E Pocket IV, Mayur Vihar Phase I, Delhi 110 091
Phone : 011 2279 5505 Telefax : 011 2279 5641
aakarbooks@gmail.com; www.aakarbooks.com

Printed at
Mudrak, 30 A, Patparganj, Delhi 110 091

Contents

Acknowledgements

I am grateful to Professor Amiya Kumar Bagchi for his constant help and suggestions. Dr Ramkrishna Chatterjee also offered worthwhile advice and rendered assistance whenever I approached him. Titas Dasgupta did the secretary's job meticulously—I am grateful to her. Institute of Development Studies Kolkata (IDSK) and Rosa Luxemburg Stiftung (RLS) cooperated to make this project successful. I am grateful to both.

Introduction

The texts which make up this selection were presented at the international conference on 'Politics of the Left and Democratic Governance in South Asia' held at the Institute of Development Studies Kolkata (IDSK) in November, 2013. Senior scholars and academics like Aijaz Ahmad and Prabhat Patnaik brushed shoulders with young researchers like Srinivasan Ramani and Taimur Rahman, and both the groups spoke on the theme selected with vigour and insight. The countries that were focused on were India, Pakistan, Nepal and Bangladesh. Scholars from Bangladesh, Pakistan and Nepal were invited to make their presentations and along with the Indian participation they gave to the conference a truly South Asian dimension. This selection also includes a comprehensive interview with Manik Sarkar, Chief Minister of Tripura, who spoke convincingly on the advance this small state has made in the last two decades. This interview, probably the longest Manik Sarkar has given till now, was conducted by Subhanil Chowdhury and Gorky Chakraborty, academicians working at the IDSK.

The subjects that were chosen for detailed analysis and commentary covered an astonishingly wide range. While Prabhat Patnaik deliberated on the question of Identity and Marxian Politics in India, Taimur Rahman's account of marginal Left politics in Pakistan expressed the hope that the small Left groups in his country would perhaps come together to give a consolidated shape and size to the working class movement in Pakistan. Although the presentations were region or country-specific, a common thread ran through these and this was the thread of crisis. Almost all speakers underlined the fact that the Left movement in the four specific countries of South Asia were passing through a phase of severe crisis. The two most significant examples of this crisis were or are to be noticed in Nepal and West Bengal in India. In both, the Leftists or communists fared miserably in the elections. While the United Communist Party of Nepal, the Maoist wing, was soundly defeated at the beginning of this year, the seemingly invincible CPI(M) in West Bengal had to bite the dust two years ago, after ruling the state for 34 long years.

The contributors however were not prepared to accept the dramatic reversals of fortune as something final and irrevocable. They considered these defeats as a critical passing phase which would be followed by revival and reconstruction, sooner or later. Such were the hopes expressed by the Left rebel-activist Prasenjit Bose and also Manik Sarkar, Chief Minister of Tripura. But what deserves a particular mention is the candour of their admission. That is, no one wore tinted glasses to view the essentially bleak present or the uncertain future. For example, Manik Sarkar, Chief Minister of Tripura, frankly said, "There is no denying the fact that we have received a big jolt. We fared badly in the election of 2009. What is most significant is that we have lost at the state level in both West Bengal and Kerala. The defeat of the Left Front in West Bengal, which had ruled uninterruptedly for 34 years, was the greatest disaster. We were really not prepared for such an outcome in West Bengal. But this is only a bad patch or phase; this does not imply that Left politics has come to an end." Also Prasenjit Bose, who was expelled from the CPI(M) for insubordination pinpointed the cause of the sharp decline. According to him, "It is in its inability to build consequential mass movements against the neo-liberal regime in India that the decline of the Indian Left needs to be primarily located." He suggested a way out of the debacle in the following words,"What is therefore required for the revival of the Left today is a principled alliance between the radical revolutionaries, who want to replace capitalism by socialism and reformists, who want to fight for democratic reforms within the system, against the neo-liberal order. Such an alliance can actualize only when the Left initiates militant mass movements and becomes ideologically open to new ideas. Radicalism in practice and openness in theory should be the new direction for the Indian Left."

Not confining himself to the issue of probable strategic alliance, Sobhanlal Datta Gupta adopted a corrective tone layered with introspection. He proposed a thorough re-reading of Marxian texts and emphasis on thinkers who have not yet been given the worth they deserve. Moreover, he advocated a reappraisal of Lenin, who according to him, should not only be regarded as the fulcrum of a centralized party, "For the Left in India exploration of an alternative understanding of Marxism, therefore, is the need of the hour. This requires shedding of the traditional mindset, dispassionate reading of the alternative texts of Marxism, many of which are still considered as taboos by the exponents of mainstream Marxism. These include figures like Trotsky, Rosa Luxemburg, Gramsci and many others. Over and above, an alternative reading of Lenin is what is very much wanting in India. That Lenin was not just an advocate of a centralized party but something more, that he was a true advocate of revolutionary democracy, that he never endorsed the stifling of the voice of the masses by that of the Party needs to be appreciated." In short, he pleaded for a Marxian alternative in different terms.

Datta Gupta's reflective text leads directly to Aijaz Ahmad's and Prabhat Patnaik's papers which are almost philosophical in tenor. While Ahmad meticulously traced the conflicting discourse on democracy from the time of Socrates and Plato, Patnaik delved deep into the question of identity and class politics. Ahmad was prepared to agree to the dictum that "For our epoch...we could plausibly say democracy is the horizon of all politics." But he did not forget to raise the crucial query as to the nature of this horizon. Is this democracy 'liberal' in character he asked. This investigative query received the answer which read, "liberal democracy (is) more attached to oligarchic concentration of power than to democratic dispersal of it, it is the negation of that horizon." Ahmad, in fact, undertook a thorough deconstruction of the term 'liberal democracy' and pointed out that the practice of it in all the capitalist countries is "actually an oligarchy in the Aristotelian sense." He posed 'substantive democracy' as the counterpoint to 'liberal democracy', linked it with the avowed practice of genuine communism and concluded. "Communism may be accused of all sorts of things, but the idea that defeat of communism would somehow give us more democracy is at best a fantastic idea."

Exploring rigorously the quality and nature of democracy as a practice of reconciliation through negotiation, Prabhat Patnaik drew our attention to the inevitable and "gradual disenfranchisement of the minority identity group which is pushed to an ever shrinking corner." This amounted to what he called "a negation of democracy" in the contemporary perspective. Indeed, by subjecting the practice of mutual accommodation to the thesis of identity politics, he concluded, "It follows then that the perception of democracy as consisting of a process of mutual accommodation between different identity groups, i.e. as entailing mutually-accommodative identity politics, is a flawed one: if democracy is indeed practised in this manner then it will progressively atrophy and get diminished." Not only were the minority groups cornered in this practice of flawed democracy, the latter also widened the ever-increasing gap between the rich and the poor, the affluent and the deprived in this neo-liberal world whose ideological hegemony was ensured by the assault of globalized finance capital. Ultimately, identity politics and class politics in the so-called democracy enlarge and intensify the communal-fascist threat in a country like ours. This uneven reality or situation could be corrected by "shaking off the thraldom to the ideology propagated by finance capital."

A clear example of identity politics gone sour is stated and examined by Maidul Islam in his text 'Indian Muslims and the Radical Democratic Project'. He began with the categorical statement that "Poverty has remained constantly high among the Muslims during the phase of economic reforms" and then offered an elaborate analysis of this identity-based deprivation. He did not ignore the successful exploits of a few Muslim businessmen and entrepreneurs, but at the same time underlined the fact that the majority of this community is yoked to poverty. Quoting relevant figures he said that "only 2.2% of Indian Muslims who are regarded as high income category spend Rs. 2776 per month or Rs. 93 per day." It is obvious then that along with Dalits and tribals, Muslims remain as the poorest community in the country and the Left has to engage itself in a massive manner to change this deplorable condition. In point of fact, the situation in which the Muslims are entrenched prove beyond doubt that identity politics in India is scarred by vicious inequality and here too one could accuse neo-liberalism of fostering and fomenting this divide. In the words of the author, "The political appeal of the Left movement should be constructed in such a manner that marginalized groups, by and large, could identify with that political project against the common antagonistic frontier of neo-liberalism."

Not only has the Left, especially in the states where it ruled, suffered the marginalization described earlier, it also failed to respond to identity politics embedded in class issues. Ravi Kumar made this explicit in his text 'Reimagining Democracy: Radicalizing *Dialogue* and *Dissent* as an Organizational Practice within the Indian Left' in which he prompted the Left to engage in sustained 'Dialogue' and 'Dissent' to redeem the flawed situation. He stated, "It (the Marxist) needs to radicalize the idea of dialogue and dissent, take it away from the bourgeois realm and turn it into a weapon of the working class politics rather than getting trapped in the liberal bourgeois imagination itself. It can be done and shall be done otherwise the social-democratization of the Left in India won't stop at any time in the near future."

Both I, as well as the co-authors Anindya Sekhar Purakayastha and Dhritiman Chakraborty invoked Rosa Luxemburg's vision of democracy to gain ideological impulses required to motivate the Left in India. While I explored the dialectical core in her vision of democracy, the co-authors of the text titled 'From Antagonism to Agonism in the *Republic of Hunger:* Towards an Indian *Democratic-a-venir'* drew a larger ideological map which accommodated Chantal Mouffe, Antonio

Negri, Arundhati Roy, Partha Chatterjee and last but not the least Lenin and Rosa Luxemburg. At the end of their wide-ranging theoretical survey they closed down on Partha Chatterjee and Rosa Luxemburg to state, "Future scholarship in this field would address further areas of research in this respect, but at present Partha Chatterjee`s argument of political society does make a case for the subaltern Third Worldian subject who strives for a different temporality of existential battle, and a Luxemburgian intervention and direct engagement with such postcolonial ontologies would definitely infuse a new theoretic agonism in this political debate." In the midst of these theoretical forays, Ritwika Biswas offered a pragmatic piece in her text titled 'Ideas and Praxis of Socialism: The Left in West Bengal 1947-77'. It traced the complex journey of Indian communism, with emphasis on West Bengal from 1947 to 1977 from the rebellious days of B.T. Randive to the formation of the Left Front in 1977.

The six texts on Pakistan, Bangladesh and Nepal were written with the Left perspective in mind and they underlined the significance, present position and future course of the Leftists, communist and social democratic parties included, in the three countries. Taimur Rahman in his text 'The Democratic State and the Labour Movement' labelled the Pakistani bourgeoisie as the new aristocracy that is stridently opposed to both peasant and workers' movements. This new capitalist class, he holds, has also consistently opposed the progress of democracy in the country. In fact, the author has taken a crucial leap forward and suggested that the bourgeoisie is thriving in an authoritarian climate which it supports and sustains. Last but not the least, it has condoned fundamentalism as well.

Mathew Joseph C. in his paper 'Pakistan: Transition to Democracy and Challenges Before the Left' termed the election held in 1913 as 'historic ... in more than one way.' It was historic primarily because neither the military sabotaged it nor the Islamic fundamentalists disrupted it with serial acts of violence. Moreover, the voter turnout (55.02%) was much higher compared to the election that had been held in 2008. The small Leftist groups and parties working at the grassroots level, anchored around Marxist-Leninism, did not fare satisfactorily in the election. They continue to occupy the marginal space and because of the absence of powerful working class and peasant movements they are finding it difficult to forge ahead. Not that they did not attempt a revolutionary challenge (for example, the Hashtanagar peasant movement followed the Naxalbari ideology) but "the lack of objective conditions for the spread of a militant movement was largely responsible for the confinement of the peasant movement." In the present situation the functioning of a democratic set-up allows the Leftists to put forth their views in the public realm and therefore expanding the "arena of democracy is the primary political task of the Left."

The three texts on Bangladesh approach the role and positions of the Leftists-cum-Communists in that country from three different perspectives. While the doyen among Bangladeshi Leftists, the aged Badruddin Umar, straightway observed that there is not a single, genuine Leftist-secular party in Bangladesh at the moment, Meghna Guhathakurta and Srimanti Sarkar focused on the splintered nature of the Left movement divided among several small sections. After tracing the evolution of the Left from the 1940s, Umar accused the present-day Left of playing a subsidiary and ineffective role in coalitions dominated by centrist parties like the Awami League. He also seriously questioned the secular credentials of the small Leftist groups who often invoke the name of Allah in their posters and manifestos to garner votes. His conclusion is categorical, "It is, therefore, no exaggeration that the Left as a political force has long been ineffective in Bangladesh. What is known as Left, particularly the traditional Left, may be described as the Left of the ruling class."

In her text 'Democracy and Statecraft in a Neo-liberal World: Narratives and Counter-narratives in Bangladesh', Meghna Guhathakurta covers a wide area. She concentrates, first, on the decreased dependence on agriculture that has prompted a structural transformation in rural Bangladesh. This is followed by a discussion on the "increasing primacy of the non-agricultural sector in the economy" that leads to the drawing of the new global horizon or the global neo-liberal paradigm inside which Bangladesh is firmly though precariously situated.

The Left discourse has to address these new realities. It has often failed in its task because of its marginal and splintered influence and this inability has left the poor "defenceless against the representatives of a predatory state bent on pocketing the lion's share of profit from the industry." To be candid, the author in her conclusion, states that at the present juncture of neo-liberal transformation she envisages neither an idyllic Sonar Bangla (the nationalist imaginary of the Bangladesh state) nor a proletariat Bangladesh. What one can at most hope for is "an ideology of national consensus supported by the state or as the ideology of the people when the dynamics of proletarianization does set in. It is then that the actual counter-narrative to the neo-liberal paradigm will begin to take shape in the understanding and in the practice of the Left."

Srimanti Sarkar, in her paper 'The Role of the Left in Bangladesh's Democracy: Challenges and Prospects' focused on the gradual evolution of the Left, "which in spite of its considerably long political existence failed to emerge as a viable political force." It is true that its vision was to unite the downtrodden of the country into the mainstream but it failed to translate this ideal into reality. This failure led to the splintering of the Left and its turning into an appendage of the ruling Awami League. Nevertheless, in spite of its marginal influence, it has tried to attend to class dynamics and protest against the neo-liberal dispensation. What is important to note is that in a strongly class-divided country like Bangladesh which is struggling against global assaults, the Left has the chance to expand and enlarge its base if it adopts a common manifesto and resists internecine rivalry. In other words, what is required is a common strategy, horizontal cohesion and a united plan of action. The future will tell if it is going to emerge as such a coherent alternative force.

The complex political picture in Nepal following the last election has been carefully drawn by Srinivasan Ramani in his text 'The Nepal Constituent Assembly Experiment: Process, Successes, Failures and Lessons.' Describing the Constituent Assembly as "a unique experiment in Asia to create a Constitution through universal adult franchise and a popular elected Assembly", he, however, adds that strong political differences among the major political parties stood in the way of finalizing the Constitution. In fact, Nepal's transition from a monarchy to a republic was arrived through deliberations in a popularly elected Constituent Assembly (CA). This has been a distinctive model of transition in Asia and the CA process promised substantive changes in the structure of the Nepali state and political economy. Yet, despite the conversion into a republic, several other promised changes remained unfulfilled as differences between various political forces—both internal and external—resulted in a retention of large aspects of the pre-Republican status quo. Ramani's article attempts to study the reasons for these and political dynamics involved in the transition.

1

The Dialectical Core in Rosa Luxemburg's Vision of Democracy

Subhoranjan Dasgupta

Epigraph and Examination

> "Proletarian revolutions ... criticize themselves constantly, interrupt themselves continually in their own course, come back to the apparently accomplished in order to begin it afresh, deride with unmerciful thoroughness the inadequacies, weaknesses and paltriness of their first attempts ... until a situation has been created which makes all turning back impossible".[1] (Karl Marx)

The lines quoted above from Karl Marx's *The Eighteenth Brumaire of Louis Bonaparte* serve as an appropriate epigraph to my paper for the following reasons:

Reason 1: The very act of questioning and criticizing various aspects of the revolution, be it the Bolshevik crowned with success or the German which failed, prompted Rosa Luxemburg to measure, assess and define the nature of socialist democracy, which was of course the aim of the two revolutions in question. In other words, the act of revolution and its aspired-for-outcome happened to be two inseparable parts of one single discourse.

Reason 2: Like the act of the revolution itself guided by its own dialectic, the ultimate objective of 'socialist democracy' attains a synthesis at the level of theory and even vision only *after* resolving the contradictions, which provoke an intense dialectical encounter. This process of genuine, redemptive resolution is something qualitatively different from a superficial attempt undertaken to patch up irreconcilable dichotomies. While the latter was attempted by Eduard Bernstein in his articles advocating Social Reform[2] as the cardinal way—as pointed out by Rosa Luxemburg with characteristic vigour in her seminal work *Reform or Revolution*[3]—the former is a rigorous dialectical exercise holding theory and praxis, act and vision together in one inextricable pattern. Rosa herself described the essential difference between the two engagements. Whereas, in her words, "Bernstein saying goodbye to our system of dialectics resorts to the intellectual seesaw of the well-known 'on one hand—on the other', 'yes but', etc' and thereby loses 'the axis of intellectual crystallization', the steadfast dialectician uses this crucial axis around which isolated facts group themselves in the organic whole to structure a coherent conception of the world."[4] Needless to add, Rosa's understanding of democracy revolving around this dialectical axis advances towards a final vision which is both consistent and comprehensive.

Reason 3: This final virtue, nevertheless, does not conceal the battle that had to be waged at the levels of emotion and reason—the battle between contradictions—before the outcome is proclaimed in programmatic faith. Just as the flowering act of revolution criticizes and interrupts itself vigorously at every step, the aim of the revolution is similarly subjected to tenacious argumentation by Rosa who was possibly more vital and volatile than the other comrades. One of her best biographers, Peter Nettl, has underlined this remarkable trait by saying, "It is impossible to understand Rosa Luxemburg as a political person without accepting her capacity for judging everything in the form of an extreme dichotomy—words or action, hope or desire, living or dying. Mere political differences were mealy-mouthed understatements; what was happening is a miniature private dialectic of her own, the birth of a new world amid the dust and ashes of the Arbeitgemeinschaft".[5] This new world is of course Rosa's indestructible dream of social democracy, an outcome of the tirelessly self-critical revolution itself, forged by the power and insight of her dialectical commitment. Though her first cogitations on this subject were forcefully expressed in her *Reform or Revolution,* in statements like "We must conclude that the socialist movement is not bound to bourgeois democracy, but that, on the contrary, the fate of democracy is bound with the socialist movement.... He who renounces the struggle for socialism renounces both the labour movement and democracy",[6] the more incisive explorations are to be found, expectedly, in her critical engagement with the pamphlet on the Russian Revolution and in her last phase of unforgettable articles written for the *Rote Fahne* (Red Flag) when the Spartacist uprising was drawing towards a tragic close. This dual contextuality once again proves how revolution and its promised fulfilment are two sides of the same coin.

Letters and Interrogation

But what was the basic, persistent question that provoked Rosa Luxemburg to spell out her understanding of democracy repeatedly in such emphatic terms? The answer to this question is perhaps to be found in one of her sensitive replies to a letter written by Sonja Liebknecht where Sonja, herself, pronounced the query that was also Rosa's own. In that very phase when Rosa was to write her critique of the Russian Revolution, she wrote from her prison cell in Wronke to her dear, younger friend Sonja in that reply dated May 23, 1971, "Sonja, you are bitter about my long imprisonment and ask – How is it that some people may decide over the fate of others? ... My little bird, the entire cultural history of humanity, which according to some conservative estimate comprises some 20,0000 years, is based on some people deciding the fate of others, and this has deep roots in the material conditions of existence. The only way to change this is by painful upheaval; we are witnessing now one of these painful chapters."[7] This letter is crucial because it expresses the fundamental question as well as doubt and answer to the question in strikingly human terms.

No wonder, Margarethe von Trotta began her film on Rosa with Rosa uttering these words inside the bleak courtyard of the prison. Significantly, we are offered an example of this practice of a few deciding over the fate of others in the very next scene where we see political prisoners lined up against the wall being shot by guards. We can interpret this act as an illustration of monarchy, bourgeois that is class-tainted democracy, or even socialist democracy gone astray hopelessly —at murderous work.

Let us deconstruct this letter to pinpoint the basic problematic. Both Sonja Liebknecht and Rosa in their distinctive ways were disturbed by the almost ingrained asymmetry in socio-human relations. This asymmetry is built on and sustained by the thoroughly undemocratic practice of some determining the fate of others. Further, when this practice is institutionalized and made sacrosanct, it gives birth to a repressive socio-political system. What enables this anti-democratic system to continue is evidently the deep-rooted disequilibrium in the material conditions of existence. By disequilibrium we mean and Rosa meant exploitative class relations which ensure the unjust coexistence of the feudal lord and the serf, the capitalist and the worker, the imperialist and the colonized. Obviously, the three few former decide the fates of the three latter. This persistent perversion of the ideal polis, which we label democracy, can be cured and corrected by periodic revolutions or, as Rosa describes them, "painful upheavals". In a flash, thereafter, the letter-writer links the strain of her thought to the palpable present by stating, "we are witnessing now one of these painful chapters".

It would not be incorrect on our part to regard the 'painful chapter' as the Russian Revolution because the other letters which she wrote during this phase to Marta Rosenbaum, Luise Kautskyand Sonja Liebknecht pointedly refer over and over again to the turmoil the Bolshevik Revolution caused within her. Even the adjective 'painful'/'qualvolle' is carefully chosen. Like Walter Benjamin's dialectical image, it stresses the indispensability of birth pangs associated with any revolution, necessarily armed, as well as celebrates the liberation it promises, the liberation of every single being placed in the network of a liberated collective. If there is a strain of pessimism of the will in this letter, it is adequately balanced by the optimism expressed to Marta Rosenbaum in another letter written from the same prison cell barely a month ago. In this letter, Rosa wrote, "Dear Marta, well, the wonderful things in Russia affect me like an elixir of life. Isn't what comes from there a message of salvation for all of us? For this reason, I would like to hear that you are in a better frame of mind, that you are all in high spirits and a happy mood—despite all the misery and horror".[8] Indeed, these letters written from the prisons of Wronke and Breslau before her release, in their articulation of rousing hope and courage, disturbing queries, acceptance of pain and joy, and even tragic reflection evoke a structure of feeling which Raymond Williams would have called uncompromisingly dialectical.

Russian Revolution and Critique

From these letters to the text *Russian Revolution* signify a specific advance in Rosa's critical engagement with the principles and praxis of democracy, triggered as they were by the Bolshevik experience. In this text we find the light and shade, praise and denunciation, euphoria and shock wedded together explicitly in an unbreakable knot, the like of which is absent in the letters more given to heartfelt praise. At this point, I would like to advance a particular point of view that is not primarily preoccupied with the sheer correctness or not of her evaluation of the Bolshevik revolution in isolation. It is true that Clara Zetkin stressed that Rosa was not adequately informed about the events in Russia and that is why perhaps her criticism, at times, sounded as intense as her eulogy. Moreover, according to Clara Zetkin, Rosa revised her former assessment of the mixed achievement of the Bolsheviks, Lenin and Trotsky in particular, in the light of her later do-or-die participation in the German Revolution.[9] Without underestimating the historical importance of such revisions and reassessments, could we not also approach the entire question from the epistemic-ideological perspective and claim that, notwithstanding the fallibility of her evaluation, she regarded the Russian Revolution as a highly relevant example to (i) establish an intrinsic link between socialist revolution and socialist democracy and (ii) to highlight the preconditions of a socialist democracy per se. In other words, the most appropriate example of the time offered her the opportunity to delineate the spirit of socialist democracy which can be only ensured by the dictatorship of the proletariat. The pressing palpability of the Bolshevik Revolution gave to her language in the text an urgent fervour which we can discern even more clearly in Alfred Doblin's epic-novel *Karl and Rosa, November 1918*. Almost echoing the sentences of Rosa's political text we have all read, Doblin wrote with the help of a slight creative colouring:

> Yes, the events in Moscow had attracted her attention. This was what engaged her most intensively, excited and challenged her.
>
> For Lenin was out there working like a battering ram, hammering against the turrets of the old society, toppling one wall after the other. The edifice trembled. It could not be long now until the whole thing crashed to the ground with a thundering collapse that would awaken the whole world.
>
> How the drama intrigued Rosa. She read how they were attacking Lenin. She defended him. What were these Mensheviks thinking, tainted with their bourgeois ideas? How was Lenin supposed to act? These foolish utopians and weaklings. They thought he would just sit back and wait while the Whites prepared a military dictatorship with all its terrors for the proletariat.
>
> She began to take down notes again, alert and aggressive.
>
> In this situation the Bolshevik wing has proven its historical worth by proclaiming from the very beginning those tactics that alone could save the revolution and by acting upon them systematically. All power in the hands of the masses of workers and peasants, that was the sword stroke that slashed the Gordian knot, leading the revolution out of its constricted passage and opening for it the free plain of uninhibited development.
>
> But then Lenin's face was revealed to her, his cynical smile. He was betraying democracy. He was setting it aside. For what purpose? To create without disruption what he called revolution.
>
> But we are not generals commanding armies. We do not command, we battle side by side on towards the same goal. Lenin versus bourgeois society, what is he then? A general, a dictator, a man of the past, whose methods are those of the past, he is no socialist but a bourgeois. Rosa became impassioned by the ups and downs of the conflict with the man. What? To have thousands shot in retaliation for an attempted assassination? To shoot them down summarily, cold-bloodedly, all the while pretending to be inaugurating a socialist society? It was enough to make you long

for the days of the czars, may they rest in peace, when every case was investigated and each guilty party hanged or exiled on his or her own.

She sat with paper before her and thought. We have had a great many discussions about the dictatorship of the proletariat and its relationship to democracy. Just look at him, how simply he solves the problem. The solution is: Lenin. Goethe, a German, said, "Moral man's greatest treasure remains the individual personality." Not the man who smashes it, the dictator.

I am the dictatorship of the proletariat, Nikolai Lenin has decreed. But why? Just ask my Latvian Rifles and the Red Guard. You will receive a bang of an answer. But what do you need all that grand rhetoric for then? Let's simply call it war and victory and defeat.

In what way is his war different from that of the Germans against the French and the English? His is fought out between civilians, the other between uniformed soldiers. The brawl has moved to the home front, the illness has spread to the homeland. What magnificent progress.

Rosa jotted it down angrily.

With the suppression of political life throughout the country, the political life of the Soviets must likewise languish. Without general elections, without unhampered freedom of the press and assembly, without free debate of opinions, life will die out in every public institution. It will only seem to live, while only one single effective pulse of life will remain—the bureaucracy.

It is at its base an oligarchy. Most certainly a dictatorship—but by a handful of politicians. In effect, a bourgeois dictatorship.

She brooded for a while before she dashed it off:

Real dictatorship, our dictatorship, consists in the application of democracy, not in its abolition.[10]

I have deliberately quoted this extract in full because its vibrant prose not only recreates the emotional turmoil of Rosa caught between the inseparable contradictions of the momentous event but also etches her unsullied vision of what socialist democracy should be. Once we deconstruct the passage, the dialectical tug of war between the positives and the negatives emerge unambiguously.

First, the positives

(1) Rosa applauds Lenin for working like a battering ram.

(2) Rosa is more than aware of the dubious role of the Mensheviks and, more importantly, the terrible threat posed by the White reaction.
(3) In fact, by combining 1 and 2, Rosa underlines the historical worth of the Bolshevik Revolution. It is as if this Revolution—neither a putsch nor insurrection carried out by a Blanquist minority—has attained the worth of a lasting model, albeit not without flaws.

Now, the negatives:

(1) By directing the assassination of many as a reply to the assassination attempts made on him, Lenin is indulging in that practice of terror which is opposed to the vaunting ideal of socialist democracy. This is plain killing which cannot be legitimized.
(2) Instead of practising or trying to practise or trying to prepare the ground for the dictatorship of the proletariat, which, as Rosa stresses over and over again, is the synonym for socialist democracy in the making, Lenin has arrogated all power to himself. As if he and his trusted few represent the solution, or better still, the ideal synthesis between the capture of power and the practice of power.
(3) Once we combine (1) and (2) we find that the Bolshevik experiment is hurtling towards a reality where the freedom of the press, assembly, general elections, etc. are destined to disappear.

To conclude, the dictatorship of the proletariat as asserted by Lenin and Trotsky does not correspond to her vision of dictatorship which is, by definition, based not on the abolition, but thriving application of democracy down to the very pores of the social reality. The positives and negatives bound together by the simultaneity of the sharply clashing dialectic may only be resolved by a bottom to top, grassroot-based, ceaseless and vigorous interaction between the vanguard and the masses. That precisely is Rosa's shining vision. But whether this unsullied vision is at all realizable in the hurly-burly of the revolution is positing another question that calls for another discourse. Suffice it to say here that her text on the Russian Revolution embodies her vision of socialist democracy and serves as the culminating point of her cogitations which began from *Reform or Revolution*, and is heard again in *Organizational Questions of Social Democracy, The Mass Strike* and the *Junius Pamphlet*. The essence of this vision is, in Rosa's words, heard yet again in her article on National Assembly which appeared in the *Rote Fahne some* months later, "Today it is not a question of democracy or dictatorship. The question that history has placed on the agenda is: bourgeois democracy or socialist democracy? For the dictatorship of the proletariat is democracy in a socialist sense. It is not a matter of bombs, coups d'etat, riots or 'anarchy', as the agents of capitalist profit dishonestly make out; rather it is the use of all the means of political power to realize socialism, to expropriate the capitalist class—in the interests and through the will of the revolutionary majority of the proletariat, that is, in the spirit of socialist democracy".[11]

What mattered to the visionary is the redemptive spirit of the socialist system which demolishes the unbridgeable dichotomy between the form and content plaguing all expressions of bourgeois democracy. The content of class exploitation encased in the supposedly faultless form of parliamentary democracy cannot be the goal of socialist democracy whose form and content should hold the individual and the collective in one indivisible digit of harmonious liberation.

It goes without saying that any other Revolution, along with the overwhelming Bolshevik, would have provoked the same reaction from Rosa had its practice led to a similar compromise or even betrayal. The practice, real or imagined, constructed the antithesis which Rosa attempted to counter and challenge by her synthetic vision. But what would have been her response, had she been engulfed in the Revolution itself? Imagine Rosa in the shoes of Lenin or Trotsky. Her dependable comrade-in-arms, Leo Jogiches, provided a reply to this query voiced by Rosa herself. When Rosa asked, "But how can Josef Dzierzynski be so cruel?"[12] Leo answered, "If the need arises, you can do it too". In a different vein, Leszek Kolakowski sharply criticized the 'mythical faith' Rosa nurtured in the purificatory process of the revolution. Questioning Rosa's unreal idealism, he said, "Rosa Luxemburg, on the other hand, seemed to believe that the Bolsheviks could have held on to power by democratic means under a system of popular representation. This strange notion could only be based on her mythical, unshakeable belief in the innate revolutionary character of the masses, which, left to themselves, were bound to evolve socialist forms of public life. Lenin and Trotsky were a good deal more circumspect and realistic than this."[13]

Rote Fahne and Resolution

Do the comments of two radically dissimilar figures like Leo Jogiches and Leszek Kolakowski open another though related terrain of dialectics, this time between the carefully nurtured ideal and the rough and tumble of actual politics experienced every moment? To put this question squarely, how and to what extent did the living encounter with the German Revolution (November-December 1918) alter Rosa's discourse on revolution and its offspring, socialist democracy? Did her understanding undergo a radical change, as some would prefer to believe?

If one analyses the stirring articles of this ultimate phase and compares its themes interrelated with those examined earlier in the other tracts I have already mentioned, one finds that a clear and cogent subterranean link binds the past with the foreboding present. The arguments and counter-arguments clash, basically, within the same dialectical frame though their fervour and fire increase manifold under the awful pressure of the uprising going awry. In fact, the maximum that occurs is the compelling emphasis on some specific aspects, which in a different context in the past were not accorded that comparable importance, although neither rejected nor denied altogether. These turns and shifts, twists and stresses, fill the earlier gaps and fired as they are by the raging battle doomed to defeat, invest the debate with an exemplary passion, tragic and sublime at the same moment. Clara Zetkin did not indulge in any exaggeration when she compared Rosa's role as a commentator in this period with that of Marx pouring himself out in the pages of the *Neue Rheinsche Zeitungin* 1848 when another revolution confronted defeat.[14]

Let us highlight some of the running or continuous themes which culminate in the *Rote Fahne.*

(1) Rosa's lifelong war against the weak-kneed and evasive reformism of German Social Democracy, under-standably, reaches its apex here when the majority of SPD and the UPSD in their own ways ensure the death of the uprising. Rosa's unforgiving assault against these duplicitous comrades is steeled by two connected factors: (i) they have betrayed the proletariat's uprising, no matter how premature it was (ii) as a result, they have annulled the birth of socialist democracy, its natural offspring. Rosa appears like a defiant Cassandra here, for what she had claimed about Eduard Bernstein in 1899 was fulfilled to the word by his successor, the Ebert-Scheidemann duo.

(2) Like Lenin and Engels, Rosa, even in this very difficult period, believed that revolution could not be tailor made one fine morning. It is true that she was an intrinsic part of the abortive uprising—her commitment prescribed no other course—nonetheless, her eloquent critique of the 'Acheron set in motion' in 'Order reigns in Berlin' reasserted the importance of painstaking groundwork, preparedness, inspired leadership and rockhard organizational strength—elements which are required to cement the success of any mass-based, spontaneous outburst.

(3) Even in her last days, she opposed the method of Louis Auguste Blanqui wedded to armed insurrection by small groups as well as the ultra centralism of the party-apparatus, by underlining the inestimable importance of the revolutionary majority. Her eagle's eye mapped the correct contours of the socialist revolution and the socialist state with undiminished vigour. Indeed, the best explication of this vision, after *Russian Revolution* is read in *What Does the Spartacus League Want*? Crystal clear and determined, these lines chart her final dream: "In all previous revolutions a small minority of the people led the revolutionary struggle, gave it aim and direction, and used the mass only as an instrument to carry its interests, the interests of

the minority, through to victory. The socialist revolution is the first which is in the interests of the great majority and can be brought to victory only by the great majority of the working people themselves ...

From the uppermost summit of the state down to the tiniest parish, the proletarian mass must therefore replace the inherited organs of bourgeois class rule—the assemblies, parliaments and city councils—with its own class organs—with workers' and soldiers' councils. It must occupy all the posts, supervise all functions, measure all official needs by the standard of its own class interests and the tasks of socialism. Only through constant, vital, reciprocal contact between the masses of the people and their organs, the workers' and soldiers' councils, can the activity of the people fill the state with a socialist spirit."[15]

Now, let us underline the changing shifts and emphases which do not constitute any radical 'break'—to borrow Althusser's term—but certainly sharpen and deepen the process of dialectics.

(1) Rosa always advocated the overthrow of the bourgeois capitalist system in uncompromising terms. She did not, like any misty-eyed liberal, accuse Lenin and Trotsky of applying force and violence. However, her allegiance to revolutionary violence received the most ardent expression in her articles in the *Rote Fahne*, precisely because the Spartacist uprising revealed fully and nakedly to what extent the enemies could possibly go. Categorical statements like 'The violence of the bourgeois counter-revolution must be confronted with the revolutionary violence of the proletariat' (What Does The Spartacus League Want); 'Arming of the entire male adult proletarian population as a workers' militia' (Ibid); 'The fight for socialism is the mightiest civil war in history'[16] bring her close to the militant position of the Bolsheviks.

(2) At the same time, in spite of her unqualified denunciation of bourgeois democracy which she labels 'parliamentary cretinism', she advocates participation in the elections to the National Assembly. This fine-tuning of the principle of acceptance and rejection, which is the basis of dialectical praxis, is in a sense a continuation of her criticism of the Bolsheviks'

dissolution of the Constituent Assembly, though it is much more focused and penetrating. In point of fact, the vision of Rosa as depicted earlier is sharpened here by her grasp of the suitable revolutionary strategy. While her ideology unmasks the essential inefficacy of parliamentary politics, yet again, her growing sense of real politik prompts her to support the minority's move for participation in the election. One of the most remarkable passages exploring this dialectical complexity is found in her speech in the debate on the National Assembly. In one single breath she demolishes the absolutism granted to bourgeois democracy by Bernstein et al. and, ironically, proposes its tactical utilization, "We all agree that the National Assembly is a bastion of counter-revolution... we want to blow up that bastion from within".[17]

(3) Finally, the glaring drawbacks of the uprising made her acutely conscious of the imperative role of the leaders, of the party and the organization. She did not minimize by any measure the importance of spontaneous mass assault but then this was simply not enough. Possibly, for the first time, the unguided and impulsive nature of the uprising led her to realize that a strong, mutually reinforcing revolutionary contract had to be forged between the proletariat and its vanguard. Her indictment of the leaders in the article 'What are the Leaders Doing?' attest to her acknowledgement of this indispensable bond. She wrote, "On their own spontaneous initiative they (workers) occupied *Vorwarts* and seized the bourgeois editors and the WTB (Wolff's Telegraphic Bureau) and, so far as possible, they armed themselves. They are waiting for further instructions and moves from their leaders.

And meanwhile, what have these leaders done? What have they decided? Which measures have they taken to safeguard the victory of the revolution in this tense situation in which the fate of the revolution will be decided, at least for the next epoch? We have seen and heard nothing."[18]

As we read and reread these articles, we realize the limitless dedication of Rosa to the dialectics of liberation. At one level, her uncompromising critical insight fortified by experience exposes the gaps and fissures of the 1918 uprising; at another level, her uncompromising commitment to the cause provokes her to throw all caution to the winds and join the battle. Why? Simply because, as Karl Liebknecht said, 'the proletariat is on the march'. In a word, she inhaled and exhaled dialectic with her brain and blood every second.

The articles in *Rote Fahne* also indicate Rosa's revised estimate of the Bolshevik Revolution. By contrasting the triumph of the former with the impending defeat of the latter in 'The Debate on the National Assembly' she paid her final compliment to her Russian comrades, Lenin in particular. Rosa's repeated arguments with Lenin did not deter the latter from writing a glowing obituary on her where he compared her with the soaring eagle whose life and message would inspire Communists of future generations. The eagle's sharp eye pinpointed the differences between the two uprisings in the 'Speech in the Debate on the National Assembly'—a flawless realization that dawned a bit too late, "When the National Assembly was rejected in Russia the situation there was somewhat similar to the one in Germany today. But have you forgotten that before they rejected the National Assembly, something else had happened in November: the proletariat had taken power. Do you already have a Socialist Government today? Do you have a Lenin-Trotsky Government? Russia had a long revolutionary history, whereas Germany does not. The Russian Revolution did not begin in March 1917, but much earlier in 1905. Their most recent revolution is nothing but the most recent chapter, preceding it lies the entire period that began in 1905. It produced a level of maturity in the masses very different from what exists in Germany today. You have nothing behind you except the pitiful half revolution of November 9."[19]

Conclusion

The synthesis in Rosa's context could only be aspired-for. Its most eloquent expression is recorded in Alfred Doblin's novel where Rosa and Karl read Karl's last declaration which proclaims, "We have not fled and we are not vanquished.... The long road to Golgotha for the German working class has not reached its end, but the day of salvation nears" and then

Rosa responds by asserting, "How true Karl, how true that is, what you have written ... Perhaps from that they will finally realize what the class struggle means for us: much, much more than just a struggle of classes".[20]

With these words the great narrator Doblin strikes the right chord. The unspoken in the last words refers unerringly to that emancipatory core, to that vision of socialist democracy, which invests the struggle of classes with a higher dimension, human and redemptive.

NOTES AND REFERENCES

1. Karl Marx, *The Eighteenth Brumaire of Louis Bonaparte* (Moscow: Progress Publishers), p. 14, 1986.
2. Eduard Bernstein, a series of articles in *Neue Zeit*, 1897-98, and *Evolutionary Socialism* (London), 1909.
3. *Reform or Revolution*, Rosa Luxemburg, in *Rosa Luxemburg Speaks* ed. by Mary Alice Walters (New York: Pathfinder Press), 1986, pp. 33-90.
4. Ibid., pp. 85-86.
5. *Rosa Luxemburg*, Peter Nettl (Oxford: Oxford Paperbacks), 1969, p. 408.
6. *Reform or Revolution*, p. 76.
7. Rosa Luxemburg, letter dated May 23, 1917, *Briefeausdem Gefaengnis* (Berlin: Karl Dietz Verlag), 2000, p. 48. Translated by the author.
8. Letter to Marta Rosenbaum dated April 1917, *The Letters of Rosa Luxemburg*, ed. and tr. by Stephen Eric Bronner (New Jersey: Humanities Press), 1993, p. 195.
9. Clara Zetkin—mentioned by Sobhanlal Dutta Gupta in his book *Rosa Luxemburg and Her Critics* (Calcutta: Pearl Publishers), 1994, p. XVII.
10. Alfred Doblin, *Karl and Rosa—November 1918: A German Revolution*, tr. by John E. Woods (New York: International Publishing Corporation), 1983, pp. 74-75.
11. 'The National Assembly'—Rosa Luxemburg's article in *Rote Fahne*, November 20, 1918. Reproduced in Sobhanlal Datta Gupta's book, p. 186.
12. Peter Nettl's book, p. 486.
13. Leszek Kolakowski, *Main Currents of Marxism-2* (Oxford: Oxford University Press), 1978, pp. 87-88.

14. Mentioned by Sobhanlal Datta Gupta in his book, p. XX.
15. 'What Does the Spartacus League Want?' Article by Rosa Luxemburg in the *Rote Fahne*. Reproduced in Sobhanlal Datta Gupta's book, p. 169.
16. Ibid., pp. 171-172.
17. Ibid., in the article, 'The Debate on the National Assembly', pp. 184-185.
18. Ibid., in the article, 'What are the Leaders Doing?'
19. Ibid., in the article, 'The Debate on the National Assembly', pp. 182.
20. Alfred Doblin, Ibid., p. 472.

2

Thinking the 'Liberal' in Liberal Democracy

Aijaz Ahmad

Liberalism is quintessentially Anglo-American. No wonder, then, two centuries or more of first the British and then the American empire have ensured that liberal democracy would come to be seen eventually as the ultimate horizon of all democratic thought. This has been particularly so since the collapse of the Soviet system—the actually existing socialism, as it came to be called.

We of course know the sort of democracy—and the sort of capitalism, liberal democracy's twin—that dawned in all parts of the former Soviet bloc. But that was not the only consequence. There was also a more generalized dimming of colours. As Michel Foucault would put it: Revolution has been the horizon of all modern politics; with that horizon disappearing it is difficult to say what politics would now mean. Fukuyama's End of History disquisition inverted that interrogation into a celebration: History had finally found its vocation—and its terminus—in the global, final triumph of liberal democracy. In short, 'Democracy' itself would now be where 'Revolution' once had been: ultimate content of all political desire.

We witnessed this, for instance, in the narrowing of horizons within which the finest of the insurgent thought in the recent Arab rebellions was able to think of itself and its aims. The famous slogan: "People Want to Overthrow the Regime" simply meant End to Dictatorship; Dawn of Democracy. In short, elections! From Tunisia to Bahrain, countless people were willing to die for—well, to use the American term—regime change. Far too many did die. Alain Badiou, flamboyant as ever, gave this re-naming of 'Revolution' as 'Democracy' a name: The Rebirth of History. Thus, the global triumph of liberal democracy is the End of History (Fukuyama) and further outbreaks of liberal-democratic demand would also be the Rebirth of History (Badiou). The left-right convergence here is quite remarkable.

That is the real triumph of liberal democracy: obliteration of all else that the word 'Democracy' has ever meant.

2

Democracy is one of humanity's oldest aspirations but one that has caused much fear and agitation in some of the greatest minds. Consequently, democracy has not had an easy time of it through its long history. Raymond Williams quotes Herodotus who is at least equally fearful of the oligarch and the democrat: of 'the insolence of a despot' as much as of the 'insolence of the unbridled commonality'. "Unbridled" is here the operative word; the idea that democracy may be a good thing but the further idea that the "commonality" has to be bridled, guided, tutored by the elect is also ancient, and it is this idea of a 'guided democracy' that eventually takes hold of the bourgeois imagination in the form of liberal, representative, electoral democracy.

There are also other accents in this discourse. In *Politics* Aristotle seems to draw the line not on the issue of despotism but of property, in a rather beguiling maxim that has the air of being merely descriptive and definitional: "An oligarchy is said to be that in which the few and the wealthy, and democracy that in which the many and the poor, are invested with the power of the state." Plato, by contrast, gets Socrates to say in *The Republic* that "Democracy comes into being after the poor have conquered their opponents, slaughtering some and banishing some, while the remainder they give equal share of freedom and power." No wonder, then, that Democracy comes rather low in Plato's classification of state forms, well below

Aristocracy and Oligarchy.

Little did Plato know that a bureaucratic trinity—civil, military and political bureaucracies—would eventually come to run the liberal state. He seemed to have had an inkling, however. In a speech embedded in the allegory of the Sea Captain in Book Six of *The Republic* Socrates describes statesmanship as a "professional calling" and an "expert art," not something one could make up as one goes along. Herein perhaps lies the origin of the preference for representative/electoral democracy, in opposition to what came to be called "direct democracy." Fear of the multitude thus has its opposite: the cult of expertise.

By and large, and right into the 20th century, most kinds of dominant Anglo-American thought tended to view democracy as a very risky affair, raging against it as an incitement for revolution, popular insurrection, unruly rule of the multitude, and with the fear, already expressed by Plato, that the poor would simply "slaughter or banish" some of the wealthy and impose Equality on the rest. Daniel Defoe, one of the architects of the English novel, fumed against Democracy because it violated what he called "the Great Law of Subordination" and Disraeli, the famous British politician, described the coming of democracy as "a leap into the dark" because it would incite the mob to mutiny, with unforeseeable consequences. Electoral democracy was quite correctly perceived as the right antidote for this revolutionary core of 'substantive' democracy. It was safest to restrict the arena of politics to the parliament of the propertied; a sense of danger and subversion still hangs, therefore, around the term "extra-parliamentary." So, when one comes upon Edmund Burke castigating "a perfect democracy" as "the most shameless thing in the world" one wonders if he had any foreboding that there would one day be the likes of Karl Marx who would describe socialism itself as a "perfection of democracy."

For our own epoch, then, we could plausibly say: Democracy is the horizon of all politics; liberal democracy, more attached to oligarchic concentration of power than to democratic dispersal of it, is the negation of that horizon.

3

At the turn of the century, in 2000-01, I published a series of seven reflections on the 20th century in *Frontline,* calling it the "Century of Democratic Demand." What did I mean? For illustrative purposes, I isolated the following instances which had in the long run proved decisive: (1) the workers' and peasants' struggles against the rule of property that were generally waged under the banner of, at least the inspiration from, socialism; (2) anti-colonial movements against the rule of the European bourgeoisie over the rest of the world, which held Europe accountable not only for its cruelties but also to the idea of Equality enunciated by its own Enlightenment that had got shipwrecked on the shores of capitalism and colonialism; (3) women's struggles for equality and emancipation that all the bourgeois revolutions, all the bourgeois projects of democracy and nation-building, had betrayed; (4) a global struggle against slavery, racism, caste oppression, religious persecution, destruction of all ways of life that contradict capitalist value systems; (5) the struggles over the contradiction between humanity's natural habitat and the very logic of capitalist accumulation, which necessarily requires abolishing bourgeois privilege of over-consumption and the re-founding of an unalienated life as originally conceived by Marx in his early writings which then provided the foundations for his later writings and for the communist conception in general.

Democracy means nothing if it does not mean the totality of all this—and much else, besides. Liberal democracy is a denial of the very principle of totality that undergirds this conception of democracy, a conception that seeks to re-unite, in the context of our time, the word 'democracy' with its original meaning: *demos* (the people) plus *kratos* (rule), meaning 'rule by the people' (what 'the people' mean changes from time to time, in contexts of class and historical time). Aristotle's definition of *demokratia* is based squarely on the opposition, the unbridgeable distance, between the demos and the oligarch. As Ellen Wood quite correctly argues, liberal democracy as practised in all the capitalist countries is actually an oligarchy in the Aristotelian sense.

4

As 'representative' democracy became the norm in 'democratic' polities, the question of who has the right to represent became paramount: men, property owners, the properly educated, racially superior ones, etc. Attention shifted increasingly towards the creation of proper institutions that would guarantee law and order, rule of property, etc. Hence a certain fissure at the very heart of modern politics: while socialism associated democracy primarily with the well-being of the people as a whole, with a distinct emphasis on Equality, in what came to be called 'substantive democracy', liberal thought associated democracy with the proper functioning of institutions designed to safeguard certain rights—primarily rights to freedom of assembly, association, election, belief, and speech—rooted in certain notions of Liberty, with far greater preoccupation with what has come to be known as 'procedural democracy'. I might add that this distinction between "substantive" and "procedural" is not a mere figure of thought. It refers, rather, to how liberal democracy in fact works, subordinating the substantive to the procedural: agreement on the substantive is minimal—basically, freedoms of speech, etc. on the model of the freedom of the market, plus the right to be represented through periodic voting—while the networks of procedure and institution are elaborate and endless. And, these rituals of voting are themselves controlled by the market. Witness the amount of money that gets spent on getting someone elected to parliament, not just in the US but also in India itself.

Of course, in the wake of the Soviet-style communist states, one may well have to inquire yet again just what that "perfection of democracy" would look like, in Marx's sense: what kind of rights and institutions would have to be embedded within a socialism of the future. With a century of socialist struggles and states behind us, it is perhaps time to start asking just what a socialist democracy— historically new kind of substantive democracy with all the instruments of procedural democracy at its disposal—would look like.

5

The question that has motivated political thought since the very outset, across the globe and not just in the West (or what came to be called 'the West'), is simply this: who has the right to rule, and what kind of government is good government? Mencius, the Chinese philosopher, was as comfortable with the cult of expertise in matters of state power, indeed with aristocratic distinction, as was Plato:

Why then should you think . . . that someone who is carrying on the government of a kingdom has time also to till the land? The truth is, that some kinds of business are proper to the great and others to the small.... True indeed is the saying, 'Some work with their minds, others with their bodies. Those who work with their minds rule, while those who work with their bodies are ruled. Those who are ruled produce food; those who rule are fed."

Mencius of course takes this distinction between rulers and the ruled as an iron law of nature. Marx would not approve of the phenomenon, would locate it not in nature but in the history of class struggles. He would nevertheless emphasize that that the distinction between the mental and the manual is the most ancient basis for division of labour, at the origin of all the rest. Development of the mandrinate at the heart of the Chinese state form is obviously related to this phenomenon, and it is significant that the Chinese mandrinate was the model that the British colonial government sought, more or less half-heartedly, to replicate in the form of the Indian Civil Service ('the iron frame of empire' they called it). Nor is it surprising that some variant of this form would be maintained in communist China as well as neo-liberal India right into these post-modern times. Conversely, the prohibition on the study of Sanskrit for women and the Shudras in Brahminical India, as much as the prohibition on the study of the Bible for the slaves in the American South, was emblematic of the conviction that what the European 19th century called "the dangerous classes" can only become more dangerous and unruly if they come to possess what was generally called "book learning"—i.e. if the distance between the mental and the manual was to be systematically abridged.

On the question of the fitness of women to make political judgement at least two quick observations can be made. Distinction between mental and manual came to be closely associated with other distinctions: between Mind and Body, Reason and Emotion, Sciences and the Arts, Masculine and Feminine. With the passage of time, and especially after the Renaissance, what we now know as the sciences, namely the forms of knowledge that are mathematically grounded and give us the magic of numbers, came to be acknowledged as superior while the poetic, the artistic, the imaginative came to be regarded as realms of aesthetic and intuitive pleasure but cognitive unreliability. Masculinity came to be identified as the seat of Reason and Science, and could therefore be trusted with management of property as well as political judgement. As the seat of emotion and imagination trapped in its wayward sexuality and fecundity, the feminine could not be trusted with such skills of management and judgement. Hence, for instance, the fact that in France itself—the home of Reason, Revolution and the Rights of Man—women were not to be given the right to vote till after the Second World War, even though Mary Wollstonecraft had already posed to Tom Paine the question: what, then, is the gender of this Citizen, this bearer of the Rights of Man?

No wonder that as idea and as practice, and throughout its entire history from Greek origins up to its current fetishization, democracy has had a very hard time conceding equal rights to slaves, workers, women and the colonized—virtually anyone who did any kind of productive (or/and, in case of women, reproductive) labour. And this denial of democratic rights was of course premised on a prior denial that those who did productive labour could think as competently as those who did not. There was always the charge of cultural inferiority and incapacity for self-governance against the colonized, deficiency of Reason among women, evolutionary retardation among African slaves, vice and mendacity among workers.

6

One of the intriguing facts about the lies that liberal democracy tells about itself in our time is that in the course of the 20th century, and especially since the Second World War, the word 'dictatorship'—with its cognate cousins such as 'Totalitarianism' —has emerged as virtually the only great opposite of 'democracy'. Not so with the great thinkers of earlier epochs. In *Suppliants* of Euripides, for instance, it is said that among the blessing of a free people is not only the rule of law and freedom of speech but also the right of the worker to the products of labour, whereas in despotic states people labour only to enrich their masters. One finds some variant of this statement in a number of those plays of Greek Antiquity. The strand in Greek thought that associates democracy with free labour and oligarchy with concentration of wealth resonates well with the thought of Karl Marx who came to believe that the great antagonist of democracy in his own time was Capital itself, and more generally the system of private property and what he called wage slavery. The idea is quite simple: where there is wage slavery, there can be no democracy. Or as Rousseau puts it: those who are unequal in their access to material goods can never be equal in the eyes of the law. For Max Weber, popular freedoms were to be weighed against the bureaucratic structure of the modern capitalist state with its instrumental rationality. It was by combining these two strands of thought, the Marxist and the Weberian, that the Critical Theory of the Frankfurt School came to two conclusions: first, that the fundamental structures of the liberal democratic and the fascist states had far more in common than is commonly supposed, precisely because both were variants of the capitalist, technocratic, oligarchic state ; and that, once capital had been expropriated in the USSR, what defeated popular democracy was neither the rise of a new capitalist class nor even the personal dictatorship of Stalin but the bureaucratic character of the Soviet state; the so-called 'Cult of Personality' was simply the mask necessary for that bureaucratic rule.

Oligarchy, dominion of property over labour, wage slavery,

permanent bureaucratic authority hidden behind electoral rituals—not personalized dictatorship—have been historically understood as deep structures that negate democratic possibility. By the same token, therefore, the question of democracy in this tradition of thought was associated with the abolition of oligarchic power, emancipation of labour, and redistribution of bureaucratized functions of the state among masses of people and their popular organs. Not the pomp and show of Westminster but the Paris Commune was the model of democracy for Marx, and "withering away of the state" was the phrase he shared with Bakunin, his great antagonist; the two could of course never agree on what this "withering away" would entail in practice.

Liberal democracy's preoccupation with dictatorship and what it called totalitarianism got shaped in a particular context, when challenges to it arose both from the left, in the shape of communism, as well as the right, in Nazi and fascist forms. Structural reasons for the rise of Nazism could be best suppressed, and the emancipatory logic of the Bolshevik Revolution could be best denied, if figures of Hitler and Stalin could be made to appear as men of the same fibre, both of them dictators, both psychopaths, and both incarnations of pure evil; furthermore, both antagonists, the fascist and the communist, could then be tarred with the same brush of 'totalitarianism'. It is only in the era of US hegemony, when even social democratic theory has itself become the subordinate half-sister of liberal democracy, that apparatuses and routines of the capitalist state—elections, parliaments, mediatic mixes of news and entertainment, the fraudulent discourses of human rights, etc—came to be accepted as democracy as such, even among large sections of the communist left, gradually but surely in the aftermath of the defeat of the Soviet system. It is in this circumstance of the defeat of the socialist project that liberal democracy arises as a universalized desire, across the political spectrum, and as an overarching fetish in the realm of ethics and politics, while, under the shadow of this improvised fetish, the real fetish of the commodity becomes all the more invisible, all the more pervasive as it deepens and expands its hold over humanity across the planet. Just as neo-liberal globalization abolishes the very idea of a national economy, promotion of democracy abolishes the very idea of national sovereignty; all markets can be opened up, all countries invaded, in the name of the one or the other. Commodity fetishism and democracy fetishism are in our time two faces of what I call capitalist universality.

7

What about democracy in its imperial home? Voluminous commentary is easily available on the issue. One of the more recent ones I have read is by Wendy Brown, so I will quote her at some length:

> Democracy has historically unparalleled global popularity today yet has never been more conceptually footloose or substantively hollow... like Barak Obama, it is an empty signifier to which any and all can attach their dreams and hopes. Or perhaps capitalism, modern democracy's non-identical birth twin and always the more robust and wily of the two, has finally reduced democracy to a "brand," a late modern twist on commodity fetishism that wholly severs a product's saleable image from its content .... Berlusconi and Bush, Derrida and Balibar, Italian communists and Hamas—we are all democrats now. But what is left of democracy?

Somewhat later, she answers her own question:

> It is not simply a matter of corporate wealth buying (or being) politicians and overtly contouring domestic and foreign policy, nor of corporatized media that makes a mockery of informed publics or accountable power. More than intersecting, major democracies feature a merging of corporate and state power: extensively outsourced state functions ranging from schools to prisons to militaries; investment bankers and CEOs as ministers and cabinet secretaries; states as non-governing owners of incomprehensibly large portions of finance capital; and above all state power unapologetically harnessed to the project of capital accumulation via tax, environmental, energy, labour, social, fiscal, and monetary policy as well as an endless stream of direct supports and bailouts of all sectors of capital.... democracy's most important if superficial icon, "free" elections, have become circuses of

> marketing and management... It is not only candidates who are packaged by public relations experts more familiar with brand promulgation... so also are political policies and agendas sold as consumer rather than public goods ... perhaps democracy, like liberation, could only ever materialize as protest and, especially today, ought to be formally demoted from a form of governance to a policy of resistance.

I shall offer only three quick comments after so lengthy a quotation. First, when Professor Brown wrote of "merger" between corporate power and state power in today's democracies, she may well have thought of Mussolini's definition of fascism as a system in which government and corporations become one; modern liberal democracies are hard to distinguish from fascist states in that specific sense. Second, she of course limits her remarks to conditions now prevailing in the advanced Euro-American zones, it is well to recognize, however, that versions of these same maladies are, if anything, more extreme in the more backward zones of capital, under dictatorships as much as in liberal democracies.

My third comment is rather longer. It is certainly true that democracy should now be conceived not as a form of government but as a politics of resistance. But resistance to what, and how? And, more crucially: in the name of what? There was a time when capitalism was criticized, denounced, fought against—but in the name of an alternative, which went under the names of socialism, communism, etc which were anchored in some alternate idea of property relations, of justice, of freedom and so on, and some sense of an active social agency—an alternative class project, in communist definitions—that might be mobilized to overcome that which we reject so resoundingly. Now, dissent and protest are construed as sufficient 'resistance', thus affirming the impossibility of anything more than the democratic right of dissent. The difficulty with thinking of 'democracy' as 'resistance' is that so many manifestations of even the most spectacular resistance in our times are themselves in thrall of the fictions of liberal democratic desire—as we have seen in so much of the Arab rebellions over the past couple of years.

Wendy Brown is right. 'Democracy' is a brand, a contentless fetish, usable for all and sundry. The democratically elected government of the Muslim Brotherhood collected vast sums of money from the Emir of Qatar to institutionalize their brand of democracy in Egypt. The subsequent unelected regime that arose out of the military coup and claimed to represent even a larger majority than the previous elected one, went on then to collect even larger sums of money from kings and sheikhs of Saudi Arabia, Kuwait and the UAE, to the satisfaction of the US Secretary of State, John Kerry, for whom the whole charade was a "restoration of democracy." These same people are busy restoring democracy in Syria, through the agency of hundreds of Islamist militias and crime gangs, including various factions of al-Qaeda, against the Assad dictatorship (a Hitler; a Stalin, so goes the chorus). Yes, we are all democrats now: sheikhs and monarchs, Egyptian Generals, French paratroopers, secular intellectuals, NDTV, CNN, al Qaeda militants, Narendra Modi—the list is endless.

8

The three classic homes of liberal democracy, the homes of the three great bourgeois revolutions, the three countries whose constitutions are the very models for constitution-making wherever liberal democracy obtains in the Tricontinent—namely, Britain, France and the United States—have also been, logically, the three main colonialist and imperialist powers in the past and the present. Among all the advanced capitalist countries, Britain and the United States have had the most impressive imperialist record, the most uninterrupted histories of liberal democracy but also the weakest communist movements. France was different but only to a certain extent: formidable empire but smaller than British or American; the legendary home of the Rights of Man but a very chequered history of liberal democratic rule; by contrast, a communist movement of considerable scope some decades ago—and a fascist movement that is gaining momentum again.

By contrast, the European countries that actually succumbed

to Nazism, fascism and military dictatorship (mainly Germany, Italy, Spain and Portugal) were the countries that had either lost great empires (Spain and Portugal) and were made to recede into agrarian and/or semi-industrialized fringes of the continent, or countries that had tried and failed to build great empires of their own (Germany, Italy)—but all four were countries with massive working class revolutionary movements that liberal democracy was unable to contain. Germany was a special case. It had produced the most splendid philosophers of revolution and democracy, and it had surpassed Britain in industrial production by the end of the 19th century, but it failed to make a revolutionary breakthrough even though it had the largest working class movement in Europe; nor could it make a transition to a stable liberal democracy till after the great colonial empires of the others had been dissolved. It does seem conceivable that Germany's failure to build a stable liberal democracy might have had something to do with its failure to build an empire, and both these failures were probably connected with the fact that it was a late-comer to the game of building capitalist economies, empires and liberal democracies. Two world wars were fought to determine whether Germany or the United States would inherit the British and the French empires, hence inherit the globe itself. At the end of the Second World War, the liberal democratic United States in fact achieved what Nazi Germany had sought but failed to achieve: universal domination and global empire. Once it became the global capitalist hegemon, it also became the great model and promoter of liberal democracy.

Is it too much too say that there has been an intrinsic relation between liberal democracy and empire? Let us just pose a question, then, and leave it at that: why is it that the very countries that accumulated vast empires, organized the slave trade, eliminated populations across the Americas and Australia, extracted wealth from the tropical zones and mining centres of the world, leading to levels of capital accumulations not even remotely matched by anyone else, were the ones that became the fountainheads of liberal democracy? Why is it that the three primary homes of liberal democracy—Britain, France and the United States—can kill and maim innumerably more people in the name of democracy and civilization than the Nazis ever did in the name of the superior Aryan race or whatever else, and yet be considered the very epitome of civilization while the German bid for a similar sort of empire can be dismissed as an act of pure barbarity, even pure evil?

9

As the history of slave-holding constitutionalism in the United States shows, liberal democracy, in its much celebrated Jeffersonian version, could happily coexist with slavery till the Civil War settled the issue, and with racial segregation for almost another hundred years, right into the middle of the 20th century. Apartheid South Africa modelled its Bantustans very much on the American reservations for the Native American survivors of the genocide of their people, just as contemporary Israeli democracy is modelled on the racialized democracy of the United States through much of its history. And, as the history of the Suffragist movement would show, those who spoke in the name of the Magna Carta, the Declaration of the Rights of Man and the Bill of Rights were through most of their history remarkably unwilling to allow women to have even the simplest, the emptiest of all the democratic rights: namely the right to vote. There have always been the few who have had abundant recourse to the fruits of democracy but the very existence of that democracy has always rested on vast underbellies of 'un-democracy.'

And there is another story that has been sanitized out of existence. I have already made the point that in Greek philosophy and drama we find numerous passages which assert that the essential difference between slavery and democracy is that the slave has no right to the fruits of his own labour, whereas a democratic citizen has precisely such a right. The phrase Marx often uses, "wage *slavery*," is thus not merely polemical but also accurately reflects this side of classical thought. Rousseau, by no means a consistent thinker, would invoke essentially that same spirit when he raises the question: Is private property reconcilable with either liberty or fraternity, let alone equality?

Even in Hegel we find the blunt dictum: "rights of distress must supersede the rights of property"—from which it would be a very short step to say that private property must be socialized for the great good of society in general. We might remind ourselves also that the Constitution promulgated in the Second Year of the French Revolution affirmed the right of insurrection as a fundamental right. In presenting itself as the product of long centuries of classical, Christian and Enlightenment thought, liberal democracy—that is to say, the actually existing democracy of our time— has had to not only deny centuries and centuries of its oppressions and even outright crimes but also to suppress the memory of whatever was revolutionary in its own heritage.

10

The consequence—necessary and inevitable consequence— of the contraction and defeat of communism has not been a triumph of democracy, as is commonly supposed, but further decay of it. The US state was distinctly more liberal, more democratic and more invested in defending the New Deal under Kennedy and Johnson than it is under Obama. As Kennedy once put it: "if we don't support a peaceful revolution we will make violent revolution inevitable." In other words, communism could be warded off only if liberal democracy learns to be much more democratic than it has ever been. [European social democracy was the practical realization of this thought.] Obama works under no such compulsions. He therefore serves the corporations much more wholeheartedly and creates a far more authoritarian state than even Nixon could have dared to do. In Western Europe, social democracy sided with the American empire through the whole period after the Second World War and then lost its reason for existence after 1989. Not only did it surrender itself to liberal democracy, social democracy itself became a tool in that neo-liberal, corporate capture of government whose only function is to facilitate massive transfer of wealth upward, from the poor to the rich.

Communism may be accused of all sorts of things, but the idea that defeat of communism would somehow give us more democracy is at best a fantastic idea.

3

Democracy, Identity Politics and Class Politics

Prabhat Patnaik

A common perception of democracy is of an arrangement where the claims of different identity groups, whether caste groups or linguistic groups or religious groups[1], are reconciled through negotiations, with the state's role being either to facilitate such negotiations if they do not occur on their own, or to arbitrate skilfully between different groups to produce solutions to everyone's satisfaction, should mutual negotiations fail to provide such solutions; for this the state may even have to enlarge the domain over which solutions can be explored (with concessions to one group in one domain being matched by concessions to another in quite another unrelated domain).

This view, even when not explicitly articulated, is certainly held implicitly, not just by state personnel, but even by many practitioners in the Indian political arena. The behaviour of the various state organs over the Babri Masjid issue exemplifies this view. The Rajiv Gandhi administration allowed the worship of the Ram idol, which had been illicitly installed within the Babri Masjid structure by breaking open its lock; but it sought to obtain the minority community's acquiescence in this act by "balancing" it with a concession to conservative Muslim elements over the Shah Bano issue. Likewise, the Allahabad High Court judgement over the Babri Masjid dispute was an attempt on the part of the judiciary to act as an arbitrator in the matter, trying a "balancing" act that could be generally acceptable.

The notion of a democratic society as one that is characterized essentially by mutual accommodation by the different identity groups, whether spontaneously arrived at or imposed by the state, thus runs quite deep. Indeed the superiority of democracy as an arrangement over other arrangements is often seen to lie in the fact that it is based on negotiated settlements and hence entails mutual accommodation, in contrast to other arrangements where one group's interests tend to override those of others.

To be sure, individuals enjoy multiple identities, so that the particular identity groups whose claims are in the forefront at any point of time keep shifting over time. But that does not negate this view of democracy as constituting at all times a regime of negotiations and mutual accommodation.

This view of democracy however is fundamentally wrong, for if democracy amounted merely to an arrangement where the interests of the different identity groups were reconciled by mutual accommodation effected either through negotiations or through state intervention, then it would be necessarily self-negating, in the sense of resulting in a *de facto* disenfranchisement of large segments of the population, for at least two reasons.

The first reason is that "mutual accommodation" necessarily works over a period of time against minority interests. If every round of conflict is resolved through "mutual accommodation", then the "base positions", i.e. the positions occupied by the majority and minority identity groups, keep shifting at the start of every round of conflict in favour of the majority group and against the minority group. What was utterly unacceptable, for being anti-minority, at the beginning of the rounds of conflict become gradually more and more acceptable through these rounds. In short there is in effect a gradual disenfranchisement of the minority identity group, which is pushed into an ever shrinking corner. This amounts to a negation of democracy.

The second reason arises from the fact that this whole exercise in "mutual accommodation" occurs within the framework of an economy engaged in developing capitalism. Capitalism, as Marx had pointed out long ago, is a *spontaneous system*, in the sense of being self-driven, through its own immanent tendencies. Even the capitalist, supposedly the hero of the system, is an alienated entity, "capital personified" to use Marx's words. Through the actions of the capitalist, with regard to which he himself has very little freedom of choice, engaged as he is in a Darwinian struggle with other capitalists, the immanent tendencies of capital work themselves out. State intervention in the realm of the economy, though pervasive, plays by and large the role of facilitating and hastening the operation of these immanent tendencies.[2]

Undoubtedly in certain exceptional conjunctures the state may be forced to intervene in ways that run contrary to such immanent tendencies, as happened for instance in the immediate aftermath of the Second World War when both decolonization and the institutionalization of Keynesian demand management through *inter alia* a set of welfare measures (and not just American-style "military Keynesianism") were effected.

But intervention of this sort makes the system dysfunctional, offering a choice between either carrying intervention further forward in the direction of the transcendence of the system, or rolling it back to conform to the logic of the system. Even the way this choice is resolved is not left entirely to the volition of the state, and hence, by inference, to the balance of merely political forces: centralization of capital, itself a result of an immanent tendency of the system, which brings ever larger aggregate capitalist entities onto the stage, tilts the choice in favour of the second option, i.e. of progressively rolling back state intervention that runs contrary to the logic of the system.

The fate of the post-war "reformed capitalism" makes the point amply clear. It first brought the system to an inflationary crisis at the end of the 1960s (an instance of its becoming dysfunctional), and produced through centralization of capital a new entity, viz. "globalized" or international finance capital, that ensured the overcoming of that crisis through the pursuit of neo-liberal policies: these overturned Keynesianism and restored in a new manner colonial-style hegemony over Third World economies (a hegemony with which the Third World big bourgeoisie itself became complicit).

A major immanent tendency of capitalism is the production of wealth at one pole and *absolute poverty* at another (a fact not often recognized because this production of poverty has occurred historically in the colonies, semi-colonies, and, more generally, in the distant "outlying regions" of the Third World that have not been very visible to the metropolis). Now, any arrangement of "mutual accommodation" among different identity groups, if it occurs in the context of an economy developing capitalism, and hence within a process that is producing poverty at one pole and wealth at another, will necessarily mean either that some groups gain while others bear the brunt of the "immiserization" process, or that within the groups themselves some gain while others get immiserized.

This latter fact, viz. the production of inequalities within any identity group, results either in class differentiation within the group, or in a proliferation of ever newer and smaller identity groups, each of which then starts engaging in its own identity politics. But such smaller and newer groups can be more easily suppressed, more easily ignored, and more easily made quiescent, so that democracy, perceived as mutual accommodation among identity groups, ends up actually marginalizing segments within the earlier identity groups, and hence gets subverted for this reason as well.

It may appear at first sight as if our two arguments about democracy perceived in this manner, namely that it will progressively enfeeble minorities, and that it will lead to a proliferation of identity groups each of which as a result is increasingly enfeebled, act against one another. In what sense, it may be asked for instance, can we meaningfully talk of a "majority" and "minority" if identity groups themselves are getting fractured all the time? Such fracturing however will not prevent the diverse fractured units from coming together in particular contexts, such as those involving conflicts with minorities. (The fact that Dalits, constituting the most acutely socially-oppressed segment, have often been mobilized to be active participants in communal riots is noteworthy in this context). It follows then that the perception of democracy as consisting of a process of mutual accommodation between different identity groups, i.e. as entailing mutually-accommodative identity politics, is a flawed one: if democracy is indeed practised in this manner then it will progressively atrophy and get diminished.

II

This however is not the perception of democracy informing the Indian Constitution. The alternative perception of democracy that underlies the Constitution, sees it as a political arrangement in which a new collectivity, whose members have transcended their specific caste, religious and linguistic identities, becomes the active subject in the realm of the polity. The very preamble of the Constitution refers to "We the people of India". The "people of India" in short constitute a new collectivity that has transcended its specific caste, religious and linguistic identity. The democracy that the Constitution visualizes is one where people participate not as members of particular identity groups but as a collectivity transcending their particular identities.

The Karachi Congress resolution of 1931 which forms the basis of the Indian Constitution and which had promised basic civil rights; free and compulsory primary education; universal adult franchise; equality before law irrespective of caste, creed or sex; and "neutrality" of the state with regard to all religions; had already visualized a new India whose citizens would be actively politically engaged on a footing of equality, without getting submerged in their specific identities. Implicit in the Karachi vision was also a path of development that, at the very least, restricted the development of capitalism: the resolution had provided explicitly for "state ownership of key industries, mines and means of transport", for it was clear to the framers of that resolution that the "people", as a collectivity, would be undermined by the development of capitalism.

There are two obvious unsustainable dichotomies however that can mar such a conception of democracy where the people are visualized as rising above their specific identities to constitute a "citizenry" that collectively decides its destiny through political intervention. The first is the implicit dichotomy between their private and public personas. As long as specific identities continue to remain etched in their minds, to expect that people should cultivate these identities only in their private lives while in their public lives they must rise above such identities as "citizens", is to expect of them a split personality that is utterly unrealistic. In other words, unless the specific identities themselves wither away over time, or get reduced at best to what characterizes for instance the supporters of rival football clubs, keeping such identities out of the political arena becomes difficult.

The second dichotomy arises in the context of a bourgeois society. In such a society people are presumed to act in the realm of the economy as self-seeking individuals each exclusively pre-occupied with his or her own particular material interests. Even if this is not an accurate description of the actual behaviour of individuals, there is no gainsaying that the interposing of money in human relationships, which bourgeois society carries to an unprecedented level, has the effect of introducing self-seeking behaviour in people. To expect the same people in the realm of the polity, as "citizens", to rise above their particular interests and decide collectively how the state should act in the social interest, is again to expect a split personality in them, which is unrealistic.

These dichotomies imply that two necessary conditions must be fulfilled if democracy, seen as an arrangement where the people as a collectivity constitute the political subject, is to be meaningful. The first is a progressive withering away of the existing particular identities; and the second is a rising above individual interests in the realm of the economy itself. And society moves closer to the fulfilment of both these conditions to the extent that "combinations" of participants in the economy, of members of the *working people*, come into being.

Of course the coming into being of such combinations suffices neither to make people rise above their *existing* particular identities of caste, religion or linguistic group, nor even to prevent the formation of *new* particular identities, such as for instance as members of particular trade unions or of particular peasant organizations, and the pursuit of self-interest via such membership. Besides, the coming into being of such combinations within bourgeois society does not overcome the "spontaneity" of capitalism that undermines the efficacy of any intervention that the "people", as a political collectivity, may undertake via the instrumentality of the state in certain conjunctures. But the coming into being of such combinations, and of combinations of such combinations, is nonetheless a *necessary* condition for an advance towards the realization of the second conception of democracy, and hence of authentic democracy itself.

But focusing on the mere coming into being of such combinations is misleading. What is crucial is the practice of *an alternative politics* which can be understood as follows.

The spontaneity of capitalism implies that even if some group, not just an identity group but even a trade union gets some concessions for itself, the burden of that concession is *spontaneously* shifted on to the shoulders of some other group. Given for instance the tendency towards immiserization immanent in the system, if some particular group manages to escape this tendency then some other group becomes its victim in an even more concentrated form[3]. *The essence of the alternative politics is that the struggle conducted on behalf of the first group which leads to an improvement in its condition must then give rise to a struggle on behalf of the second group on whom the burdens of the first group's improvement are shifted, and so on.* It is politics in which there is a series of ever-widening inclusions, instead of a closure with the advancement of a particular group. The latter type of politics which characterizes identity politics is necessarily exclusionary. The former is necessarily inclusive; I call it "class politics" because the active pursuit of this politics is what has always been visualized by the revolutionary Left.

According to this argument, the distinction between identity politics and class politics is altogether different from what is commonly supposed. This distinction lies not necessarily in the fact that identity politics is concerned with the interest of an identity group, while class politics is concerned with the interest of some supra-"identity" combination of individuals. Nor does it necessarily lie in the fact that identity politics is concerned with "identity issues" while class politics is concerned with "class issues", which typically have an economic character. These ways of identifying 'class politics" undoubtedly do fall within the rubric of class politics, *but they do not constitute its defining characteristic.*

The real distinction lies in the fact that identity politics is concerned with the interests of some particular identity group *to the exclusion of any concern for other groups,* while class politics, even if it starts with advancing the interests of some particular group, *including of some particular identity group,* keeps widening its ambit to include the interests of others on whose shoulders the spontaneity of capitalism may unload the "burden" of the advancement of the initial group. *Class politics therefore is ipso facto a struggle against the spontaneity of the system, and hence against the system itself.* The advance towards the realization of authentic democracy, which is democracy in the second sense we have discussed, is possible only through the practice of class politics.

To say this is not to make the obvious point that is implicit in what has been said till now, namely that a transcending of capitalism is necessary for the realization of authentic democracy. This conclusion simply follows from the fact of the spontaneity of capitalism: if any attempt at collective political intervention by the people to shape their own destiny gets frustrated by the spontaneity of the system, a fact that is so evident in the contemporary era of hegemony of finance capital as to need no further elaboration, then clearly overcoming this spontaneity, and hence transcending the system that produces such spontaneity, becomes a condition for the realization of authentic democracy. But while this is clear, the point being made here is a somewhat different one, namely that the struggle for the advance of democracy, and against the rolling back of whatever democracy exists, *within a bourgeois society itself,* is dependent upon the practice of class politics.

III

An implication of the foregoing argument should be explicitly underscored here. Once we get rid of the *simpliste* notion that class politics is concerned primarily with economic issues or primarily with issues affecting supra-identity-group interests, while identity politics is concerned with a wider range of issues, including social and cultural issues affecting particular identity groups, it follows that *class politics must also concern itself with the social and political discrimination against, and exclusion of, particular identity groups.*

An obvious example is the discrimination against the Dalits. The distinction between Dalit identity politics and class politics is not that the latter is concerned only with Dalits *qua* workers or *qua* agricultural labourers, and hence only with their economic misery, while the former is concerned with their social oppression. Class politics must also be concerned with their social oppression. The distinction between class politics and Dalit identity politics then lies in the fact that the former ensconces the struggle against their social oppression within the larger context of a struggle against the spontaneity of the capitalist system, and hence against the capitalist system itself, while the latter treats this struggle as an exclusive struggle not connected with this larger struggle. *The difference in short lies in the fact of ensconcing, not in any difference in the attitude towards social oppression.*

Indeed, according to this argument, if class politics does not take up social issues of caste oppression, then that constitutes *its weakness as class politics*; it is not because of any conformity with class politics. If the votaries of class politics have not taken up issues of caste oppression in India (which they can with some justification be accused of not having done adequately), then the reason lies not in the fact that they are votaries of class politics, but rather in the fact that they have been inadequate practitioners of class politics.

Put differently, the difference between class politics and identity politics, even in the form of Dalit identity politics, has nothing to do with the point of intervention, i.e. the point where praxis begins. Class politics too, in a society like ours, must focus its praxis on the struggle against the social oppression of the Dalits. *The difference has to do with what such intervention has as its objective and what it leads up to, whether to exclusive Dalit politics which does not aim at transcending the capitalist system characterized by spontaneity, or to an inclusive mobilization with the aim of transcending this spontaneity.*

Just to take an example, while class politics must support and demand affirmative action in the form of reservation for Dalits in educational institutions, it cannot remain confined only to this; it must simultaneously fight to ensure that the necessity for reservations itself withers away, through an overcoming of the scarcity of opportunities that capitalism entails.

Precisely because Dalit identity politics remains confined to an adjustment within the bourgeois system, it is incapable of improving in any fundamental sense the condition of the Dalits. Even if it brings them *formal* social equality, and even some advance towards *real* social equality, the spontaneity of capitalism in generating wealth at pole and misery at another will keep the bulk of the Dalits at the pole of misery, and hence thwart their progress towards real social equality. It may at best produce a class differentiation within them (as is happening at present among the blacks in South Africa through the emergence of a black bourgeoisie, although the Dalits in India are still far from such a *denouement*). But it will not overcome their social and economic exclusion, and hence their *de facto* disenfranchisement.

To say this is not to cast aspersions on Dalit identity politics which has played a remarkable role in the struggle against the millennia-old social oppression of the Dalits. The idea is merely to point out its inherent limitations and why it must be ensconced within a more inclusive class politics if the Dalit cause itself is to be carried forward.

IV

Two questions may be raised immediately. First, what is the agency for *consciously* pursuing class politics? This question however is not germane to the issues being raised here, which are concerned with the *conceptual* distinction between two different kinds of politics. Besides, it is a question to which if a specific answer is given that is supposed to be valid for ever, then that answer must necessarily be a metaphysical one. In other words, the pursuit of class politics is a matter of praxis, and no particular agency can be identified as being forever the custodian, as if by divine right, of the correct praxis dictated by class politics.

The Leninist Party, conceptualized as a self-correcting vanguard, was supposed to pursue, through such self-corrections, a more or less correct praxis in conformity with the requirements of class politics; but in practice there is no reason why a group of persons calling themselves Marxist-Leninist should, despite their attempt at self-corrections, necessarily be the custodian of such correct praxis.

The second, related, question is whether the term "class politics" refers only to some desirable kind of politics that *ought* to be pursued, or whether it refers to some actual politics, like identity politics, that *is* pursued in real life. It will be difficult to sustain the claim on behalf of *any particular agency* that the politics it has actually been pursuing constitutes pristine class politics; hence it would be difficult to identify the reality of pursuit of class politics *in that way*. But in society at large, not necessarily systematically, not necessarily always consciously, the multiplicity of political agencies in their aggregate do also pursue class politics (spurred on no doubt by the initiative of particular agencies committed to the pursuit of class politics).

In other words, we should not divide the political agencies in society at any time into those who pursue exclusively identity politics and those who pursue exclusively class politics. Undoubtedly, some agencies design themselves specifically to pursue class politics, while others design themselves to pursue identity politics. The Left in particular makes a serious attempt to remain committed at all times to the pursuit of class politics. But even those committed to class politics cannot absolve themselves of the charge of lapsing into identity politics on occasions; and even those committed to identity politics can also stray into the pursuit of class politics on occasions. The distinction between the two kinds of politics must not be identified exclusively with a mere distinction between two sets of agencies.

We have already referred to the Karachi resolution of 1931 which constitutes an example of an attempt towards the pursuit of class politics by a political party that on other occasions has engaged in identity politics. Likewise, even political parties founded with the goal of pursuing identity politics, occasionally come together, as they did recently in passing the food security legislation, to pursue a political course that would constitute a bow towards class politics. In other words, the pursuit of class politics, if only in a non-systematic, non-conscious manner, is as much a feature of the actual political life of the country as the pursuit of identity politics.

Indeed the real democratic process at any time is characterized by a tussle between these two contending elements, the pursuit of identity politics on the one hand and the pursuit of class politics on the other. The institutionalization of a neo-liberal economic regime however, by opening the country to the free flow of globalized finance, and hence by forcing the state, which is a nation-state after all, to cater necessarily to the caprices of globalized finance, reduces the scope for class politics (since the state ceases, to an even greater extent than before, to be usable as an instrument for the realization of universal material gains by the people, or even of ever-widening material gains by several different groups of people, one after another). Neo-liberal regimes therefore are characterized by a substantial fillip to identity politics.

This is a paradoxical phenomenon, since it means that the era of "globalization" also becomes the era of pervasive pursuit of identity politics. The roots of this paradox, which is readily observable in our contemporary political life, lie in the dialectical inter-play between class politics and identity politics, whereby constraints upon the former provide a fillip to the latter.

But precisely because the strengthening of identity politics entails, for reasons discussed earlier, an attenuation of democracy, neo-liberalism is associated with such an attenuation. The attenuation of democracy under neo-liberalism in other words occurs for a reason quite apart from the one that is usually emphasized. This usual reason is that the state, in thraldom to the caprices of globalized finance, and hence of the corporate-financial elite that is closely integrated with globalized finance, becomes largely impervious to the demands of the people: all elected governments, as long as they do not take the country out of the orbit of globalized finance, are more or less constrained to pursue the same policies, viz. policies approved by globalized finance, thereby making a mockery of the people's electoral choice. But in addition to this, there is also an attenuation of democracy arising from the fact that identity politics becomes far more pervasive under this dispensation. And this acts in particular to the detriment of the minorities and of other excluded sections.

V

The ideological hegemony of globalized finance capital, superimposed on this situation, also plays an important role. The fact that hunger, abysmal living conditions and homelessness characterize vast segments of the population to this day, after almost seven decades of independence, is a remarkable feature of Indian social life, especially when we bear in mind that these could be so easily eliminated through a redistributive process. Such a redistributive process of course is anathema for the bourgeois order, but one would have expected that it would be attempted by those committed to class politics, and even those committed to Dalit identity politics (since Dalits are among the poorest).

Indeed a fierce commitment to a redistributive agenda had brought the Left into prominence in West Bengal in the late 1960s when it had simply allowed the landless peasants to move into the ceiling-surplus land of the rich landlords. Why has such a redistributive agenda come to a halt?

True, since the Left and the Dalit movement have succeeded in coming to office only at the level of states, the only redistribution that could have been put into effect was at the state level. But why has this not happened in the last several years? Why for instance has a programme of taxing the rich and using the resources for a massive housing scheme for the poor not been put into effect to overcome homelessness? (Kerala remains the sole exception in this respect as in others, since it has for long put a redistributive agenda into practice). And if in answer fingers are pointed to the limited taxing powers of the state governments, then the question could be simply reframed: why has there not been a diversion of public expenditure from those benefiting the rich and the affluent segments to those benefiting the poor?

Indeed, on the contrary the typical policy pursued by state governments under neo-liberalism has been to provide tax concessions to the rich and the corporates for enticing them into the state to undertake investment and accelerate the state's growth rate. Since such acceleration scarcely benefits the poor[4], why have state governments which one would have expected to be more concerned with the poor persisted nonetheless with such policies?

There are undoubtedly powerful class forces, including especially the pressure from an urban middle class, that drive state government policies in this direction. But one cannot ignore the role played by the ideological hegemony of finance capital. This has been an important contributory factor even in shaping these class forces.

Shaking off thraldom to the ideology propagated by finance capital (not an easy task in view of the corporate-financial elite's control over and manipulation of the mass media), and reviving class politics in a strong manner, are essential for rolling back the attenuation of democracy that is all too evident at present, of which the communal-fascist threat confronting the country is a major ingredient.

NOTES AND REFERENCES

1. Gender is kept out of the ambit of identity politics as defined in this paper, though some of the paper's conclusions may retain their validity even in the context of gender politics.
2. A discussion of "spontaneity" under capitalism and its implications is contained in Prabhat Patnaik, *Re-envisioning*

Socialism, Tulika Books, Delhi, 2011.

3. It has often been argued for instance that the burden of wage increases obtained by workers through trade union struggles tend to get passed on "spontaneously" to the "unorganized sector" of primary producers who constitute "price-takers". J.K. Galbraith, *Economics and the Public Purpose*, Houghton, Boston, 1973, argues along these lines. See also Prabhat Patnaik, *Accumulation and Stability Under Capitalism*, Clarendon Press, Oxford, 1995, which extends this argument to the world economy.
4. Utsa Patnaik has shown that precisely during the period of high GDP growth in the Indian economy, the extent of both urban and rural poverty, defined in terms of the proportion of the population falling below 2100 calories per person per day, and 2200 calories per person per day respectively, has increased significantly. See her "Poverty Trends in India 2004-5 to 2009-10", *Economic and Political Weekly*, October 5, 2013.

4

The Left in India and the Issue of Democracy: A Theoretical Inquiry

Sobhanlal Dattagupta

I

Following the rise and coming to power of the Am Admi Party in Delhi in the closing days of 2013, a question that has been plaguing the Indian Left in the recent past has again come alive. Has the Left lost its relevance in India altogether? The question becomes pertinent for a very specific reason. This issue that the ideology of the Left, which broadly comes under the rubric of Marxism, has become irrelevant, that it has lost its magical appeal, that the cause which it defends has ceased to be important—all these questions suddenly opened up in a big way in Europe in the early 1990s when the Soviet Union collapsed and the East European regimes crumbled as its after effect. Civil society movements, dissident voices symbolizing the spirit of pluralism, alternative versions of Marxism, as distinct from the rhetoric of mainstream Marxism, opened up new frontiers, sparking off debates that were unheard of in the era that preceded the 1990s, that is, the age of official Marxism. These new challenges were manifest on two levels: in practice they were expressed through a series of popular movements across the USSR and Eastern Europe, directed against the authoritarian systems that had been in power for decades. On the intellectual level, this spirit was manifest in a series of philosophical interventions in the realm of Marxist theory, reviving interest in the ideas of many forgotten thinkers of the Marxist tradition.

In India nothing of the kind of happenings that the Soviet Union and Eastern Europe witnessed took place. While it is true that the fall of Soviet socialism had a demoralizing effect on the Indian Left, as it happened all over the world, this cannot explain the steady decline of the Left in India over the last two decades. There are two tricky questions involved here. First, while in the post-Soviet era the electoral performance of the Indian Left at the national level, that is, in the Lok Sabha elections has been pretty good, the seats that the Left gained were primarily from West Bengal and a few from Kerala and Tripura. In other words, in terms of seats gained, although the performance did look impressive, it was actually quite hollow, being not at all representative of the national scenario. Over the years some of the old bastions of the Left, namely, Bihar and Andhra Pradesh, have witnessed steady erosion of the Left. Second, while the Left, guided, again, by electoral considerations, has struck up alliances with non-Congress and non-BJP parties, this has hardly been reflected in the electoral gains of the Left. The reason is not difficult to understand. And this refers to the second question. The electoral gains of the Left have not been matched by corresponding political gains. On the contrary, in the political sphere the Left had to cede to the strategies as well as demands of the numerous regional and casteist parties, with whom it approached for electoral alliance. While it gained electorally, by yielding ground to these new forces, it lost politically, its traditional class support base being taken over by its allies, which had far-reaching consequences. Having no ideological congruence with these parties, except such vague slogans that they believed in democracy and secularism, the new social spaces that emerged since the late 1980s and the major players being the dispossessed, the socially deprived lot, represented mostly by the Dalits, the landless and the tribals, these were appropriated not by the Left but by its allies. This mismatch between electoral gains and political retreat constitutes the core of the crisis of the Left in India.

II

For an explanation of this growing marginalization of the Left one has to go back to the historical origins of Indian communism. To cite the words of P.C. Joshi, it was M.N. Roy's flawed understanding of Indian communism which was largely responsible for the failure of Indian communism to emerge as an hegemonic force.[1] Although Joshi did not elaborate it, two explanations are possible. First, Roy's understanding of Indian communism was largely Eurocentric, as he believed that industrialization had been attained in India under the aegis of British colonial rule, resulting in polarization of classes. The classic illustration of this position was Roy's Supplementary Theses, accepted with some modifications effected by Lenin in 1920 at the Second Congress of Comintern, which was adopted as a parallel document together with Lenin's Colonial Theses. The outlook of Roy, as reflected in his Supplementary Theses, was further elaborated in his *India in Transition* (1922). In other words Roy, like many of his European counterparts, believed that the Soviet model of revolution, with the industrial proletariat at the helm, was fully applicable to India. Second, in this understanding, which was essentially class-oriented, there was no place for categories like caste, community, religion with the help of which one has to understand the ground realities of Indian society. Most importantly, in Roy's understanding nationalism was a spent force, which had joined hands with the British imperialism, Gandhi, Nehru, Bose its spokespersons.

Roy could emerge as the unrivalled spokesman for India in the Comintern and thereby the doyen of Indian communism for the success he gained in weeding out the challenges posed by a number of Indian revolutionary groups, organizationally as well as ideologically. Roy's meteoric rise in Comintern made it possible for him to project his viewpoint as the sole expression of Indian communism and declare a closure on other alternative positions, represented by these groups who were looking for the Comintern's support. With the opening of the Comintern archives it is now clearly established that Roy made every effort to stop any such support from Moscow to these groups, resulting in the recognition of Roy's voice as the one single authoritative voice of Indian communism. This is evident in the way the Indian Revolutionary Association (IRA), represented by M.B.P.T. Acharya and Abdur Rabb Barq, among others, which was active in Tashkhent even before Roy's entry, as well as the Berlin group of Indian revolutionaries, headed by Virendranath Chattopadhyaya, Pandurang Khankhoje and Bhupendranath Datta, to name a few, were marginalized by the Comintern. While organizationally, Roy was not prepared to accept the existence of any alternative leadership which might threaten his own, ideologically too their positions were quite irreconcilable. Very briefly, despite differences, the IRA and the Berlin group, while declaring their faith in socialism and revolution, were not in favour of complete rejection of nationalism in working out a strategy of anti-imperialist struggle in India. While their position on the issue of nationalism was relatively positive, for them the complexities of Indian society could not be grasped simply with reference to class. Thus, for them, by ignoring factors like caste, religion, untouchability the problem of the Indian revolution could not be properly grasped.[2] Understandably, this was a position which implicitly questioned Roy's industrialization and class polarization thesis. As Roy succeeded in declaring a complete closure on these alternative positions, the communist groups operating from India had no access to these viewpoints and, thanks to their total dependence on Roy for material and moral support of the Comintern, especially after the formation of a Communist Party on the Indian soil in 1925, the mindset of Indian communism became grounded in Roy's outlook from the time of its birth.

The tragedy of the Communist movement in India has been that, historically, there were certain possibilities which, if recognized, could have introduced an alternative Left perspective in the anti-imperialist struggle. But Roy's virtual declaration of closure on these alternatives decided the destiny of communism in India, as the CPI's understanding of India's history and society became anchored in Roy's position from its very birth.

To put it briefly, one can have a sense of these alternative positions if one considers the documents of the Berlin Committee, some of which could be communicated to Lenin and the Comintern but could not be officially placed on the agenda for discussion. But what also remained unknown for decades was what transpired between this Berlin group of revolutionaries and Lenin in their very brief meetings. While many of these young revolutionaries were greatly inspired by the October Revolution and looked upon the October model to be replicated in India, Lenin had no such illusion. In a document sent to Lenin on the occasion of the Third Congress of the Comintern in 1921, by Bhupendranath Datta, a member of the Berlin Committee, the accent was on the organization of communist groups in India for accomplishment of socialism through a social revolution after the victory of political revolution against British imperialism. Lenin's reply, known many years later, was that instead of discussing social classes what was necessary was to gather 'statistical facts about Peasant leagues if any exist[ed] in India.'[3] Years later, Datta recalled this comment and admitted that the importance of the peasant question, as emphasized by Lenin, for the first tine made him aware of the role of the peasantry in India's anti-imperialist struggle.[4] But the death of Lenin, together with Roy's industrialization thesis, completely obscured the importance of the peasantry and the agrarian question in the CPI's perception of the anti-imperialist struggle and it is precisely this space which was appropriated by Gandhi. The Communists' traditional tirade against Gandhi is, therefore, self-explanatory.

Then there was the 'Thesis on India and the World Revolution', prepared by Virendranath, Luhani and Khankhoje, for consideration by the Comintern in its Third Congress, but which remained ignored. The text of this long document, which now is known for the first time after the opening of the Comintern archives, makes it amply clear that the understanding of anti-imperialist struggle in India in this document was quite different from Roy's understanding. Unlike Roy's unilinear understanding of India in terms of one single category, namely, class, this document highlighted three distinct issues: (a) India was described basically as an agrarian country with a feudal structure; (b) the Indian society was believed to be divided not just vertically along class lines but also horizontally along the lines of religion and caste; (c) without mentioning Roy's name, it was stated that the argument put forward from certain quarters that the Comintern's assistance to bourgeois-democratic and national-revolutionary movements would prove counter-productive was hardly tenable.[5] That carrying out a revolution in India involved a proper understanding of its cultural pluralities and social complexities like caste and religion and that this required a different kind of strategy which recognized its agrarian character was what differentiated the position of the Berlin group from that of Roy. Khankhoje, for instance, states in his memoirs that he felt that the plurality of religions, languages and cultures that characterized India could not be simply swept aside, since these had struck deep into the consciousness of the masses.[6] Again, while the Berlin group was in favour of building up contacts between the Comintern and the national-revolutionary elements in India, Roy was strongly opposed to it. However, since, ultimately, it was Roy's position that prevailed and the Berlin group of Indian revolutionaries virtually came to be considered as persona non grata by the Comintern[7], this alternative perspective got completely erased. It is, therefore, not surprising that a strong undercurrent of left-extremism, which was dismissive of nationalism, intolerant of categories other than class, characterized the mindset of Indian communism from the very beginning. When the Comintern launched its new line of class vs class in 1928, following the Sixth Congress, it fitted in quite well with the CPI's orientation, despite some initial confusions. The consequences were disastrous, as the Party, following its characterization of nationalism and the nationalist leaders as counter-revolutionary, burnt its boats, got completely isolated from the anti-imperialist struggle and embraced the self-destructive line of left-adventurism. Later, after 1936, in the aftermath of the publication of the Dutt-Bradley thesis, which was reflective of the position of the Comintern's Seventh Congress, it became almost an insurmountable problem for the

CPI to convince its ranks of the justification of the shift towards the united front strategy, envisaging alliance with the Indian National Congress, that is, bourgeois nationalism. The problem became particularly complicated in the period thereafter, when the CPI joined an alliance with the Congress Socialist Party (CSP). While the CSP had within it quite a number of elements who were opposed to communism, the CPI too was heavily dominated by a trend which was sharply sceptical of this alliance with the CSP. Bouts of sectarianism and left-adventurism, which have plagued the CPI on repeated occasions since its birth, have been the logical culmination of a flawed understanding of the anti-imperialist struggle, resulting in its isolation from the national mainstream. This was manifest, first, in the early 1930s, when the call for establishment of a 'Soviet republic' in India was given, followed, again, in 1948-1950, when the successive calls for armed proletarian revolution and agrarian revolution, drawing inspiration from the Russian and the Chinese path respectively, ended in disaster. The split of the CPI in 1964, further split in 1969, primarily between the 'Right', the 'Left' and the 'Extreme Left' and the consequent weakening of the Marxist Left in India have been the symptoms of an organic crisis of Indian communism, the roots of which are essentially historical, to be explained by the peculiar circumstances in which it was born.

III

The Left in India has cared very little for the crucial distinction between the art of organization of the Party and that of governance when in power. While organization entails centralism and sometimes often as a short-term measure democratic norms are violated, when in power, this mindset ultimately becomes self-destructive, because this involves the question of negotiating with the larger masses beyond the periphery of the Party. The Gramscian distinction between hegemony and domination and Gramsci's notion of viewing the Communist Party as the hegemonic "Modern Prince", which he projects as the symbol of the "national-popular-collective", become extremely relevant in this context.[8] That the state in India is not simply a coercive institution which rules simply by use of naked force but that it is, indeed, a state that rules by a judicious use of coercion and consent has never been seriously discussed by the parties of the Left. One possible reason is that in the discourse of the Indian Left the Gramscian vocabulary is completely missing. Many of the populist strategies and programmes of the Indian state can be explained in this light.

Thus, as the neo-liberal regime has set in, corporatization of the Indian economy has led to withdrawal of the state and opening of some of the core sectors to market in the name of reforms, development and governance. Consequently, this has led to the emergence of a vast strata of marginalized poor, the majority of which belong to the informal sector, which has been paralleled by the growth of an affluent new middle class, leading to the "India vs. Bharat phenomenon" . The state-market negotiation has led to the following contradictory situation. (a) Protection of corporate capitalism by the state in the name of development has led to intensification of violence and repression, which is most starkly manifest in the tribal areas, leading to the phenomenon of what has come to be known as "Maoist" violence and the rise of civil society as a critique of state repression. (b) To offset these effects the state has undertaken a series of poverty alleviation programmes like the NREGA, in the implementation of which the NGOs, bureaucracy as well as the political parties are at work. These two faces of the Indian state, violent and welfarist, can be viewed in this light. It is the dialectical understanding of Gramsci which would enable us to understand why in the history of post-independence India we are passing through a time when the Indian state is simultaneously so violent and also so welfarist. The moment the authority of the state is frontally challenged or defied, violence of the highest scale is being unleashed, as the state acts as the defender of corporate capital. Again, the moment the state gets the sense of burgeoning unrest and discontent, which may threaten the stability of the state in future, the state doles out a slew of packages and welfarist schemes.

Like Gramsci, Althusser's notion of the state too becomes

especially relevant in this context. Since in India armed seizure of state power is at least in the present situation passé, the Althusserian distinction between state power and state apparatus[9] becomes very important and the struggle not just for capture of state power, which involves formulation of electoral strategies with all its limitations, but for hegemonization of the state apparatus becomes even more crucial. This is an issue that is directly relevant for how the Left can address the issue of governance. In India what the Left has in mind is how to take over state power. But that it is a two-step strategy, namely, capturing state power (however partial it has been at different moments, namely, Kerala, West Bengal and Tripura), to be followed up by the capture of state apparatus, has never occurred in the theoretical thinking of the Left in India. The nuanced understanding of Althusser that (a) the state apparatus is not just repressive but also ideological and that (b) the state apparatus functions somewhat autonomously in relation to the class that is in power provides interesting clues to the understanding that the apparatus with its structure, culture and style may outlive state power and simply by packing the state apparatus with dozens of party loyalists without caring for their ability, efficiency and vision of an alternative perspective will not do. In India, in the Left-run regimes what has mostly happened is the packing of the different wings of the state apparatus with party men at different levels, political loyalty being the main consideration. Thus, like Gramsci's strategy of establishing hegemony in the sphere of civil society, the Althusserian understanding too calls for hegemonizing the state apparatus, thus breaking new grounds in the understanding of state.

IV

A closely allied question that is deeply relevant in this context is the notion of vanguardism. The Left continues to be guided by the argument that the Party is always right, that it can never do any wrong, the presumption being that the Party represents the masses. It is this understanding that went into the coinage of the dreaded term "Enemies of the People" in the erstwhile Soviet Union, when Stalinism reached its zenith. It legitimizes every act of violence and coercion in the name of the Party, while silencing the voices of difference. It has been the experience of the larger public that, guided by the notion of vanguardism, the Left parties are masters of agitational politics in their deft handling of organizational questions, while steering a mass movement. But the track record of the Left in governance has not been that impressive in India except for rather short spells. In West Bengal, for example, the coming to power of the Left Front in 1977 was full of promises, but its performance, especially in the field of governance, was not at all impressive. After all, people vote the Left to power not for short-term agitational politics but for long-term governance, which would be not only good but also be different from traditional bourgeois style of rule. This needs to be appreciated and given priority, that is, how an alternative model of people-centric governance, which would address the burning problems of administration that plague the daily life of the common man, with focus on efficiency and service, can be worked out. In other words, quantitative growth of the Party and Party control at all levels would ultimately prove counter-productive, because people will ultimately judge the Left in terms of the service they render to the masses. This is what reminds one of Lenin's slogan, 'Better fewer but better" in the closing years of his life.

This, in turn, brings into focus a closely related question, namely, the issue of pluralism or recognition of the voice of difference. The answer to this question as to why the Left parties are by and large allergic to the idea of pluralism lies probably in a wrong reading of Lenin, the latter being considered as a defender of centralism in absolute terms, his *What is to be Done?* (1902) being the classic text in defence of this position. The weakness of this argument is that Lenin's text was the product of a situation that was extraordinarily difficult for a revolutionary party which was forced to work in illegal conditions. That the Party which Lenin himself had created can emerge as a monstrous force and thereby kill the initiative of the masses, reducing the latter as appendages of the Party and thereby endanger the very existence of socialism was starkly manifest in his "Letter to the Congress", in 1922 commonly known as his *Last Testament* the focal points of which were: (a) induction of more workers in the Central Committee, (b) activating the mechanism of Workers' Inspection whereby workers' control over the Party would be facilitated, (c) encouraging inner-party democracy by bringing out discussion bulletins, etc and (d) forging links with the non-party masses.[10] This was very clearly a call for recognition of pluralism and diversity. Nikolai Bukharin, one of the key figures who prepared the blueprint of Soviet socialism in Lenin's time, strongly believed that without the recognition of pluralism socialism would be turned into a monotonous, lifeless mediocrity. He wrote in one of his prison manuscripts, namely, *Socialism and its Culture*, "It would be absolutely absurd to imagine human beings of the future as impassive calculating machines that walk. There will be different kinds of people with passions for all sorts of different things. Socialism, growing over into communism, eliminates the exploitative forms of diversity altogether. But this by no means signifies a return to primitive communism, nor does it regard the latter as a bygone 'golden age'...And in its structure it is not by any means a return to the undifferentiated and articulated whole, that is to a high degree a diversified and articulated community that at the same time is not a community based on ties of 'blood' but ultimately a community of an order that is absolutely different from all previous ones."[11]

However, in the Marxist vocabulary the notion of pluralism has never been given due weightage, as it has traditionally been considered a pejorative expression. It is high time that, as against monolithic party control at all levels, Rosa Luxemburg's famous phrase "Freedom is the freedom to think differently" needs to be projected in cultivating the notion of recognition of diversity and difference. It is the lack of this understanding that the mainstream Indian Left is plagued with, what Achin Vanaik has categorized as "Parliamentary Stalinism"[12] that is, taking all the advantages of parliamentary democracy by being its beneficiary, while harbouring a stolid silence in regard to the question of democracy. It is now being argued by Marxists themselves that in the name of democratic centralism, a principle that was accepted as the guiding spirit of party organization in the prevailing conditions of Czarist Russia, democratization of the Left movement has been obstructed, blocking off fresh air and new blood.[13]

This also brings into focus a larger question relating to the social composition of the leadership of the Leftparties in India. Class being the central axis of Left thinking, other hard core ground realities like caste, community, gender, etc have not been seriously taken into consideration in the past notwithstanding the fact that the close interconnection between low caste and oppressed communities on the one hand and the downtrodden masses on the other is undeniable. It is, however, an established fact that the representation of the adivasis, women and the minority communities in the leadership of the Left parties has never been at all impressive. The question of negotiating the class question and that of caste, community and gender without being trapped by the idioms and vocabularies of casteist and communal forces is a big challenge before the Indian Left, since this issue is yet to be addressed satisfactorily.

For the Left in India exploration of an alternative understanding of Marxism, therefore, is the need of the hour. This requires shedding of the traditional mindset, dispassionate reading of the alternative texts of Marxism, many of which are still considered as taboos by the exponents of mainstream Marxism. These include figures like Trotsky, Rosa Luxemburg, Gramsci and many others. Over and above, an alternative reading of Lenin is what is very much wanting in India. That Lenin was not just an advocate of a centralized party but something more, that he was a true advocate of revolutionary democracy, that he never endorsed the stifling of the voice of the masses by that of the Party needs to be appreciated.

NOTES AND REFERENCES

1. Labour History Archives and Study Centre.Manchester University. CPGB archives. CP/IND/MISC/3/7 'Indian Communism—Years of Formation: 1917-1925. An Outline for

Discussion by P.C. Joshi.' Typescript.

2. For details of these differences between Roy, the IRA and the Berlin group, see Sobhanlal Datta Gupta, *Comintern and the Destiny of Communism in India 1919-1943*. Second revised and enlarged edition (Kolkata: Seribaan, 2011), pp. 284-314.
3. V.I. Lenin, 'To Bhupendranath Datta', *Collected Works*, Vol. 45 (Moscow: Progress Publishers, 1960), p. 270.
4. Bhupendranath Datta, *Dialectics of Land-Economics of India* (Calcutta: Mohendra Publishing Committee, 1952), p. iii.
5. Document 48, "Thesis on India and the World Revolution. Presented to the ECCI and the Congress Commission on Oriental Questions by V. Chattopadhyaya, G.A.K. Luhani and P. Khankhoje on the occasion of Comintern's Third Congress', in Purabi Roy et al (eds.), *Indo-Russian Relations 1917-1947: Select Documents from the Archives of the Russian Federation, Part I: 1917-1928* (Calcutta: The Asiatic Society, 1999), pp. 116-125. The original file no. in RGASPI, Moscow is 495/68/37/54-67.
6. Savitri Sawhney, *I Shall Never Ask for Pardon. A Memoir of Pandurang Khankhoje* (New Delhi: Penguin Books, 2008), p. 219.
7. Khankhoje has described it in detail in Sawhney, *I Shall Never Ask for Pardon. A Memoir of Pandurang Khankhoje*, pp. 211-225.
8. Antonio Gramsci, *Selections from the Prison Notebooks* (New York: International Publishers, 1971), pp. 262-263.
9. Louis Althusser, 'Ideology and Ideological State Apparatuses (Notes Towards an Investigation), in Louis Althusser, *Lenin and Philosophy and Other Essays* (London: New Left Books, 1971), pp. 131-141, 149-173.
10. V.I. Lenin, "Letter to the Congress", *Collected Works*, Vol. 36 (Moscow: Progress, 1971), pp. 593-597.
11. Nikolai Bukharin, *Prison Manuscripts. Socialism and Its Culture* (Calcutta: Seagull Books, 2006), pp. 111-113.
12. AchinVanaik, "Subcontinental Stratgies", *New Left Review*, July-August, 70, 2011.
13. Javeed Alam, "Can Democratic Centralism be Conducive to Democracy?" *Economic and Political Weekly*, September 10, 2009.

5

Indian Muslims and the Radical Democratic Project

Maidul Islam

"There is no future for the Left if it is unable to create an expansive universal discourse, constructed out of, not against, the proliferation of particularisms of the last few decades...The task ahead is to expand those seeds of universality, so that we can have a full social imaginary, capable of competing with the neo-liberal consensus which has been the hegemonic horizon of world politics for the last thirty years. It is certainly a difficult task, but it is one which, at least, we can properly formulate. To do so is already to have won a first important battle."

—Ernesto Laclau[1]

"One of the central tenets of *Hegemony and Socialist Strategy* is the need to create a chain of equivalence among the various democratic struggles against different forms of subordination...[W]e insisted that the Left needed to tackle issues of both 'redistribution' and 'recognition'. This is what we meant by 'radical and plural democracy'. Today, such a project remains as pertinent as ever—which is not to say that it has become easier to realize...What is at stake is the building of a new hegemony. So our motto is: 'Back to the hegemonic struggle'."

—Ernesto Laclau and Chantal Mouffe[2]

Contemporary Situation of Indian Muslims

Recently, a central government appointed expert committee report has shown that Muslims along with Dalits and Tribals are the poorest communities in India and poverty has remained consistently high among the Muslims during the phase of economic reforms.[3] According to the above report, 84.5% of Indian Muslim households spend no more than Rs. 20 per day and Rs. 609 per month and belong to 'extremely poor', 'poor', 'marginal' and 'vulnerable' sections of the Indian population. If we also take into account the 'middle income' group as per the parameters set up by the above report, then 13.3% of Indian Muslim households only spend Rs. 1098 per month or Rs. 37 as daily per capita consumption expenditure (DPCE), which is actually low given the high persistence of inflation in the economy. Only 2.2% of Indian Muslims, who are regarded as high income category by the report, spend Rs. 2,776 per month or Rs. 93 per day.[4] It is difficult to argue that Indian Muslims are an economically heterogeneous community when only a meagre 2.2% of them belong to the high income category. The above report also shows that Muslims and SC/STs have high concentration among unorganized sector workers.[5]

Today, Indian Muslims neither own the major means of production nor control the policy-making decisions of the state. However, there are some exceptions that constitute the 2% high income Muslim elites in India. According to the latest Forbes list published in October 2013, only 5 Muslims have a place in the top 100 richest persons in India: Wipro chairman, Azim Premji (Rank 4), Cipla chairman, Yusuf Hamied (Rank 28), NRI businessman from Kerala—M.A. Yusuff Ali (Rank 40), who is the managing director of Abu Dhabi-based Lulu Group International that owns a fast growing retail chain and has investments in Catholic Syrian Bank and Federal Bank in Kerala, Irfan Razack (Rank 88), the managing director of the Bangalore-based property developers, the Prestige Group and Wockhardt chairman, Habil Khorakiwala (Rank 89). One can also add to the list the names of the Ansari family, which is the only Muslim owner of a major newspaper in the country, *Mid-Day*, and B.S. Abdur Rahman, a Tamil Muslim who is currently the Vice-

Chairman of the Dubai-based ETA Star Group and has significant investments in real estate, maritime and urban infrastructure in Tamil Nadu.[6] One can also add a few Muslim businessmen like Badruddin Ajmal, who backs the All India United Democratic Front in Assam and a few Kerala Muslim entrepreneurs who have been benefited from the Gulf economy and 'have adopted the business and labour practices of global capitalism.'[7] Similarly, Shahrukh Khan, the founder of Red Chillies Entertainment along with several Muslim film stars and sports personalities belong to the upper class elite Indian Muslims. There are also several traditional Muslim merchants and traders in many small towns of India.[8]

The successful Muslim businessmen in India seem to come from the medium-sized capitalist families of Gujarati Muslims including Azim Premji (a Khoja Muslim), Habil Khorakiwala (a Dawoodi.Bohra Muslim) and Yusuf Hamied (a Kutchchi Muslim). As Aakar Patel notes:

> [B]ecause few Indian Muslims are converted from trading castes, they are not particularly good at business...The Indian exception is the Shia from Gujarat. Though it is a tiny community, perhaps no more than a half a million people, it totally dominates India's other 160 million Muslims in matters of business. So it isn't so much religion that makes a difference so far as the ability to trade is concerned, but the linguistic community an Indian belongs to, and his caste...There are also Sunni businessmen in India, but few. The dominant community here is again Gujarati, like the Memons of Kutchch, who do business around the world. Bollywood's Muslim producers also tend to be Gujarati, like the Nadiawalas... I can only think of one non-Gujarati Sunni industrialist of some scale and that is Hakim Abdul Hameed of Hamdard.[9]

However, there is no denying the fact that the Muslims are grossly under-represented amongst India's capitalist elite. Out of 1365 member companies constituting the Indian Merchants' Chamber of Bombay in the 1980s, Muslims owned some 4%, and in 1988, no Muslim-owned company featured in the top 100 corporate companies. Of the 2832 industrial units listed for monitoring in the 1990s by the Centre for Monitoring the Indian Economy, only 4 (0.0014%) were owned by Muslims. Despite the entry of new entrepreneurs, including Muslim women, and the fact that Muslims head some of the most successful and dynamic IT corporates, these are still exceptions that prove the rule.[10] One survey found just over 1% of corporate executives to be Muslims.[11] Such a situation has not changed drastically even during the period of the economic reforms of the last two decades. A glimpse of the composition of the board of directors of Indian companies listed in the national stock exchange shows a negligible proportion of Muslim board members among the corporate class in India. In a recent empirical study of the caste diversity of Indian corporate boards of the thousand top Indian companies—accounting for 80% of market capitalization of all companies listed in the major stock indices in India—shows that Indian corporate boards continue to remain "old boys' clubs" based on caste affiliation rather than on other considerations (like merit or experience).[12] The same study shows that an overwhelming majority (92.6%) of Indian corporate board members are 'forward castes' comprising Brahmins (44.6%), Vaishyas (46%), Kshatriyas (0.5%) and Syrian Christians (1.5%). On the other hand, OBCs and SC/STs account for a mere 3.8% and 3.5% respectively of the total number of Indian corporate board members.[13]

On the other hand, the presence of big landlords among Indian Muslims is also rare. The partition led to the migration of Muslim elites to the then West and East Pakistan leaving behind the majority of poor Indian Muslims. The state-enforced abolition of *zamindari* in 1952 obliterated even the minuscule number of *ashraf* elites: the absentee landowning class formed by a few traditional aristocratic Muslim families. Only a minority among the educated landowning elite, like a few in Hyderabad, Mysore and Uttar Pradesh could remain near the seats of power, obtain employment and a new status, often by successful control over their land through renting and letting. Now, even if there are a few Muslim landlords, the 'ascendancy in the relative power of the corporate capitalist class compared to the landed elites'[14] in a neo-liberal regime has weakened the latter to influence major macro-level policy-making. Thus, even a cursory glance at the living conditions of the Muslim community in India unravels the social reality of the Muslims as a socio-economically marginalized community. The Muslim political elites are almost negligible, as Muslims do not provide the economic and political leadership in the national mainstream with gross under-representation of Muslims in various legislatures of the states and at the centre.[15]

The socio-economic background of Indian Muslims disables them from getting certain rights and benefits due to their unorganized status as casual workers, among the small and landless peasants in some parts of rural India, and as a self-employed group in both urban and rural sectors.[16] On the other hand, their educational backwardness hinders them from upward social mobility in getting access to certain infrastructural benefits from the state. This form of dual hindrances is again supplemented by the communal problem which makes things worse for the Indian Muslims. All these only make us think that the Muslim question in India can be addressed from the vantage point of socio-economic deprivation albeit with some peculiarities and specificities of its own.[17] In an overall analysis, as informed by several government reports like the Sachar and Arjun Sengupta Report on one hand and academic literature on the other, one can hardly argue that Indian Muslims constitute a significant section of India's ruling classes or even form a significant section of the middle classes. Thus, Indian Muslims are *heterogeneous* in terms of language, regional affiliations, culture,[18] and caste[19] but relatively *homogeneous* by the parameters of socio-economic profile (largely concentrated in the informal sector workforce), educational backwardness and common faith in Islamic religion. Now, once Foreign Direct Investment (FDI) in retail is being implemented, it will further dampen the livelihood prospects of small traders, petty shopkeepers, petty producers, casual workers in the tobacco industry, tailors, transport workers and artisans—the major occupational groups among the Indian Muslims.[20]

Apart from educational backwardness, poor health infrastructures in Muslim localities, socio-economic deprivation in terms of income, employment, assets, and the lack of credit opportunities for the Muslim youth as reported by the Sachar Committee and other academic works, the Muslim community in India also faces several forms of discrimination. An empirical research based on surveys and interviews of Muslim ex-mill workers in present-day Mumbai reveals how the feeling of *karahiyat*[an Urdu term for nausea, disgust, hate, etc.] combined with suspicion of terrorism and underworld mafia, creates barriers for employment opportunities of Muslims in the city.[21] Moreover, in Mumbai, about 70% of the Muslim population feels discriminated in the public sector while in the private sector, 18% Muslims feel discriminated apart from the Muslim localities being severely underserved by both private and public sector banks and repeated denials of loans to Muslim families by the banks.[22] The fear of communal violence impedes Muslims from choosing their residence in non-Muslim localities in Mumbai. To add to this, the spiralling property prices hinder Muslims from opting for separate flats for each family unit; thus forcing them to reside in overcrowded rooms and houses within a joint family.[23] Even in Kolkata, a city known for its secular credentials and cosmopolitanism, Muslims are marginalized in their urban slums with limited educational and employment opportunities, poor physical infrastructure in Muslim localities and living in abject poverty with added victimization of innocent Muslim youths in false cases of alleged terrorist activities.[24]

The deep prejudice of the police and the media against Muslims in suspecting this minority community as potential terrorists remains.[25] The overrepresentation of Muslims in jails[26] reveals a clear link between the criminal justice system and the discrimination and marginalization faced by the Muslim minorities in India.[27] Indian Muslims also face social exclusion, ghettoization, biased stigmatization, housing distress, and violence from both the state and non-state actors not only during communal riots but also in other situations in their everyday lives.[28] Except Kozhikode in Kerala, Muslims face almost the same kinds of problems in most Indian cities such as ghettoization due to perpetual denial of housing in non-Muslim localities, anxieties of communal violence and poor infrastructure in Muslim localities.[29] Then there are specific problems of Muslim women who are relatively more deprived in socio-economic terms than Muslim men owing to structural and institutionalized forms of inequality and discrimination.[30] Moreover, Muslim women in India also face special disadvantages, disparities and disempowerment due to several conservative and patriarchal provisions under the Muslim Personal Law.[31] The fact that Indian Muslims by and large do not own the major means of production, apart from being persecuted by majoritarian communalism, and facing a number of disadvantages, makes the community a natural ally of the Left. However, merely such objective conditions do not necessarily ensure political mobilization of the Muslim minorities behind the Left wing project.

The Muslim Question: Queries for the Indian Left

In this respect, the queries and tasks before the Left in dealing with the Muslim question in India are twofold. First, the Left has to theoretically deal with the Muslim question not only from a class perspective but also in order to make a chain of equivalence between class and Muslim identity. Secondly, it has to grapple with the specifics of pragmatic politics in mobilizing the Muslim minorities behind a cluster of democratic demands that are both particular in nature, having traction to a particular identity group like Muslims, Dalits, and Tribals, as well as to articulate a more general universalist agenda that can rally the Indian people at large. Let us first deal with the first challenge before the Left in the realm of theoretical articulation.

Arguably, there is wide agreement that the Left wing political project in contemporary India is in crisis. Issues like caste, minorities, gender and environment have emerged to inform and shape the political and policy-making discourses in the country. Accepting and acknowledging such relevant issues by the Left requires a reformulation of the older versions of the socialist ideal. In this respect, an extension and deepening of the democratic project needs to be foregrounded by the Left. However, there are serious disagreements on the theoretical and political strategy that need to be adopted by the Left to carry out such a task. Some prefer to prioritize 'class struggles' over any other forms of 'non-class struggles'. On the other hand, some are more interested in focusing on identity-based 'non-class struggles'. In the terminology of political philosophy, we can summarize that although both are concerned with an emancipatory project for particular constituencies like the workers (class) or marginalized identity groups (Dalits, Tribals, Muslims, Women, etc), the focus on 'class struggles' is anchored around the ideas of *distributive justice* and *equality*. However, those who argue for struggles of marginalized groups are more concerned with *social justice* and *identity*. In such cases, as Nancy Fraser argues, we encounter the 'either/or choice: redistribution or recognition? Class politics or identity politics? Multiculturalism or social democracy?'[32] However, such decoupling of cultural politics from social politics, of the politics of difference from the politics of equality, of the philosophical idea of egalitarian distribution from the politics of recognition is a 'false antithesis'. As Fraser correctly argues, redistribution and recognition converge together despite their divergent philosophical provenances.[33] The argument for social justice and identity not only asks for recognition of various democratic demands of marginalized groups but also calls for equal opportunity. In this respect, the idea of equality is expressed in the social justice discourse in terms of 'equal recognition', 'equal opportunity' and 'equal treatment'. Thus, the apparent point of departure between the two schools of justice and the apparent distinction between *equality* on the one hand, and *diversity* and *difference* on the other, is not a fundamental distinction. The challenge of the Left in this regard is to initiate and establish a dialogue between these two philosophical positions.

Here we can ask a pertinent question: can *difference* and 'identities' commensurate with the project of *equality*, evidently one of the cherished core principles of the Left? Here, the argument of a noted political theorist, Ernesto Laclau holds some merit:

> (T)he proliferation of differences is the precondition for the expansion of the logic of equality. To say that two things are

> equal—i.e. equivalent to each other in some respects—presupposes that they are different from each other in some other respects (otherwise there would be no equality but identity). In the political field equality is a type of discourse which tries to deal with differences; it is a way of organizing them.[34]

Similarly, in the Indian context, Dalits, Tribals, Muslims and Women have *different* identities, but they can be equivalent in terms of say, conditions of poverty, oppression, exploitation, deprivation, discrimination, exclusion, etc and furthermore negatively affected by the neo-liberal policy regime. Thus, their 'enemy' is also common, namely 'neo-liberalism'. The identification of the 'enemy' creates conditions of possibilities for a further equivalential bond between these marginalized groups to come together to emerge as the collective political actor of the 'people' to fight the antagonistic frontier of neo-liberalism. But how can such a construction of the 'people' be made at the level of political praxis? In this respect, an insightful example given by Laclau is impressive:

> In a situation of extreme oppression—the Tsarist regime, for instance—workers start a strike demanding higher wages. The demand is a particular one, but in the context of that repressive regime it is going to be seen as an anti-system activity. So the meaning of that demand is going to be split, from the very beginning, between its own particularity and a more universal dimension. It is this potentially more universal dimension that can inspire struggles for different demands in other sectors—students for the relaxation of discipline in educational establishments, liberal politicians for freedom of the press, and so on. Each of these demands is, in its particularity, unrelated to the others; what unites them is that they constitute between themselves a chain of equivalences in so far as all of them are bearers of an anti-system meaning. The presence of a frontier separating the oppressive regime from the rest of society is the very condition of the universalization of the demands via equivalences (in Marx's words: a social sector has to become a general 'crime' for the aims of society as a whole to emerge).[35]

So far, the Left has failed to understand that both 'identity' and 'identity formation', related to socio-political, cultural and psychological processes, are important political categories without which any politics is impossible. In fact, the 'class identity' of a person is revealed by his/her specific membership to a particular class like that of a worker, peasant, capitalist or feudal landlord. But the process of *identification* of that particular person whether (s)he is a Dalit, Tribal, Muslim, worker, peasant, capitalist, feudal, Punjabi, Indian, etc depends both on the outside agency (how 'others' identify him/her) and the inside agency (how s/he is identifying herself/himself, how s/he is asserting/emphasizing his/her identity, how s/he wants to be identified). As philosopher Akeel Bilgrami argues, there are both 'objective' and 'subjective' identities where '[y]our subjective identity is [that which] you conceive yourself to be, whereas your objective identity is how you might be viewed independently of how you see yourself. In other words, your objective identity is who you are in the light of certain biological or social facts about you.'[36] The psychoanalytic category of 'identification' in the making of identities[37] is also important in this regard and identity construction is definitely a hegemonic socio-political and cultural construct; something which the Indian Left has traditionally overlooked. Moreover, the Indian Left has also failed to understand that the marginalized and excluded groups like the Dalits, Tribals, women, and Muslims constitute the overwhelming majority of the working classes and the peasantry as there is a significant overlap between 'marginalized group identities' and '(working) class identities'.

A Plea for Leftwing Populism: Towards a Radical Democratic Politics in India

In the concrete context of India, the Left might reformulate the concept of 'people' and 'people's democratic front' in order to mobilize/rally different particularist groups by articulating different particularist demands. In this respect, the term 'people' can be theoretically used in a Laclauian sense that is different from the usual meaning in the dominant political discourses that equate it with the 'population' as a whole. As Laclau incisively points out, 'traditional terminology—which has been translated into common language—makes this difference clear: the people can be conceived as *populus*, the body of all citizens;

or as *plebs*, the underprivileged.'[38] Laclau's further clarification regarding 'people' and 'populism' conceptually differs from the usual meaning in the dominant political discourses: "in order to be the 'people' of populism,...we need a *plebs* who claims to be the only legitimate *populus*—that is, a partiality which wants to function as the totality of the community."[39] This is because those sections of the population who are responsible for the underprivileged conditions of the *plebs* cannot be a legitimate part of the same community ('people' in this case) since the *plebs* are in an antagonistic relationship with a frontier made up by the rest of the population which are part of the power bloc and thus the chasm between them is 'irretrievable'.[40]

Thus, the Left also needs to make an equivalential relation among varied particularist demands with a popular agenda of transforming the current neo-liberal regime, whose victims are none other than the working class, peasants, Dalits, Tribals, Muslims and Women—all those who have a plebian and underprivileged status and are negatively affected by the neo-liberal power bloc. Thus, several class and non-class oriented demands of particular marginalized sections of the society might be articulated in Left wing political discourses with a radical democratic strategy of Left wing populism in order to fight out neo-liberalism. Therefore, regarding the future of emancipatory politics of the Indian Left, there could be a normative ethico-political project, implicit in the radical democratic strategy of Left wing populism to achieve *normative* ideals of 'justice' and 'liberation' from the oppressive neo-liberal regime.

In Left wing political discourses, it might be helpful to see the terms 'popular' and 'populism' in the same sense as Laclau has used in his several evocative works. To summarize: *it is a hegemonic formation of the underdogs constructed through an equivalential articulation of various particularist demands challenging an antagonistic frontier of the power bloc.* As Laclau observes "in the case of populism: a frontier of exclusion divides society into two camps. The 'people', in that case, is something less than the totality of the members of the community: it is a partial component which nevertheless aspires to be conceived as the only legitimate totality."[41] Thus 'populist claims', 'populism' or 'popular demands' in Left wing political discourses need not necessarily be used pejoratively as often used in dominant political discourses. Rather 'populism' should be regarded as a *strategy of political mobilization*. We can further elaborate by saying that today Left wing populism as an effective strategy of political mobilization might be an important political task of the Left, particularly in the wake of the current crisis of the Indian Left, reflected in the electoral debacle in its own citadels. The question that still haunts is: Is 'populism' always necessary in a world of globalized capitalism? Laclau gives an insightful answer to this question:

> Capitalist development creates many others: ecological crises, imbalances between different sectors of the economy, imperialist exploitation, etc. In that case, the subjects of an 'anti-capitalist' struggle are many and cannot be reduced to a category as simple as that of 'class'. We are going to have a plurality of struggles. Struggles in our society tend to proliferate the more we move into a globalized era, but they are less and less 'class' struggles.[42]

In contemporary India, the Left has clearly and correctly identified the current neo-liberal regime as the prime enemy of the Indian people. The party programmes of major communist parties in India also have a political imaginary of building a 'people's democratic state' followed by a 'people's democratic revolution'. For this purpose, it has also correctly identified the need to build a 'people's democratic front' (PDF). The communists also acknowledge the necessary struggle of Dalits, Tribals, women and Muslims, but the concept of the 'people' and the 'people's democratic front' in the communist party programmes, is essentially *class defined*. That is to say, who would be part of PDF is essentially recognized by the kind of 'class identity' a person is identified with.

Theoretically speaking, the Indian Left is struggling with its own theoretical contradictions between choosing either the working class as the universal emancipatory class, or the 'people' as a universal political actor. That is to say, the Left lacks clarity on the issue of who would lead the politics of emancipation. This is precisely because of its *emphasis on the centrality of the working class* and the *working class party playing the role of a vanguard*. Therefore, the Left's contradiction can be conceptualized as the contradiction of non-identification and misconstruction of the universal emancipatory political actor, namely the 'people'. In this connection, the basic questions that the Left has to theoretically resolve are the following: in an era of various particularist struggles, can the working class *alone* become the universal political class which can represent and articulate the voices of other marginalized and oppressed sections of the population? Can we say that the 'people', in the Indian context, is a much broader and comprehensive political category, and an *inclusive collective political actor* which can encompass varied plebeian and underprivileged groups? Can we argue that the working class itself has become a form of particularism like other marginalized groups such as the peasantry, Dalits, Tribals, Muslims and women?

Since the collective political actor called 'people' is a result of an equivalential bond between several identities which are plebian in character, it can accommodate both class and non-class particularist identities into its Universalist construct. In this context, Simon Critchley and Oliver Marchart's summary of Laclau's vision of constructing the universal: 'political alliances had to be constructed not along class lines but *beyond* class lines in a constant effort to hegemonize a larger universal task'[43], holds merit. Therefore, the current task of the Indian Left might be to *reconceptualize* the notion of the *people* and in this sense, *people's struggles, by* constructing a radical democratic alternative. This might perhaps help the Left's cherished political programme of *people's democracy* as the goal of Indian revolution where the discursive appeal of the *people would* be *inclusive* in its form and content. The *inclusion* of Dalits, Tribals, women, and Muslims into the Leftist notion of the *people*, both in its theoretical premise and the practical performance of making an equivalential chain between the particularist demands of varied marginalized groups, might be useful for an optimistic political future of Left wing populism. However, such an emancipatory project of Left wing populism has to also be complemented by protracted militant extra-parliamentary struggles of the Left.

Now, let us focus on the specifics of pragmatic politics that the Left must concentrate on in order to mobilize the Muslims behind its political project. First, in a neo-liberal regime when the public sector vanishes and the organized working class shrinks, the political system still tries to address the issues of exclusion, deprivation and backwardness of marginalized groups through varied forms of affirmative action and *reservation* in education and jobs. In the case of Muslims too, *affirmative action* and reservation has often been repeated within policy debates in neo-liberal India as in the recommendations of the Sachar Report and the Ranganath Mishra Commission Report. Now, the public sector and the organized working class have been the backbone of traditional Left wing mobilizations. Once, these two sites of the Left bastion crumble, the Left has to invent new ways of organizing the unorganized or informal sector workforce. Organizing the informal sector labour force is also crucial for mobilizing the Muslims since the community is largely concentrated in the unorganized sector. Due to the reservation of Hindu SCs and OBCs in the public sector, the private sector is much more attractive for the Muslim youth. As a result, the chance of getting influenced by Left trade unions in the public sector is relatively less for Indian Muslims.

Secondly, the policy of affirmative action including reservation is only a *relief* than a *transformative change* in the affairs of excluded groups. The *normative position* of a progressive politics cannot afford to argue against the policy of affirmative action. Rather, it can only evoke the *limits* of affirmative action that perfectly abide with the negotiated terms of the existing political system. Thus, affirmative action can benefit, empower and give relief to certain sections of the population but until and unless an alternative society is built around the normative ideals of equality and distributive justice, the *emancipation* of the people would only be restricted to a utopian idea.[44] Even if positive discrimination continues, the simultaneous persistence of the neoliberal regime in India would cause havoc for the people. The nature of contemporary neo-liberalism in India marked by a job-loss and jobless growth trajectory, along with income inequality and forced displacement, inexorably worsens the living conditions of the Indian people including an overwhelming majority of Indian Muslims.

Therefore, any fundamental resolution of the socio-economic deprivation of any particular marginalized identity group like Muslims, Dalits, Tribals, and women cannot just rely on social justice politics that would argue the case for such groups in and around affirmative action and reservation. But in order to address the socio-economic backwardness of these marginalized groups, one has to think about the question of distributive justice in a possible post-neoliberal order. This is why the specific politics of *particularist demands* for and around affirmative action, and the fulfilment of the same, are nothing short of a politics of *appropriation* and *accommodation* by the power bloc in order to close down the possibility of a politics of radical alternative that seeks to alter the power relations of the prevalent society in favour of the people with a popular demand of challenging an existing political system. However, at the same time, the Left also needs to formally address various grievances of Muslim minorities and *recognize* specific problems of Indian Muslims that were noted in the first section of this essay apart from foregrounding its oppositional politics to neo-liberalism.

Finally, the Left has to deal with the specifics of political leadership of the Muslim community. Since Indian Muslims lack a progressive political leadership, it is the historic task of the Left to provide that political leadership in directly addressing the socio-economic issues of the Muslim community. If class agenda is the cornerstone of Marxist politics then in the present context, a future of Marxist politics cannot be imagined without addressing the class aspects of marginalized groups. Both the Left as a political group and the Indian Muslims as a 'community' need to rethink a possible political solidarity among them while forging out an alliance based on the common interests of the Left movement on one hand, and the Muslims as a deprived socio-economic group on the other. The Left movement also needs serious introspection about its attitude towards Muslim minorities, especially in making an in-depth analysis of the contemporary Muslim situation and understanding the genesis of Indian Muslims and its peculiar minority psyche. For these initiatives, the Left has to continuously engage and dialogue with members of the Muslim community on a daily basis at a very local level of its political operation. After all, political mobilization of the Muslims behind a progressive Left movement cannot be possible with merely focusing on token representational politics that many political parties in India practice, whose strategy is to woo Muslim support by promoting a selective Muslim leadership in its organization and fielding Muslim candidates in elections. However, this is not to discard the issue of representation. For a fundamental resolution of the socio-economic and political problems of various marginalized groups including the Muslim minorities, and for an effective and sustained political mobilization from those groups, the Left has to surpass representational politics and carry forward the agenda of both social justice and distributive justice apart from defending the strategic vision of transcending the neo-liberal status quo.

In this respect, a progressive politics of the Left has to offer something positive and better to the marginalized groups than the existing political parties in India. Thus, the *political appeal of the Left movement should be constructed in such a manner that various marginalized groups, by and large could identify with that political project against the common antagonistic frontier of neoliberalism*. On the other hand, Indian Muslims also need to understand that only by greater participation in the Left movement can they address the socio-economic problems of the community since Left politics prioritizes the interests of the working people apart from negating the oppressive and exploitative policies of neo-liberal power bloc. The emancipation of the Indian people from the clutches of neo-liberal injustices can be only possible if there is united opposition from the heterogeneous sectors of the Indian people, including the overwhelming majority of Indian Muslims, to transcend the contemporary phase of neo-liberal capitalism for a relatively just order in a possible people's democracy. In order to realize such a political vision, the project of Left wing populism with a radical democratic politics of making equivalential relations with various marginalized sectors of the population namely, workers, peasants, Dalits, Tribals, women and Muslims is more relevant than ever. Such a project seeks to organize a united people's resistance against all forms of subordination, against all dominant social formations, and against the multifarious structures of power. Such a task is certainly difficult to pursue. It has to essentially be a collective effort. Let us hope that we will be able to achieve this objective.

NOTES AND REFERENCES

1. Ernesto Laclau, 'Constructing Universality', in Judith Butler, Ernesto Laclau and Slavoj Žižek, *Contingency, Hegemony, Universality: Contemporary Dialogues on the Left* (London: Verso, 2000), p. 306.
2. Ernesto Laclau and Chantal Mouffe, 'Preface to the Second Edition' of *Hegemony and Socialist Strategy: Towards a Radical Democratic Politics* [1985] (London: Verso, 2001), pp. xviii-xix.
3. Arjun Sengupta, K.P. Kannan, G. Raveendran, 'India's Common People: Who Are They, How Many Are They and How Do They Live?', *Economic and Political Weekly* (March 15, 2008), pp. 49-63.
4. Ibid., pp. 51-52.
5. Ibid., pp. 58-59.
6. For some successful business companies owned by Muslims, see Harish Damodaran, *India's New Capitalists: Caste, Business, and Industry in a Modern Nation* (Delhi: Permanent Black and New India Foundation, 2008), pp. 302-306.
7. Filippo Osella and Caroline Osella, 'Muslim Entrepreneurs between India and the Gulf', *ISIM Review*, No. 19 (Spring 2007), pp. 8-9; Filippo Osella and Caroline Osella, 'Muslim Entrepreneurs in Public Life between India and the Gulf: Making Good and Doing Good', *Journal of the Royal Anthropological Institute*, Vol. 15, Issue Supplement 1, Special Issue: *Islam, Politics, Anthropology* (May 2009), pp. 202-221.
8. Mattison Mines, *Muslim Merchants: The Economic Behaviour of an Indian Muslim Community* (New Delhi: Shri Ram Centre for Industrial Relations and Human Resources, 1972); S.M. Akram Rizvi, 'Kinship and Industry Among Muslim Karkhanders in New Delhi' in Imtiaz Ahmad (ed.), *Family Kinship and Marriage Among Muslims in India* (New Delhi: Manohar, 1976); Elizabeth A. Mann, *Boundaries and Identities: Muslims, Work and Status in*

Aligarh (New Delhi: Sage, 1992); Omar Khalidi, *Muslims in Indian Economy* (Delhi: Three Essays Collective, 2006); Asghar Ali Engineer, 'Muslim Middle Class and its Role', *Secular Perspective* (May 16-31, 2001).

9. Aakar Patel, 'The Muslim Businessmen of India', *DNA* (May 16, 2010).
10. Barbara Hariss-White, *India Working: Essays on Society and Economy* (Cambridge: Cambridge University Press, 2004), pp. 142-143.
11. S. Goyal, 'Social Background of Indian Corporate Executives' in Francine R. Frankel and M.S.A. Rao (eds.), *Dominance and State Power in Modern India*, Vol. II (New Delhi: Oxford University Press, 1990), pp. 535-544.
12. D. Ajit, Han Donker and Ravi Saxena, 'Corporate Boards in India: Blocked by Caste?', *Economic and Political Weekly*, Vol. 47, No. 31 (August 11, 2012), pp. 39-43.
13. Ibid., p. 41.
14. Partha Chatterjee, *Lineages of Political Society: Studies in Postcolonial Democracy* (Ranikhet: Permanent Plack, 2011), p. 218.
15. Iqbal A. Ansari, *Political Representation of Muslims in India: 1952-2004* (New Delhi: Manak, 2006).
16. Maidul Islam, 'Mapping Socio-Economic Status of Indian Muslims: A Factual Analysis', Working Paper Series I, Vol. 1, No. 2 (2009) published by the Programme for the Study of Discrimination and Exclusion, School of Social Sciences, Jawaharlal Nehru University, New Delhi.
17. Maidul Islam, 'Posing the Muslim Question in India: A Leftwing Perspective', *Journal of Humanities and Social Sciences*, Issue 6 (September 2009), pp. 66-79.
18. Imtiaz Ahmad, *Family, Kinship and Marriage Among Muslims in India* (Delhi: Manohar, 1976); Imtiaz Ahmad, *Ritual and Religion Among Muslims in India* (New Delhi: Manohar, 1981).
19. Imtiaz Ahmad (ed.), *Caste and Social Stratification Among Muslims in India* (Delhi: Manohar, 1973); Sachar Report also recognizes three principal castes of *Ashrafs* (Muslim upper castes), *Ajlafs* (Muslim OBCs) and *Arzals* (Muslim SCs with just 1% of total Muslim population in India). See *Sachar Report*, pp. 186-216.
20. *Sachar Report*, p. 103, pp. 329-341.
21. Sumeet Mhaskar, 'Indian Muslims in a Global City: Socio-Political Effects on Economic Preferences in Contemporary Mumbai', MMG Working Paper, 13-04 (Göttingen: Max Planck Institute for the Study of Religious and Ethnic Diversity, 2013).

22. Ranu Jain and Abdul Shaban, 'Socio-economic and Educational Status of Muslims in Mumbai', *Report Submitted to Maharashtra State Minorities Commission* (Mumbai: Government of Maharashtra, 2009).
23. Abdul Shaban, *Mumbai: Political Economy of Crime and Space* (New Delhi: Orient BlackSwan and TISS, 2010), p. 41.
24. Jeremy Seabrook and Imran Ahmed Siddiqui, *People without History: India's Muslim Ghettos* (New Delhi: Navayana, 2011).
25. Sharib Ali, 'Politics of Terror: The Mecca Masjid Blast Case', *Economic and Political Weekly*, Vol. 48, No. 34 (August 24, 2013), pp. 36-46; EPW Editorials, 'Blaming Muslims', *Economic and Political Weekly* (March 16, 2013); "'Witches' Brew in Hyderabad", *Economic and Political Weekly* (December 1, 2012); 'Fifteen Minutes of Infamy', *Economic and Political Weekly*, (January 19, 2013).
26. Seema Chisti, 'The Missing Muslim: Part-III', *Indian Express*, October 29, 2006.
27. Vijay Raghavan and Roshni Nair, 'Over-Representation of Muslims: The Prisons of Maharashtra', *Economic and Political Weekly*, Vol. 48, No. 11 (March 16, 2013), pp. 12-17.
28. Abdul Shaban (ed.), *Lives of Muslims in India: Politics, Exclusion and Violence* (New Delhi: Routledge, 2012) and Abdul Shaban and Saqib Khan (eds.), *Muslims in Urban India: Development and Exclusion* (New Delhi: Concept Publishing, 2013).
29. Laurent Gayer and Christophe Jaffrelot (eds.), *Muslims in Indian Cities: Trajectories of Marginalisation* (New Delhi: Harper Collins, 2012).
30. Zoya Hasan and Ritu Menon, *Unequal Citizens: A Study of Muslim Women in India* (New Delhi: Oxford University Press, 2004); Zoya Hasan and Ritu Menon, *Educating Muslim Girls: A Comparison of Five Indian Cities* (New Delhi: Women Unlimited, 2005)
31. Zoya Hasan and Ritu Menon (eds.), *In a Minority: Essays on Muslim Women in India* (New Delhi: Oxford University Press, 2005); Hajira Kumar (ed.), *Status of Muslim Women in India* (Delhi: Aakar Books, 2002).
32. Nancy Fraser, 'Social Justice in the Age of Identity Politics: Redistribution, Recognition, and Participation', in Nancy Fraser and Axil Honneth, *Redistribution or Recognition? A Political-Philosophical Exchange* (London: Verso, 2003), p. 8.
33. Ibid., pp. 8-11.
34. Ernesto Laclau's Reply to Judith Butler: Butler and Laclau, 'The Uses of Equality' (Appendix I) in Simon Critchley and Oliver Marchart (eds.), *Laclau: A Critical Reader* (London: Routledge,

2004), p. 331.

35. Laclau, 'Constructing Universality', in Butler, Laclau and Žižek, *Contingency, Hegemony, Universality*, p. 302.
36. Akeel Bilgrami, "Notes Towards the Definition of 'Identity'," *Daedalus*, Vol. 135, No. 4, On Identity (Fall, 2006), p. 5.
37. Ernesto Laclau, 'Introduction', in Laclau (ed.), *The Making of Political Identities* (London: Verso, 1994), p. 3.
38. Ernesto Laclau, *On Populist Reason* (London: Verso, 2005), p. 81.
39. Ibid.
40. Ibid., p. 86.
41. Ibid., p. 81.
42. Ernesto Laclau, 'Ideology and Post-Marxism', *Journal of Political Ideologies*, Vol. 11, No. 2 (June 2006), p. 112.
43. Simon Critchley and Oliver Marchart, 'Introduction', in Critchley and Marchart (eds.), *Laclau: A Critical Reader*, p. 2.
44. Maidul Islam, 'Rethinking the Muslim Question in Post-Colonial India', *Social Scientist*, Vol. 40, Nos. 7-8 (July-August 2012), pp. 61-84.

6

Reimagining Democracy: Radicalizing *Dialogue* and *Dissent* as an Organizational Practice within the Indian Left

Ravi Kumar

When the Left Front lost assembly elections in West Bengal after a long rule of 34 years while the bourgeois press as usual portrayed it as "the fall of communism" there was a sense of despair among the parliamentary Left. The anti-parliamentary politics had already committed a blunder by its alliance with Mamata Bannerjee. This despair was visible in different forums but the Communist Party of India (Marxist), which lost the elections admitted through its Central Committee Resolution of June 11-12, 20011 that

> The organisational aspect is also an important factor. The image of the Party amongst the people has been dented by manifestations of highhandedness, bureaucratism and refusal to hear the views of the people (emphasis mine). The existence of corruption and wrong-doing among a small strata of Party leaders and cadres due to the corrosive influence of being a "ruling party" and running the government for a prolonged period was also resented by the people. All these have affected the Party in the elections.
>
> The erosion of support amongst the working class and the rural and urban poor indicates the failing to consistently take up the class issues. The independent role of the Party and the mass organisations was impaired due to the dependence on the administration (CPI(M), 2011, p. 4).

The above realization indicates not only towards an increasing substitution of party by the state (through dependence on the administration) but also that the workings of the party had developed tendencies of undemocratic nature when it came to its interaction with the masses. This obviously raises questions about how would one place the idea of democracy within the context of Left politics.

The question of democracy within party and between party and the masses has been a long debated one. We had debates within the Indian context and some of them not long ago (Alam, 2009; Karat, 2010; Purkayastha, 2010).However, thesedebates do not develop as inner-party ideological struggles in a way that would supplement the larger revolutionary politics. In many cases, in fact, it gets reduced to branding of cadres/leaders as 'trotskyites' or 'Maoists' or 'Orthodoxists' and so on. This symbolizes the failure of the Left so far as developing a democratic culture of dialogue and dissent is concerned. In fact, more than that it indicates towards absence of innovation within the Left politics when it comes to imagine/reimagine the idea of democracy itself from a working class politics. And this absence creates a vacuum at the level of ideas and, hence, at practice not allowing it to go beyond the notion of liberal bourgeois order. The liberal bourgeois notion of democracy for obvious reasons does not allow possibilities for challenging its own existence, which by its very nature is undemocratic and limiting. It is based on a rule of law that is created through forms and content that maintains the status quo of the system (with changes, if and when they happen, that do not challenge the basic premise of the system). Hence, as a term it is used not only in a relative sense but also to provide a colourful cloak to the hideous rule of capital. For instance, the brutal murder of tribals in Chhattisgarh by the police forces becomes a 'collateral damage' for the torchbearers of democracy whereas the murder of a few Congress leaders in the same state becomes the 'murder of democracy'. It, as a liberal bourgeois concept, primarily refers to a way of governance where "socio-economic inequality and exploitation coexist with civic freedom and equality" (Wood, 2000, p.201).In other words, there is a "separation of civic status and class position" under capitalism, where while capitalism coexists with formal democracy "civic equality does not directly affect class inequality" (Wood, 2000, p. 201). By defining and operationalising democracy this way it becomes an ethos, a way of life to be imagined within contexts of exploitation and deprivation. The elaborate system that is created by thisform of democracy creates an illusion of giving it a look of the best possible systemic framework available and we all repose our faith in it and its instruments in different ways at different points of time.

Democracy as a Political System and as Everyday Structure of Life

It is important to make a distinction between democracy as a political system and asan everyday structure of our life though they intersect and act upon each other. By doing so one is confronted with the dilemma of whether we can repose faith in the form of democracy that we have or we have to listen to Marx when he says that

> We have seen... that the first step in the revolution by the working class is to raise the proletariat to the position of ruling class to win the battle of democracy (Marx and Engels, 2010, p. 26).

In a sense Marx is hinting at the fact that one cannot imagine democracy as a possibility within capitalism. It will be possible only when the rule of proletariat replaces the rule of capital. One of the reasons for this is the existence of private property, which sets in motion relationships, which are hierarchical and unequal.

This is emphasized by Engels when he writes that

> Democracy would be wholly valueless to the proletariat if it were not immediately used as a means for putting through measures directed against private property and ensuring the livelihood of the proletariat (Engels, *The Principles of Communism*, 1847).

This paper relates to democracy as a possibility and as a way of life that is based on the idea of *dialogue* and *dissent* and thereby becomes a tool of subversion and challenging the status quo. These two aspects can be seen acting dynamically within our everyday lives as well as organizations/parties. It creates a dynamic interface between masses as active subjects and the politics for systemic transformation (which is the end). This idea of locating democracy within the context of everyday life is distinguished from the ideas of democracy which has existed within the left formations though cannot be termed completely alien to the left political praxis.

The Left parties worked around the principle of Democratic Centralism, which is obviously a combination of Democracy and Centralism. Javeed Alam argues that while the concept of centralism was paid attention "the component of democracy was never, and has not been yet, systematically concretized, nor has it been given a clear definitional sense" (2009, p. 37). He furthers his argument by saying that

> By now it seems to me quite clear, that DC, in the way it stands, provides one such struc-tural condition for the throttling of democracy inside the CPs. In itself there may not be anything necessarily wrong with the principle—its working remains corrigible and can still be the basis for organising revolutionary activities in society—but the way it has come down historically, there is a serious imbalance in its internal features (2009, p. 37).

Karat (2010, p. 5) on the other hand argues about the significance of Democratic Centralism as an organizational principle within the Left. He writes that

> The exigencies of class politics require an organisation which is able to change the forms of struggle according to the prevailing situation. This requires a centralised party. Democratic centralism is best suited as the organizational principle for a party based on Marxism and class struggle. Class struggle is a collective act. Democratic centralism promotes collective decision making and collective activity; it allows for freedom of thought and unity in action.

He brings in the question of 'majority' versus the 'minority' and important it is to develop a collective functioning of a revolutionary party, which "requires going beyond the democratic method of decision-making by majority opinion to bind the entire collective into implementing that decision". The minority has to "abide by the majority and the individual to submit to the will of the collective" (Karat, 2010, p.5). It is difficult to disagree with this especially when one is talking of a revolutionary party and its role in a transcendental politics. However, what remains cryptic here is how to arrive at the 'majority opinion'.Use of ethnographic details become relevant here. In past there have been innumerable instances of conferences of mass organizations, where the majority present in the conference did not like what the Party proposed as the leadership but it is eventually forced as the will of collective whereas that is merely the will of the Party. The elections therefore do not remain democratic but rather an exercise in imposing the will of the Centre to the organization and the majority.

It is important to have an organization that would present an united voice of collective, however, that united voice has to be arrived at through debate, processes of *dialogue* and *dissent* and agreeing by majority rule to work towards transcending the rule of capital. Pluralities of voices cannot be restricted and ability and openness to experiment cannot be termed problematic at such a political juncture. Though elections at all levels represent a semblance of representative democracy but in actual terms the power of the Centre is so overwhelming that in the name of losing the cadres or to control 'deviation' the organizations over-centralize the operations.

This paper is an effort to critically examine the possibilities of exploring alternatives ways of democratizing the left organization politics within the country. Hence, it is located in the context of party/organization/politics of the left and the paper does not talk about democracy in context of bourgeois political forces assuming that they will not have democracy or notion of democracy that would contribute to the transcendence from capitalism.

To explain it further, the notion of democracy that the paper puts forth is based on the principles of dissent and dialogicity, as two primary principles that ruptures the possibilities of a hierarchised relationship that feeds not only on the vast mass of people not ready to organize on account of insecure life but also in absence of a movement/assertion that is rendered so because of the divisions within the workers and the misconceptions including that certain segments are not workers.

Dialogue and Dissent as Essentials of Democracy

This paper looks at the idea of *dialogue* and *dissent* as concepts that are not necessarily liberal bourgeois notions as many of us have come to believe but they can be reimagined as working class concepts that become effective tools in the struggle of emancipation.

What happens when one engages in *dialogue*. It implies a host of things and had wider ramifications. By agreeing to engage with the other it demolishes the idea of hierarchy and opens up new vistas for the involved parties to learn from each other. This process of learning may require some of the existing notions to be unlearnt while it may also in the process of engagement allow modification of opinions, views and understandings of the situation.

If one has to look at it in the context of movements what it does is that it initiates a relationship between the organizational structure, which historically evolved out of struggles, and the toiling masses. *Dialogue* continues to provide inputs to the organizations about the changes required in strategies of struggle. It also results in altering theoretical positions of the organisations. In other words, this process also presupposes that the struggle against rule of capital involving organizations and the masses are in continuous flux and open to changes. It is a historical process through which the party/organization becomes the leader of the movement. The right to lead is not bestowed by the God as religious sects think and propagate. These organizations are not permanent as the Indian Left has come to imagine its role and this has been shown by experiences of societies in different parts of the world. Marta Harnecker (2007) argues in the context of Latin America but something that suits the Indian context equally that the parties do not understand

> that being the vanguard is not something bestows upon itself but something that is earned through struggle and that there cannot be a vanguard without a rearguard.

> They certainly failed to understand the distinct Lenin established between the moment in which the party and the revolutionary organization is formed—during which the leadership cadres are rained—and the moment when it manages to acquire the authentic ability to lead class struggle... Each organization fought over the right to be called the most revolutionary, the most just, and all the accolades: what mattered most was the sect, the T-shirt, and not the revolution. That's how sectarianism arose and most parties fell prey to it (p. 50).

The moment the organization/party begins to think itselfas the vanguard of the working class struggle it develops rigid hierarchies and an ethos that is non-dialogic, mechanical and not open to criticisms. These tendencies generate an ethos that assumes of an all-powerful 'centre' within the organization, which is untouchable and over and above the vast mass of working class. It also allows for lesser and lesser critical space of engagement with the masses. The character of organization/ party is destroyed as it creates classes of 'knowledgeable' and 'non-knowledgeable' people. The Party leaders, however ignorant, become the pundits and the cadres appear as Dalits. The status gathered through various factors such as being members of Parliament, or members of the Central Committee, etc., defines the hierarchy that is there within the organization. Rosa Luxemburg (2005) while responding to Bernstein wrote that

> It is, therefore, in the interest of the proletarian mass of the Party to become acquainted, actively and in detail, with the present theoretical controversy with opportunism. As long as theoretical knowledge remains the privilege of a handful of "intellectuals" in the Party, it will face the danger of going astray. Only when the great mass of workers take in their own hands the keen and dependable weapons of scientific socialism will all the petty-bourgeois inclinations, all the opportunist currents, come to naught (p. 130).

She is concerned about the way organization/party is institutionalized with assumptions that certain people know/ understand the working class politics while the others do not. In fact, she argues that the whole distinction between the 'intellectuals' and 'non-intellectuals' within the party needs to be done away with. She, hence, writes

> No coarser insult, no baser defamation, can be thrown against the workers than the remark "Theoretical controversies are only for intellectuals". Lassalle once said: "Only when science and the workers, these opposed poles of society, become one will they crush in their arms of steel all obstacles to culture." The entire strength of the modern labour movement rests on theoretical knowledge (Luxemburg, 2005, p. 130).

This attitude leads to degeneration of the organization, which becomes a hurdle for the revolutionary politics. It acts against the principles of self-reflexivity, internal critique as well as alienates the masses. It creates mathadhishes (satraps) ignoring what Marx meant when talked of people as "not static" and "that the struggle for material needs can produce new people with new, 'radical' needs". Lebowitz (2003) clarifies this idea when he writes that

> Just as every activity of the worker alters her as the subject who enters into all activities, similarly the process in which workers struggle for themselves is also a process of production, a process of purposeful activity in which they produce themselves in an altered way. They develop new needs in struggle, an altered hierarchy of needs. Even though the needs that they attempt to satisfy do not in themselves go beyond capital, the very process of struggle is one of producing new people, of transforming them into people with a new conception of themselves—as subjects capable of altering their world (2003, p. 180).

Combining what Harnecker argues about vanguardism and what Lebowitz puts forward one finds the organization/party as situated in a dynamic context. The fixated, permanent existence of the party also becomes questionable and as has been shown by historical experiences. However, the Left politics in India is yet to come to terms with this. All of them assume that they need to be there at whatever cost, a cost that has largely detrimental political consequences for the working class politics. And in this process they forget that the organizational structure needs to demonstrate an ethos, which is dialogic.

The dynamic character of the production process produces

newer forms of labour relations as capital reinvents techniques/ ways of exploitation and surplus accumulation. Hence, the people (or the masses) do not remain static but their character also alters, many a times creating illusions of newer kind hampering the process of building a working class consciousness. In this situation it is important that the organization also reinvent itself and, one of the ways would be to enter into a dialogic relationship with the masses in order to bring the 'non-static people' and hence, the ever changing analysis of labour-capital relationship within the organisationsal fold. This has somehow evaded the organizational design of the Left.

Another ramification of a non-dialogic model of revolutionary politics is its inability to contribute to the sharpening of class contradictions by enlarging its political influence through combination of theory and practice. It becomes nothing more than an organization that whenever close to power draws support of people of different kind for the simple reason that it virtually becomes and acts as an instrument of the state. The ideological preparedness that strengthens the everyday struggle of massesno longer constitutes an important component of its politics. Therefore, the moment the organization gets out of state power the allegiance of people, which was never ideological, also shifts away from it.

It is a dilemma of the Left politics to reflect on the kind of relationship it envisages between the party/mass organisations and the state while in power. In absence of a critical reflection on this relationship it the dominant liberal bourgeois paradigm becomes a practice for it. Hence, it mistakes the bourgeois notion of community participation and decentralization to be a symbol of democracy and once implemented it becomes a insignia of the party. A critical reflection combined with dialogic ethos would allow democracy to be redefined in a different sense. It would separate the Left government from a liberal bourgeois government in the sense of its everyday operation. Hence, even when it holds state power it is in a sort of contestation with the bourgeois order. Simultaneously, it also keeps strengthening the mass base and the spirit for a larger battle ahead.

In absence of these distinction it was no surprise that overnight the allegiance of trade unions changed in the state of West Bengal when Trinamool Congress (TMC) came to power. The same trade unionists who were with the CPI(M) became TMC workers. In other words, the engagement of the CPI(M) kind of politics always lacked the element of a dialogic relationship with the masses. Either there was a difficulty discerning the two parties along their ideological understanding on issues or there was no difference at all. In any case, it would need a lot of explanation why this happened.

The same could be seen in the resistances across the state of West Bengal. If an organization ruled the state for 35 years it obviously enjoyed support in terms of vote among masses. If one probes the reasons behind its decimated electoral result to 40 seats in State Assembly from nearly 176 one would be compelled to look into the alienation of people from the party. The connect it had with the masses somewhere ruptured and that happened gradually and not suddenly. Where and why did the disconnect between the masses and organisations happen? Why did not the organization realize that the masses were not with them? And the party itself says that

> It is evident from the results that the trend against the Left Front which emerged partly in the panchayat election in 2008, continued in the Lok Sabha polls in 2009 and the 2010 municipal polls got further momentum in the Assembly elections. The people have voted determinedly for a change (CPI(M), 2011).

As an organization claiming to represent the working class politics it needed to probe deeper into the very functioning of the organization-mass linkage. The structure of an organization historically emerges due to the need to sustain the movements. This structure is also determined by the way the organizational politics imagines its role. In revolutionary struggles one may imagine the organizational structure as organized at two levels —at level of functioning within the party and at the level of interaction with outside bodies. At the level of functioning within the party the structures need not be vertically split, they should be organized horizontally. The horizontal organization allows each structural unit to engage with the other on different issues. It has not worked this way in the Indian Left politics largely. There is a vertical regime of organizational structuring which renders the village/panchayat/block level units 'powerless'. And this was reflected when I asked the CPI activists in the erstwhile Jehanabad district of Bihar as to why they do not initiate a dialogue with the 'centre' the response was that 'we act according to the circular that we get from the 'centre' or the state'. One may disagree with the idea of 'autonomy' of units but that disagreement largely emanates out of the insecurity of the organization to lose hold over its members and therefore bind them through rigid structures which replicate many other structures of the society that one is supposed to fight against.

Marta Harnecker (2007) argues in another spatial context that

> The vertical style of leadership—which translated into an attempt to lead from above, handing down to the rank and file lines of action drawn up by the political leadership—was common practice. The leadership cadres were the people who knew where to go, and therefore decisions about everything that was done were handed down ready-made from above. It was assumed that anything the leadership though was right, and therefore that the members simply had to carry out the instructions handed down. Such leaders took no trouble to convince people of the correctness of their proposals.
>
> Those who determined the line were the leadership cadres, and the tendency was to create mechanisms which allowed them to keep control in their hands by, in practice, denying access to new blood (p. 51).

What happens in the Nandigram or Singur does not merely happen because other organizations become more active but it also happens because the revolutionary politics was ill-prepared to engage with the masses for quite sometime on the questions of class struggle and issues central to labour-capital conflict.The absence of this engagement was reflected through nearly negligible organizational resistance put up by the CPI(M). A revolutionary working class resistance emerges strongly and fights at all costs if it is clear that the attacking party represents the rule of capital and would act against the interests of the workers.This happens when the organizational principle of dialogue is extended to the outside world and the party/ organisationsbegins to have a dialogue with the masses. The failure lay in the non-dialogic relationship that had become norm of the organizational politics of the Left. A sustained engagement on the issues would have meant that the organization would have got a sense of the issues that the area faced and would have developed terms of engagement with people accordingly.

The absence of a dialogic organizational form is generally absent because it contains within itself the possibilities of dissent. And dissent demands not only an engagement with the issue raised and with the people raising the issue but it contains seeds of challenging the power that has been created gradually with the few within the party. A new leadership might emerge through this process and hence, the old leadership will have to live with the new people and abjure the politics that they claimed to stand for. In other words, dissent, potentially, ruptures the processes that create and sustain a power centre and destabilize the possibility of an undemocratic organizational set up.

Once this aspect of organizational reality becomes part of everyday life of political activism it gets translated into the engagements with the masses as well. The ability to dialogue and accept the existence of a dissenting voice within the masses allows the revolutionary politics to create a relationship that transcends the limitations of 'lured connection'that people develop with the party holding state power. In other words, democratic functioning as an everyday practice of dialogue and dissent has a potential to further the revolutionary struggle rather than getting reduced to social democratic tendencies that get caught in the electoral battlefields and assume that they have contributed to revolutionary struggles.

The tragedy, however, is that there is a fear of dissent and this fear denies the possibility of sustaining the working class politics as a dynamic and vibrant practice representing the working class interests. By not allowing to dissent the organization impedes a robust working class imagination to transcend capitalism from evolving. It hampers the possibility of a counter-hegemonic idea to emerge because spaces of voicing a counter-point do not exist.

Today for the Left politics to exist it is important to reimagine the organizational politics in a drastically different way. It needs to radicalize the idea of dialogue and dissent, take it away from the bourgeois realm and turn it into a weapon of the working class politics rather than getting trapped in the liberal bourgeois imagination itself. It can be done and shall be done otherwise the social-democratisation of the Left in India won't stop at anytime in near future.This would also mean that the Left needs to get out of its endless amnesia that democracy is an impossibility under capitalism which flourishes on the principle of competition, private property and inequity of different kinds and therefore, unless socialism is build on the debris of capitalism one will have to wait for the new system to come into existence. Yes, when it comes to looking at democracy as a form of governance translated through the state power it cannot happen under capitalism but when it is about everyday life within the context of Left organization it is a possibility and that alternative can be built. Through conceptualizing and practicing democracy in everyday life of the party an alternative programmatic agenda that represents the working class aspirations has to be generated—by going among people, sharing with them and contesting theirs if they have anti-working class orientation as is the possibility. This would allow a process of working class *consciousness* to set in, make people ideologically committed and contest the rule of capital.

NOTES AND REFERENCES

CPI(M) (2011), *Review Report of the Assembly Elections* (Adopted by the Central Committee at its June 11-12, 2011 Meeting), available at http://www.cpim.org/documents/2011-June-election%20review.pdf (Accessed on January 10, 2013).

Ellen Meiksins Wood (2000), *Democracy Against Capitalism: Renewing Historical Capitalism* (Cambridge: Cambridge University Press) (Indian edition: Aakar Books).

Frederick Engels (1847), *The Principles of Communism*, available at https://www.marxists.org/archive/marx/works/1847/11/prin-com.htm (Accessed April 15, 2011)

Javeed Alam (September 19, 2009), 'Can Democratic Centralism Be Conducive to Democracy?', *Economic and Political Weekly*, Vol. XLIV, No. 38.

Karl Marx and Frederick Engels (2010/1848), *Manifesto of the Communist Party*, Marxist Internet Archive, available at http://www.marxists.org/archive/marx/works/download/pdf/Manifesto.pdf (Accessed on 10th March 2012).

Marta Harnecker (2007), *Rebuilding the Left* (London and New York: Zed Books).

Michael A. Lebowitz (2003, Second Edition), *Beyond Capital: Marx's Political Economy of the Working Class* (New York: Palgrave Macmillan).

Prabir Purkayastha (August 15, 2010), 'The 2009 Elections and the Challenges from the Left', *The Journal*, Vol. I, Centre for Policy Analysis.

Prakash Karat (January–March 2010), 'On Democratic Centralism', *The Marxist*, XXVI No. 1, pp. 3-20.

Rosa Luxemburg (2005), *Rosa Luxemburg Reader*, Hudis, Peter and Anderson, Kevin B. (eds.), (Kharagpur: Cornerstone Publications).

7

The Indian Left at a Time of Crisis

Prasenjit Bose

At a time when a crisis is gradually embroiling the Indian economy and polity, the mainstream Left in India appears to be in a state of decline. The crisis symptoms in India are quite similar to the ones afflicting neo-liberal regimes across the world: currency depreciation triggered by outflows of speculative finance capital, debt distress faced by the private corporates and the sovereign, deceleration in economic activities and persistently high inflation. As is always the case under capitalism, the burden of crisis is being shifted on to the working people by the ruling classes and the state. The worsening economic plight of the people has combined with mega-corruption scandals and obtuse governance to produce not only a credibility crisis for the Congress-led government of the day, but a crisis of legitimacy for the entire array of liberal democratic institutions in India.

Crises faced by neo-liberal regimes around the world in recent times have not necessarily led to the growth of the Left everywhere. But in Latin America, the recurrent crisis of the last decade of the 20th century did trigger a continental shift towards the Left in the past decade and a half. Radical Left governments were formed in Venezuela, Bolivia and Ecuador and more moderate Left governments came into being in Brazil, Argentina, Uruguay and Peru. In the backdrop of the sovereign debt crisis and austerity measures being implemented in Europe, the elections in Greece in 2012 also propelled a radical Left force from the margins to becoming the major national opposition. It is noteworthy that these recent success stories of the Left have all followed from big mass movements against neo-liberal regimes. It is in its inability to build consequential mass movements against the neo-liberal regime in India that the decline of the Indian Left needs to be primarily located. In the absence of an ascendant Left, the right-reactionary BJP, with an unapologetic fascist at its helm, is seeking to aggressively hegemonize the opposition space. The revival of the Left is an imperative to rein in and defeat the communal-fascist forces. Such revival, however, can happen only when the ideological-political reasons underlying the Left's decline are identified and addressed.

I

A major problem confronting the mainstream Left in India relates to its approach towards neo-liberal globalization and its impact on the economy and society. Since the initiation of neo-liberal economic reforms in India in the early 1990s, the Left has always adopted an oppositional approach towards it at the national level. The Left-affiliated trade unions have been at the forefront of working class strikes and protests against the government's economic policies. However, the resistance put up by the Left against these policies has mostly been defensive struggles, against privatization of public sector enterprises and deregulation of various sectors. Despite facing occasional resistance, the overall process of liberalization and deregulation has proceeded apace in India as in the rest of the world over the past two decades.

Big capital in India has been the main driver as well as the biggest beneficiary of the process of neo-liberal reforms. With their assets and wealth growing manifolds, the Indian corporates have emerged as one of the most powerful capitalist class within the developing countries. Given its global interests, the Indian corporates have also forged close links with international finance capital and have strategically allied with the big business class of the United States and its allies. The Indian state has also undergone a transformation from being a major player in the economy and regulator of economic activities to becoming a 'facilitator' for private capital, both domestic and foreign. This has resulted in fast-paced capitalist development in India with primitive accumulation of capital occurring on a large scale, through corporate expropriation of natural resources, cronyism and corruption. Such developments have posed serious challenges for the Left.

The programmatic understanding of the Left had evolved out of the freedom struggle and was shaped through the debates in the 1960s/1970s over the class character of the Indian state, the relationship between the Indian capitalist class and imperialism, the nature and extent of capitalist development in agriculture, etc. Despite theoretical differences, there was broad agreement that capitalist development in India was constrained by the feudal/semi-feudal agrarian relations on the one hand and subservience of the capitalist classes to imperialism on the other. It was on the basis of this understanding that Leftist programmes accorded centrality to the agrarian revolution/ land reforms and advocated state-led macro-economic and industrial policies to pursue self-reliant economic development. The international context in which such a programmatic understanding was evolved was marked by the Cold War between the US-led imperialist bloc and the socialist bloc led by the USSR and China. Neo-liberal globalization has altered this setting in many ways. The Cold War ended with the collapse of the socialist regime in the USSR. The socialist regime in China underwent major transformations, introducing market-oriented reforms and integrating itself with the globalized world economy. The neo-liberal reforms in India were initiated within such a global context, where socialism had ceased to exist as a major countervailing force to global capitalism, dominated by international finance capital and US imperialism.

The capitalist development witnessed in India under the neo-liberal regime has also transformed the Indian socio-economic landscape. Because of the fragmentation of landholdings due to demographic change, landed property has ceased to be the principal source of economic and political power in the rural areas.[1] Feudal/semi-feudal landlordism has weakened and given way to the development of capitalist interests in myriad forms. Struggles against coercive land acquisition for industrial, infrastructure or commercial projects have acquired centrestage in the place of struggles for land redistribution. Over half of the rural workforce continues to be engaged in agriculture, but peasant agriculture is itself in a crisis owing to the withdrawal of state support, exposure to the global market and gradual corporate penetration into agriculture. The major questions confronting the peasantry today relate to prices of output, availability of cheap inputs, credit and the very viability of small-peasant agriculture.

This is not to argue that neo-liberal capitalism has ushered in a revolutionary transformation of social relations. Rather, since capitalist development is being superimposed on extant socio-economic relations without breaking them, the older forms of exploitation and oppression are getting juxtaposed with new ones. Caste and gender oppression continues to be rampant, including physical atrocities against Dalits and women. In fact, such social oppression and struggles against it has assumed much greater importance in contemporary times compared to feudal/semi-feudal economic exploitation. Moreover, while neo-liberal capitalist development has created a crisis for peasant-agriculture rendering huge masses unemployed and under-employed, it has failed to absorb that surplus labour in gainful non-agricultural activities. This has created a 'footloose' workforce, which migrates across geographies and sectors in order to survive as informalized labour. This informal workforce, comprising over 90 per cent of India's 460 million strong workforce, has mostly remained outside the purview of traditional trade union or peasant organizations. The wages and working conditions of this workforce has emerged as a major socio-economic question. Over half of this workforce is also self-employed, signifying their engagement in petty production and trade. Expansion of non-agricultural employment has been restricted to a few sectors like construction and certain services. The proportion of casualized or contract labour has increased significantly across sectors. This section also remains mostly unorganized.

The urbanization and industrialization occurring under the neo-liberal regime has also impacted the middle class. The traditional urban middle class mostly came from regular salaried employment in the organized sector, a major share of which was in the public sector. Declining public sector employment and the expansion of the private corporate sector in the post-liberalization period has contributed to the rise of a 'new middle class', which is not only employed or dependent on the private corporate sector but is also influenced by its worldview. Moreover, there is a greater stratification of the middle class, with the upper middle class setting the benchmarks for the economic, social and cultural aspirations of the middle and lower middle classes. For the lower middle class, access and quality of education, healthcare and other public services and basic infrastructure like electricity, water and sanitation have emerged as major issues alongside issues such as corruption, environmental degradation and the cornering of public resources and enclavization of spaces by the big corporates and the upper class elite.

The response of the Left parties and their mass organizations to these changes has so far been inadequate, both theoretically as well as in praxis. There have been two erroneous trends noticeable within the Indian Left. One tends to look at the changes ushered in by globalization as progressive or "inevitable" and seeks to align the Left with the neo-liberal project in the name of ushering in "modernity" and "development". This line of thinking fails to recognize the class character of the neo-liberal project, the deeply inequalizing impact of the neo-liberal processes on society and the paradoxical nature of the modernization brought about by them. The other trend seeks to turn its back on the significant changes that have occurred and clings to the orthodox tenets, vainly trying to fit the complex realities of the day to obsolete theoretical straitjackets. In praxis, the first trend has translated into brazen class-collaboration, degeneration and co-option of sections of the Left, while the second manifests itself in the stagnation of the Left movement combined with a supercilious closed-mindedness and dogmatism.

II

The trend towards aligning the Left with the neo-liberal project has been most visible in the states where the Left has been in power. Since the Left in West Bengal was uninterruptedly in power for over three decades, it is here that this trend has had its clearest manifestation. The longevity of the Left Front (LF) government which came into office in 1977 was secured through the pursuit of alternative policies like land and tenancy reforms, democratic decentralization and expansion of welfare measures for the rural and urban poor. Since 1991, however, the alternative policy trajectory of the LF government became difficult to pursue in the context of the neo-liberal policies adopted by the centre. What was attempted under Jyoti Basu's stewardship since 1994 was a pragmatic compromise with the neo-liberal order, by welcoming private and foreign investments even while attempting to continue with the pro-people policies of the erstwhile regime to the extent possible.

The mainstream Left understanding during this phase was that the compulsions arising out of running a state government within India's constitutional framework, where centre-state relations were heavily skewed in favour of the centre, necessitated some compromises with the neo-liberal order. But it was always emphasized that the rights of the basic classes, like the trade union rights of the workers or the land rights of the peasants would not be bartered away. This uneasy compromise, however, was not a sustainable arrangement. The Left had to make a choice, either to make a break with neo-liberalism or get increasingly co-opted within its structures.

Since the advent of the Buddhadeb Bhattacharya regime, the understanding of a compulsion-driven compromise with neo-liberalism was discarded in favour of an increasingly enthusiastic embrace of neo-liberal policies, particularly after the LF victory in the 2006 assembly elections. The path adopted by the nominally socialist regimes of China and Vietnam was often cited to justify the rightward shift in the orientation of the LF government. No efforts were made to seriously study the serious contradictions that have emerged in China in the post-reforms era; the increasing socio-economic and regional inequalities, the conflicts over land acquisition and labour unrests, rising cronyism and corruption and the transformation of the Communist Party of China itself, which following the incorporation of the theory of "Three Represents" in its constitution in 2002 allowed big capitalists to enter and hold positions within the party. Nor were the differences between the Chinese and the Indian situation taken into account, where in contrast to the single party rule in China, India remains a multi-party democracy.

The embrace of neo-liberal policies in the name of "industrialization" was an important reason behind the downfall of the LF government. On the one hand, big corporates like the Salim group and Tata were being wooed by offering various kinds of concessions in a non-transparent manner. Moreover, the hypocrisy of opposing SEZs at the centre and promoting them in West Bengal contributed to the confusion within the Left and created suspicion in the minds of the people. On the other hand, forcible land acquisition in Nandigram and Singur faced resistance from small landowners and alienated significant sections of the peasantry across the state. This combined with the neglect of the social sectors, with the state lagging behind in various social indicators and implementation of welfare schemes. This was particularly true of the socially deprived sections like the Muslim minorities, adivasis, Dalits and women, who had totally gone off the government's radar. It was the backlash against the LF government's policies combined with years of accumulated discontent against a three-decade-old regime that helped the Mamata Banerjee led TMC to defeat the LF on the populist plank of "*maa, mati, manush*" and capture power.

How far neo-liberalism has permeated the thinking of the Left in West Bengal can be seen from the fact that even after the landmark electoral defeat in 2011, the dominant party of the Left—the CPI(M)—has refused to accept its fundamental ideological error. There were the customary election reviews which noted the alienation of the workers, peasants and other poor sections from the Left. But such alienation was never analysed in terms of the rightward ideological shift that was effected. Rather, the dominant sections of the CPI(M) in West Bengal have always maintained that there are hardly any ideological reasons behind the loss of mass support for the Left.

The counter-argument has been made in terms of standard anti-incumbency against a three-decade-old regime alongside unfavourable electoral arithmetic caused by the coming together of the TMC and the Congress following the Left's withdrawal of support to the UPA-I government in 2008 for going ahead with the Indo-US nuclear deal. The anti-incumbency argument does have some merit, since the failings of the seventh LF government were on multiple fronts. However, the specific form that the anti-LF opposition took subsequent to the Singur-Nandigram episodes, the re-appearance of Left wing extremism in *Jangalmahal* and the populist plank adopted by the TMC point towards the importance of the ideological factors. The argument of the TMC and Congress coming together being decisive in the defeat of the LF has always lacked credibility, because the vote share of the LF has itself declined consistently from close to 50 per cent in 2006 to 43 per cent in 2009 and 41 per cent in 2011. Significant sections of supporters have deserted the LF and switched their loyalties to the TMC. Much of this comprises the rural and the urban poor.

Despite such evidence, however, the CPI(M) and the LF in West Bengal have remained in a denial mode. Rather than trying to rectify their ideological position and mobilizing the people on issues like price rise, farmers' suicides, atrocities against women or the chit fund scam, they have continued to criticize the TMC government for failing to "industrialize" the state and refusing to accord SEZ status to IT companies, which was promised by the LF government. Alongside, there have been desperate attempts to create a "wedge" between the TMC and the Congress, by supporting the Congress candidate in the Presidential elections in an unprincipled manner and other such tactics. Ironically, the TMC has unilaterally distanced itself from the Congress owing to the growing unpopularity of the scam-tainted government at the centre. Following that, it is the TMC which has been able to enhance its political and electoral support base in West Bengal, both at the cost of the Congress and the LF, as was seen in the recently held panchayat and municipality elections in the state. It is indeed alarming that despite its misrule and autocratic tendencies, TMC's electoral support has continued to grow in the state.

While it started as an opposition force when the UPA-II government was formed in 2009, the LF has landed in a situation on the eve of the Lok Sabha elections where it is being perceived as being soft on the discredited Congress-led government at the centre and ambivalent on supporting it again in future. It is the TMC which is raising the pitch against the Congress regime in order to channelize popular discontent. This shows how the Left can get repeatedly wrong-footed on tactics once it loses its ideological moorings.

III

The fact that the Left in West Bengal has been culpable of ideological deviations has been widely noted and commented upon.[2] The reason why such ideological errors have gone uncorrected, however, is an issue which merits serious discussion. It is not the case that the rightward ideological shift had not met with internal dissent. But such dissent could never graduate into a viable alternative position, because it was rooted in orthodoxy and dogmatism.

The inability to correct rightward deviations within a communist party lie in the problematic manner in which democracy has been historically conceived by the communist Left. This goes back to the ideological construct of "Marxism-Leninism" developed by the CPSU under Stalin. It needs to be noted here that Lenin developed the concept of "democratic centralism" for a revolutionary party which was fighting a brutal czarist dictatorship and seeking to capture state power through armed insurrection. The need for a disciplined and regimented party was widely felt by communist revolutionaries across the world after the success of the Bolshevik Revolution, which was institutionalized in the Third International held in Moscow in 1919. The basic idea was to form communist parties in countries across the world on the lines of the Bolshevik party to carry out revolution in their respective countries, to achieve the goal of a world proletarian revolution.

There have been major debates on the question of "Leninism" since its very inception. Rosa Luxemburg had underscored the importance of the spontaneous role of the masses in a revolutionary situation and had questioned the desirability of the overriding powers of the central authority within the labour movement. Later day critics, most famously Trotsky, alleged that the "Leninist" regime that was established under Stalin's leadership in the USSR was a gross distortion of what Lenin had intended or envisaged; it was rather a "dictatorship of the apparatus over the party". Antonio Gramsci developed the concepts of "hegemony" and "war of position" to delineate alternative strategies for communists to make proletarian revolutions in advanced capitalist societies. Moreover, the successful revolutionary movements of China and Cuba had never held the "Leninist" script as sacrosanct. While the CPC under Mao's leadership developed its own revolutionary strategy of peasant guerilla warfare (against Comintern advice), the Cuban revolution triumphed against the Batista dictatorship in 1959 under the leadership of Fidel Castro and Che Guevara as the 26th of July movement. It was only in 1965 that the ruling party was organized as the Communist Party of Cuba.

The short point is that the legacy of Lenin, as the first revolutionary leader of the 20th century who successfully led a revolution against the autocratic bourgeois regime in Russia and established a socialist state, needs to be distinguished from "Leninism" which was the official ideology of the USSR and emulated by socialist regimes and communist parties across the world. This proposed distinction is similar to that between "Mao Zedong Thought" and "Maoism", where the former is considered to be the teachings and insights developed by the Chinese revolutionary leader Mao from which we can all learn and draw inspiration from in our own revolutionary endeavours, while the latter is considered to be a blind imitation of his strategies irrespective of the context.

It needs to be recognized that while many of Lenin's theoretical insights, pertaining to the bourgeois state, the predatory character of imperialism, the complexities of socialist construction and the dangers posed by revisionist/reformist and left-adventurist trends within the revolutionary movement continue to remain relevant, some of his theories have also become outdated. For instance, Lenin's analysis of inter-imperialist rivalries leading to world wars has been rendered obsolete in the post-war period. The traditional imperialist powers today function as an unified bloc under the hegemony of international finance capital and US imperialism. More importantly, Lenin's notion of a regimented, vanguard party seizing power through armed insurrection could never be replicated in functional bourgeois democracies anywhere in the world. The stalwarts of the Indian communist movement had always recognized this limitation of "Leninism" and had fashioned their praxis in tandem with India's transition into a multi-party democracy in the post-independence period. That is why the more successful streams of the Indian communist movement based their strategy on a combination of "parliamentary and extra-parliamentary struggles" and an "Indian road to socialism". The relevance of an indigenous "Indian road to socialism" has enhanced manifold for the Left, in the aftermath of the collapse of the 20th century socialist regimes.

Although the collapse of these socialist regimes had complex reasons, two broad factors can be easily identified. First, over-centralized planning undertaken by these socialist regimes could not provide a sustainable and dynamic economic alternative to capitalism. Second, the bureaucratic state apparatus, the conflation of the state and the party under single party rule and the absence of political freedoms and civil liberties led to the ossification of the party and deep alienation of the working people from the socialist system. These factors have been officially acknowledged by the mainstream Left in India too. However, the official line has always been that while these mistakes had indeed taken place in the erstwhile socialist regimes, they were the results of "deviations" and "distortions" and not because there was anything wrong with "Marxism-Leninism" per se.

Such manoeuvres may have helped in tiding over a momentary crisis, like the one communist parties across the world faced after the collapse of the USSR, but in the process a peculiar duplicity got built into their ideological framework. For instance, the present constitution of the CPC states: "The Communist Party of China takes Marxism-Leninism, Mao Zedong Thought, Deng Xiaoping Theory, the important thought of Three Represents and the Scientific Outlook on Development as its guide to action." Epithets like "Deng Xiaoping Theory", "Three Represents", "Scientific Outlook on Development" have been added on successively by the CPC alongside "Marxism-Leninism" over the past three decades. These have signified an increasing thrust on market-oriented reforms and integration with the capitalist world economy, which is the exact opposite of "Marxism-Leninism", which espoused a "dictatorship of the proletariat". The CPC no longer considers itself to be the "vanguard" of the Chinese working class alone but also "the Chinese people and the Chinese nation", and which "represents the development trend of China's advanced productive forces, the orientation of China's advanced culture and the fundamental interests of the overwhelming majority of the Chinese people". Even as the class character of the CPC has changed, the political form of dictatorship has been preserved zealously. And "Marxism-Leninism" has been retained as the official ideology in order to sustain the regime's legitimacy.

The revolutionary essence of Marxism needs to be rescued from such "Marxism-Leninism", which has mutated into neo-liberal state capitalism and that too, without democracy. Does the essence of Marxism lie in the class struggle against capitalism or just in being a member of a communist party—even if that party abandons class struggle and the pursuit of revolutionary objectives in practice, but continues to nominally adhere to "Marxism-Leninism" in theory? As in China, significant sections within the Left in West Bengal too have started believing in the latter version. Commitment to the class struggle and revolutionary objectives has been replaced by nostalgia, blind loyalty towards the "leadership" and dogmatic adherence to a warped notion, which is "democratic centralism". As a result, while there has been occasional dissent from within the Left regarding specific policy errors, like that of forcible land acquisition, there has been no consistent and organized resistance against the rightward ideological shift from within the Left.

IV

The revival of the Left movement in West Bengal is a pre-requisite for the strengthening of the Left across the country and at the national level. In order to fulfil this objective, however, the Left has to: (a) make a complete break with neo-liberalism and isolate those sections which have got co-opted into the neo-liberal order (b) shun status-quoist dogmatism and creatively engage with radical alternatives outside orthodox "Marxism-Leninism". The quest should begin with the realization that Indian society and economy have changed considerably since the 1960s/1970s and the slogan for an agrarian revolution against feudal landlords has lost much of its relevance. The principal challenge before the Left in India today is to intensify the struggle against the neo-liberal capitalist regime backed by Indian big business and open up possibilities for an alternative trajectory of economic development.

Since 1991, the Left has often argued that it has a grand socialistic vision that can only be implemented when it comes to power at the centre; and meanwhile at the state level it can only pursue policies which are not much different from those implemented by non-Left parties. Such reasoning would not work any longer. People judge the Left by the policies implemented by the Left-led state governments, not by theoretical grandstanding. A crucial challenge for the Left is therefore to envisage and implement alternative policies at the state level. Such policy alternatives should address the problems of unemployment, informalization and casualization of labour, crisis of peasant-based agriculture and ensure universal entitlements of food, education, healthcare, housing, etc. The Left should resist the reckless exploitation of natural resources, privatization, land grab, large-scale displacement and environmental degradation caused through primitive accumulation under the neo-liberal regime. In other words, the Left should first demonstrate at the state level, the contours of its policy alternative which it wants to pursue at the centre.

The struggle for an alternative development trajectory also needs to be combined with a struggle for social justice and the democratic transformation of the Indian society and the state. In a society characterized by multiple forms of oppression and discrimination other than class exploitation, no emancipatory movement can advance unless the struggle for social justice is combined with class struggle. With increasing participation of women in workplaces and the public sphere, gender-based discrimination and violence against women are acquiring newer and more vicious forms. The struggle for gender equality is central to the struggle for social justice. Caste oppression continues to be a big obstacle to the democratization of Indian society. The Dalits, Adivasis and OBCs have grossly inadequate representation in formal sector employment, especially in the private sector. The Muslim minorities not only continue to suffer from neglect, discrimination and backwardness but are increasingly feeling insecure because of the way innocent persons from the community are often being victimized as "terror suspects". The advancement of the rights of minorities, including reservations, acquires significance in this context.

The Left has to make a distinction between the emancipatory politics of the socially oppressed sections and the narrow, exclusivist politics based on identities, which seek to perpetuate rather than annihilate social oppression. But to relegate identity questions to the background on the pretext of prioritizing class struggle is an anachronism. These struggles are in no way less significant than class struggle. In contrast to the identitarian mobilizations based on emotive issues, the Left should address the concerns and aspirations of the new generation among women, Dalits, Adivasis, Muslims and OBCs. This cannot be achieved unless the youth from these socially oppressed sections are provided adequate space and representation within the Left leadership.

In the backdrop of humongous corruption and plunder of resources, the restructuring of India's political system has become an imperative. Democracy in India is being subverted by money power and the strong nexus that has developed between policy-makers and vested interests. In order to dismantle this nexus, thorough electoral and political reforms are required. Accountability and transparency of the elected representatives and the state apparatus can only be ensured by institutionalizing decentralized participatory democracy. The Left had a proud record of initiating democratic decentralization in West Bengal till the panchayats started being viewed less as rural self-governments and more as instruments to control the rural masses. This needs to be reversed to ensure meaningful participation of the people in decision-making.

Before setting upon the task to democratize society, the Left should thoroughly democratize its inner structures, which have got bureaucratized. Homilies on "strengthening inner-party democracy" are no substitute for genuine introspection and opening up the organizational structures of the Left. The orthodox view holds that the only way to organize a revolutionary party is to have a top-down, regimented party structure. This militaristic and vanguardist notion of a revolution needs to be replaced by a revolutionary vision, which accords centrality to enormous mass participation.

A mass revolutionary party should be structured in a way where the party remains embedded within the masses. Since masses are bound to have different opinions on ideological and policy matters, such diversity of opinion should be freely allowed to exist and contend within the party organization. Platforms or tendencies based on ideological-political positions should be formally allowed, with provisions for free debate and voting in the decision-making fora, like conferences. In fact, such tendencies already exist as factions or lobbies within the Left parties, but they function in a hypocritical and distorted manner because of the formal adherence to a stringent notion of "democratic centralism".

The approach of the Left towards alliances with non-Left forces also needs a major rethink. The present approach has been marked by a tendency to forge alliances from above, primarily geared towards short-term electoral gains. Not only have those gains remained elusive, but the Left has lost much of its fighting character, mass base and credibility owing to these opportunistic tactics. The alliance which the Left should focus on building is one between the 'political Left' and the 'social Left', whose efficacy has been brought into the fore through the Latin American experience. The people's movements today have emerged as a significant force fighting against the adverse impact of neo-liberal policies. There is some merit in the critique that these movements are too localized and lack a universalist perspective. However, it is also a fact that with all its universalism, the Left has been absent on the ground on many issues that impact the lives of the people. The other critique of the people's movements, in terms of their being "reformist" also sounds hypocritical, since in spite of the theoretical or rhetorical revolutionism, that is what much of the Left has become in practice.

The approach of the Left towards imperialism needs fresh thinking. The days of the "progressive" or the "national" bourgeoisie are over. The interests of big businesses across the world are intricately tied up in a globalized world and they all favour US imperialism to provide stability to the world order. The crucial arena of struggle against imperialism today is the struggle against neo-liberalism. Imperialism can be defeated only by defeating the domestic ruling classes of different countries. Despite being strongly backed by the Indian bourgeoisie and international finance, the neo-liberal regime in India faces multiple contradictions. The ongoing crisis of global capitalism has exposed the fallacies of neo-liberalism and India cannot remain unaffected much longer. However, the persistence of the ruling classes can also be seen in the continuance of neo-liberal policies and austerity across the globe. Defeating this powerful bloc requires a very broad mobilization of all other classes and which can be attained only by building large social and political coalitions.

What is therefore required for the revival of the Left today is a principled alliance between the radical revolutionaries, who want to replace capitalism by socialism and reformists, who want to fight for democratic reforms within the system, against the neo-liberal order. Such an alliance can actualize only when the Left initiates militant mass movements and becomes ideologically open to new ideas. Radicalism in practice and openness in theory should be the new direction for the Indian Left.

NOTES AND REFERENCES

1. See Deepankar Basu and Debarshi Das, "The Maoist Movement in India: Some Political Economy Considerations", *Journal of Agrarian Change*, Vol. 13, No. 3, July 2013.
2. The most consistent critique of the rightward deviation of the CPI(M) in West Bengal has been Ashok Mitra, who was the Finance Minister of the first two LF governments between 1977 and 1987. See AM, "The State of the CPI(M) in West Bengal", *EPW*, Vol. XLIV, No. 30, July 25, 2009.

8

From Antagonism to Agonism in the *Republic of Hunger*: Towards an Indian *Democratie-a-venir*

Anindya Sekhar Purakayastha
and
Dhritiman Chakraborty

> Bourgeois parliamentarism has thus completed the cycle of its historical development and has arrived at the point of self-negation. Social Democracy, however, has taken up its post in the country and in parliament as, simultaneously, the cause and effect of this fate of the bourgeoisie. If parliamentarism has lost all significance for capitalist society, it is for the rising working class one of the most powerful and indispensable means of carrying on the class struggle. To save bourgeois parliamentarism from the bourgeoisie and use it against the bourgeoisie is one of Social Democracy's most urgent political tasks. (Luxemburg, 1904)
>
> Democracy today, I will insist, is not government of, by and for the people. Rather it should be seen as the politics of the governed. (Chatterjee, 2004: 4)
>
> We must democratize Democracy. (Aristride, 2000: 36)

In his book, *The Hatred of Democracy*, Jacques Ranciere has articulated the growing distrust of the liberal democratic model for its failure to serve the masses and it is now commonly held by many that democracy in its existing *avatar* serves only the wealthy and the powerful corporate elites, not the people, despite the façade of elections, which are themselves corrupted by money and special economic interests (Jayal, 2012; Crockett, 2011; Roy, 2011; Banerjee and Duflo, 2011). Democracy in the Asian and Third World context has perhaps mutated into a cannibalistic nature where the democratic state on the surface swears by the people but devours its own citizens to consolidate its sovereign power of exception. The centralization of power among the ruling elites and the diminishing status of radical political imaginaries necessitate the irruptive singularities of a revitalized left politics or an emancipatory paradigm of egalitarian politics which would make an attempt to restore power to the people or would at least strive towards the cardinal principles of democracy, which is the Luxemberian mass line or people-centric politics (Patnaik, 1996, 949). In this context, we feel that Rosa Luxemburg and her conceptual model of socialist democracy deserves serious discussion so that all forms of centralisms and programmatic doctrines can be swept aside to accommodate a reformulated framework of radical democracy which would be characterized with the everyday dynamics of the real *politics of the governed* (Chatterjee, 2004). We argue that Indian democracy requires a thorough critique of its existing norms and we do that with an analysis of the heteroglossic grammar of Indian democracy through the critical optics provided by Partha Chatterjee and Arundhati Roy and we reinforce the derived critical trajectories through the radical imaginaries of current thinkers such as Chantal Mouffe and Antonio Negri and finally we conclude our analysis with an incorporation and infusion of Rosa Luxemburg's primary concern for spontaneous participation of the people for a revolutionary future. In the process we engage with the *Luxemburg-Lenin debate* on party centralism and mass line or on the spontaneous mobilization of organizational power for a possible refashioning of a new left politics which does not shy away from democracy but translates democracy from mere proceduralism to a substantial framework of real participatory democracy. In this respect we engage with prominent contemporary observations of the neo-left (Vanaik, 2012; Ghosh,

2012; Bardhan, 2011 and Sen, 2011) and we arrive at certain futural directions for socialist/people-driven democracy in India. In the subsequent sections we would first traverse various theoretic positions and debates on these questions and would offer ways to engage with a vantage ground of coming radicalities within the framework of democracy in India.

Among prominent recent theorists, Chantal Mouffe, Antonio Negri, Jacques Ranciere and Jacques Derrida have engaged with the question of reformulating both the substance and functioning of democracy. Such critical interventions in the domains of democratic theory though have been characterized as post-Marxian which subsequently led to many debates on issues of class, social responsibility, representation and praxis. While Mouffe, Derrida and others are to be credited for their attempts in re-energizing the debates on democracy, the limitation of their theorization on democracy stems from their failure to engage with the Third World, or Europe's Other. The Third World praxis necessitates re-incorporation of pressing concerns for poverty (poor economics), state-corporate nexus, social divide and equality, etc in the democratic debate. This suggests a restoration of alternative Left models of democracy which is to be scripted in the dynamics of contemporary realities. Although the Sensex is projected as the only denominator of financial growth, farmers' suicides, malnutrition, SEZ and forceful eviction, slumification (*Planet of Slums*, Mike Davis), lack of basic amenities, price rise, unemployment, absence of health care or social security remain the everyday reality for majority of Indians. While field notes of Indian democracy convince some subaltern theorists that post-liberalization, governmental/democratic technologies have deeply penetrated the lives of the peasants in India and therefore the peasants/subalterns are in a better position today to bargain with the state for their own good (Chatterjee, 2008), the everyday grim ground realities speak of a 'demoncrazy' in India that brutalizes its own citizens in the name of democracy. The *aporias* of Indian democracy make one rethink about its real achievements and such rethinking necessitates a re-reading of the socialist democratic axioms of Rosa Luxemburg. Perhaps more than ever the paradigms of socialist democracy are highly relevant today for a world which is abuzz with anti-developmental human rights movements like the Occupy movement, the congregation in Tahirir Square, the Anti-corruption movement in India against mal-governance, economic meltdown and market fundamentalism. Even after sixty years of independence, India has failed to cater to the basic needs of all its citizens while allowing a handful to gluttonize their life to an absurd extent and that necessitates a renewed and reformulated model of the leftist path to launch a new crusade against marketocracy. Such a reformulated Leftist paradigm would require an introspective analysis of the Rosa Luxemburg-Lenin debate on socialist democracy, party centralism and other argumentative deliberations to unearth the maladies that plagued the left movement or that led to the decadent totalitarian tendencies in the leftist discourse. An agonistic discursive leftist model would guard against all reductive epistemologies and any futural enframing of socialist democracy would have to be non-transcendentalist as the coming contours of socialist democracy would cater to the needs of all and yet would not be overarchingly programmatic, keeping open the possibilities of a *democratie a venir* or a democracy-to-come that would be context-specific or praxis-oriented, ingenious, welfarist and yet operationally non-totalitarian. In what follows we would first underscore the growing absolutist nature of Indian democracy so that new radicalities can be discussed in the light of the anomalies.

Absolutist Democracy and State Cannibalism

Partha Chatterjee's idea of political society (Chatterjee, 2004) postulates a distinct domain of non-civil society population in a post-colonial society like India, which compels the state to yield to their various demands and which operates in different non-law abiding activities to disrupt the status quo so that the state is forced to deliver to the needs of the political society. In this respect governmentality assumes a crucial role in a post-colonial society like India which has sharp class and caste differences as well as regional and linguistic disparities and therefore, the real zone of political or democratic dynamics in India resides in the proper execution of governmentality or in the consolidation of constant process of bargain or negotiations of *the politics of the governed* with the bourgeois state. Different groups of political society with their different sets of demands constantly exert pressure and resort to unlawful activities only to register their voices and the operating modes of Indian democracy have to accommodate these various political passions to execute people-centric governance. Any lapses or failure on the part of the state to deliver or to go against the people would result in anti-state resentments and Arundhati Roy, the celebrated Booker Prize winning Indian author, has articulated such cases of state absolutism or state cannibalism in India where the state has gone against its own people, violating all possible norms of governmentality. In the introduction to her non-fictional work, *Listening to Grasshoppers: Field Notes on Democracy*, Roy has foregrounded the aporias of Indian democracy to reinforce the scepticism about the real nature and future of democracy in a post-colonial country like India. The 'Failing Lights of Democracy' has resulted in, as Roy said, 'Demon-crazy' in India. The pathologies or aberrations of democracy demand a critical vigilantism vis a vis the malfunction of democracy and the growing incidents of human rights violation and the repressive mechanisms of statecraft/ marketocracy in the name of democracy in India or other post-colonial countries call for a radical reformulation of existing democratic paradigms. Matters have come to such a pass that one cannot help being virtually apocalyptic about the autocratic nature of democracies in post-colonial countries and Roy's apprehensions are not unfounded when she asks, "while we're still arguing about whether there is life after death, can we add another question to that cart? Is there life after democracy? What sort of life will it be?" (Roy 2009: 2).

These anxieties and misgivings are crucial and they have valid critico-theoretical implications. Similar misgivings have been voiced by the IAC (India Against Corruption) movement in 2011 and 2012, by the Aam Admi Party, the Maoists and various other human rights organizations in India. They have asked for the dissolution of state power and for the constitution of people's power or Democracy for the Masses. Continental thinkers such as Jacques Derrida had betrayed similar concerns about current oppressive trends in democracy in the post 9/11 world and Derrida formulated his concept of the *Democratie a venir* or the future democracy-to-come to coronate a new alternative political imaginary (Mcquillan, 2009: 4). The Mouffean praxis of agonistic democracy also envisages a similar ontology of emancipatory discourse of an enlightened public sphere and participatory democracy which is empowering and averse to the mechanisms of neo-capital and non-governance. Giorgio Agamben's notion of the *coming community* (Murray, 2010: 46) and Derrida's outcry against absolutist totalitarian democracy are similar to Roy's concern about the coercive nature of the state. Recent movements in India voicing dissent against a pro-laissez faire democratic state such as the anti-eviction movement in Noida, Delhi and Maharashtra, the movement against SEZ (Special Economic Zone) in Nandigram or the anti-land Acquisition movement in Singur in West Bengal and sundry other movements raising voices against the complicity of the state with the market forces mark the robust agonism of Indian democracy which does not allow the statist status quo to settle in for its hegemonic sway.

Autoimmunity and *Democratie-a-venir*

Throughout the world, democracies are fast becoming ruthless dictatorial machines and in the post 9/11 world the American neo-imperial intentions have unveiled the heinous atrocities perpetrated in the name of democracy. The need of the hour is to sharpen our critique and to explore an alternative model of futural democracy which is not bedeviled by absolutist and totalitarian endgames. According to Agamben, the modern state under the façade of democracy has relegated the individual to a bare life of the *Homo Sacer* or the outcaste (Agamben, 1998). Democracy today has ended in lumpenocracy/corporatocracy and Roy has betrayed her positions on such modern lumpen democracies in the following way,

> So this—all these—is Empire. This loyal confederation, this obscene accumulation of power, this greatly increased distance between those who make the decision and those who have to suffer them. Our fight, our goal, our vision of another world must be to eliminate that distance (Roy, 2005: 81).

The essentialized grand narrative of traditional democracies has become overarching which is hostile to all resisting voices. Derrida in his late ethical phase coined the term auto-immunity (Thomassen, 2006: 83) which signifies the coercive mechanism by which a traditional democracy subsumes subversive forces for systemic auto-immunity in the name of democracy. In his book *The Beast and the Sovereign*, Derrida implied how the sovereign state describes the resisting forces as disruptive beasts. By foregrounding the atrocities of rogue democracies (be it the USA or India), Roy too has attempted through her non-fictional domain a reformulation of a radical *democratie a venir* or a future democracy to come (Thomassen, 2006: 268) which is free from its current rigid foundationalism and coercive profile. Roy has an apocalyptic apprehension about the present state of Indian democracy and she feels the Indian state is fast becoming an auto-immunized coercive mechanism that kills her own children with impunity in the name of marketized development or in the name of national sovereignty. Corporate aficionados and democratic diehards draw a rosy image of the Indian state and its burgeoning soft super-powerdom. On the face of it, India is cruising along and is said to be the next superpower in the making and political pandits would go ga ga about India shining and about India being poised to take the next giant stride to millennial progress, but Roy here prefers to play the spoil sport or the damp squib, making people conscious that something is in fact grossly rotten in the state of *Bharat*. Roy's dark ruminations on the lopsided nature of Indian democracy and on the genocidal proclivities of the Indian political class may invite rabid reactions but Roy has carefully called a spade a spade. Her disconcerting premonitions on the alleged state-sponsored genocidal slaughters in Gujarat and its subsequent justification by the state betray her vigilant vanguardism or agonism,

> But the Gujarat genocide is part of a larger, more elaborate and systematic vision. It tells us that the wheat is ripening and the grasshoppers have landed in mainland India. (Roy, 2009: 144)

The grasshoppers, therefore, have arrived in mainland India, but we the people, the mainstay of the democratic edifice have no idea that the blister is on, that it is going to be a cannibal democracy, a body politic where the grasshoppers/assassins are all set to pounce on the deviant, the Other at any time. The *Other* in the Indian democracy are the minorities, the tribals, and the dissidents and in the Introduction to his *Listening to Grasshoppers: Field Notes on Democracy,* Arundhati talks about the failing lights of democracy to care for the Other. She shows how the Indian democratic set up is harbouring a growing sense of hostility towards the Other/dissidents. All dissident voices are either silenced or branded as separatists, insurgents or seditious. Such a repressive democratic model fails to accommodate the necessary agonism by alienating the people as antagonists and such state hostility can occasion a perfect Mouffean analysis of the Indian scenario in terms of anatagonism and agonism. The post-Tahrir Square world needs further exploration of the democratic process and for that, new thinking in the domain of radical politics would be immensely helpful. The subsequent section would address the Mouffean hypothesis of vibrant democracy and its relevance to post-colonial contexts.

Mouffean Hypothesis and Negri's Notion of Immanent Democracy of the Multitude

Chantal Mouffe has been eager to contribute to the theoretical discussion in political theory by proposing a different model, one which she calls the agonistic model of democracy and we would show how the Mouffean agonistic line and the Negrian immanentism find a close kinship with Luxemburg's mass line and spontaneous approach to revolution. Mouffe insists that the dynamics of the political is linked to the dimension of conflict that exists in human societies, conflicts that remain as the ever-present possibility of antagonism, an antagonism that is ineradicable. This means that a consensus without exclusion—

a form of consensus beyond hegemony, beyond sovereignty, will always be unavailable in any democracy worth the name and in that way we would be able to keep away from centralism and absolute power. Mouffe has also tried to understand why in the kind of society we are living in today—which she calls a post-political society—there is an increasing dissent against democratic institutions. The Habermasian deliberative model has inspired us to believe that the aim of democratic politics is to reach a consensus and countering this consensus model, Mouffe developed a new model that she calls an "agonistic model of democracy," which postulates that the central objective of democratic politics is to transform antagonism into agonism. If we take these principles to be "liberty and equality for all," it is clear that they can be understood in many different, conflicting ways, which will lead to conflicts that can never be rationally resolved. This is how Mouffe envisages the agonistic struggle, a struggle between different interpretations of shared principles, a conflictual consensus. Conflicts that would be between adversaries, not enemies would generate "passions" for political collective identities.

In this respect Mouffe is against Hardt and Negri's idea of an "absolute democracy," a democracy which is beyond any form of institution. Mouffe is more for a concrete and engaged version of democratic vitalism, something that is more akin to Chatterjee's idea of the *politics of the governed* or the simmering tensions of a post-colonial democracy like India where the issue of institutional governmentality and its deliverance result in constant friction or agonism between the institutions and the populace or non-civil society-based political society. For Mouffe, there is democracy as long as there is conflict. If we arrive at a point where we say, "This is the end point, contestation is no longer legitimate," it means the end of democracy. We are living in a situation that, in *On the Political,* Mouffe calls "post-political," (Mouffe, 2005) in which we are constantly being told that the partisan model of politics has been overcome, that there is no more Left and Right: There is this kind of consensus at the centre, in which there is really no possibility for an alternative. Such pro-status quoist views also have a hegemonic place in contemporary post-colonial countries where the ultra right is on the rise and where statist ideology of globalization builds the univalence of the market hypothesis of neo-colonization. Refuting to yield to such ideologies of depoliticization or political Thermidorianism, post-colonial *politics of the governed* has challenged the very ethos of the market or the rise of the fascist Right. Various trade union movements in India and the rise of the Maoists have proved to be a gravel in the shoe of market-oriented globalized economy which is anti-people. The recent legislation for an anti-eviction Law in India and the significant success of the *Rights to Information Act* under which the Government of India is bound to express governmental moves transparently are marks of success for agonistic conflictual voices of political society.

The political thought of Chantal Mouffe is an interesting attempt to preserve something of the old programme of the radical Left and to adapt this to contemporary conditions and therefore radical parties like the Indian Left can have a dialogue with Mouffean theories to keep alive the left ideology through the democratic process. In India the leftist ideology has already mutated itself through its accommodation of democratic norms and countless trade unions are fighting for the cause of the political society but they still have miles to go in accomplishing their objectives and there can be a symbiotic theoretic dialogue between Mouffe and other Third World pro-subaltern political practices for the greater good of future democracy. Mouffe's passion for democracy and political radicalism aligns her to Rosa Luxemburg and in the next section we discuss Luxemburg's position for proletarian democracy to arrive at a possible consolidation of a new leftist democracy that is sustained with all these theoretic findings.

Luxembergism and Socialist Democracy

Rosa Luxemburg's vision of a socialist movement had a basic democratic character. The bourgeois character of the world war and the need for democracy against an emerging spectre of chaos inspired her in many of her formulations. Her writings and speeches over the years, as we find, evince this central strand. This leitmotif was already evident in her 1904 essay "Organizational Questions of Russian Social Democracy" where Luxemburg makes clear the fundamental difference between her basic democratic position and Lenin's ultra centralist party concept. The party centralist structure and the requisite organizational strength were not entirely ignored by her; rather she was of the firm belief that such concerting organizational effort is not alienated from the dialect of spontaneity. The essay, *Dialectic of Spontaneity and Organisation* is a discussion of this possible tandem between these two seemingly opposite ideals. To be more precise, this idea of spontaneity for Luxemburg was context generating, therefore of organic origin and not thrust from above. For Luxemburg the ultra centralist concept neglects the creativity of the proletarian masses.

According to Luxemburg, the 1917 Revolution made the biggest mistake of formulating a system of bureaucracy that initially appeared as the bureaucracy of the German Social Democratic Party and the German unions. Her 1906 booklet "The Mass Strike, the Political Party, and the Trade Unions" and the posthumous essay "The Russian Revolution" could be the point of reference to glimpse on her logic of 'spontaneism' and her detestation towards party regimentation. Her emphasis was on the spontaneous action of the proletarian masses and on a forward driving agitation for the rise of a revolutionary development and also for strengthening the workers' organization. This basic democratic orientation was also the starting point for Luxemburg's criticism of the Bolshevik policy in Russia in 1918 written down in her famous unfinished manuscript "On the Russian Revolution" (September 1918). For Luxemburg the dictatorship of the proletariat is

> the work of the *class* and not of a little leading minority in the name of the class—that is, it must proceed step by step out of the active participation of the masses...

And she confirms this view: "The whole mass of the people must take part of it [the development of a socialist society, OL]. Otherwise, socialism will be decreed from behind a few official desks, by a dozen intellectuals. And she pleads for freedom of press, of free association and assemblage as essentials for the "rule of the broad mass of the people..."Luxemburg and the Bolsheviks had in common the socialist goal but differed in the method of realization. For Rosa Luxemburg socialism could not be realized except in a process with complete freedom for all proletarians, without suppression of the ones thinking differently. This was for her the implicit prerequisite for assuring the most active and creative participation of the working class in developing a socialist society with equal social, economic and political rights for all citizens. Self-determination, democracy and the democratic socialism are placed on that palpable bias towards that subordinated strata of the society that, as she apprehends, would remain unaddressed in any democratic set-up that is not owned by this section. Therefore she was apprehensive about the role of the bourgeoisie, not of the bourgeois institution: the parliament in reconstituting the socialist democratic bedrock in a post-revolutionary social structure. The condition that she presumed as the possible panacea for lessening the oppressive mechanism against the proletariat is the "international socialist revolution" which would suffer if the democratic power is reposed or arrested by the handful of bourgeoisie. It has to be kept on board at this juncture that Rosa Luxemburg was in favour of the creation of Poland. She wrote on the "necessity to annihilate the Russian influence on Europe by the application of the right of peoples to dispose of themselves and to reconstruct a Poland on a democratic and social basis" (Luxemburg: 2009). She reiterates her point that this basis on democratic principle is context-generating, therefore it escapes the scope of any predisposed programmed overarching narrative. Lenin disagreed with this lack of generalized theorization of Luxemburg, and he counted them as "abstract" and "metaphysical". Though Lenin was admissive of context-specific approach, he was more akin towards "concentration, both political and economic, but concentration on the basis of democracy". This concentration means a more concerted, generative theorization, something that Luxemburg negated.

Rosa Luxemburg's position on Left politics can be summarized in the following ways,

1. Socialism means full democracy: not only political equality but also the economic, social and legal equality.
2. Socialism means basic democracy: decisions by full broad participation of the people not mainly by the leaders.
3. Socialism means humanity and solidarity: no indifference concerning suppression and misery all over the world and no use of suppression by socialists.

Conclusion

Luxemburg wrote her pamphlet, as we have already indicated, against a specific historicity and ruptures that saw Marxism and its various tenets reformulated by the changed geo-political scenario. Luxemburg's position was more attuned to the classical Marxist position in keeping the balance between the growing call for democracy and self-determination and the socialist promise of freedom from oppression and exploitation. She imagined a democracy between the oppressed across national boundaries and talked of the alliance between different nationalities against the common coercive structure of capitalist accumulation. However, the point is that democracy and the notions of popular control have undergone huge tectonic reshuffling in the face of highly technologized and liberalized social palimpsest and democracy is not understood today as a mere exercise of self-determination and franchise. Rather, as the discussion above has shown, it is more drawn on the basis of a sense of right and entitlement. Right is not understood against the holistic maxim of duty, it is sensed more as a pragmatic call for immediate benefit. The notion of political therefore has penetrated, thanks to several technological achievements, further deep and inculcated the knowledge of right and entitlement pervasively. The obvious outcome is a change in the perception of power not exerted from the one side of administration solely, it is mutually a negotiable understanding generated from the immediacy of sites and contexts. On both the civil society level and the political society level, this empowering knowledge of subjectivity and self-interest has infused a new sense of democratic consciousness. However, the point that requires more engagement is that even after accepting this changing topology of democracy, it is essential to remember its limitations.

It is true that democratic consciousness has grown, and the assertion of right has touched a new chord, but this assertion and exertion from the populace has taken place within a tremendously biased terrain of bourgeois interest that occludes a vast section of the society. The democratic process has remained uneven, different classes and different regions of people enjoy highly differential benefits of democratic governments and their social consequences. Apart from that, democratic politics is the domain of a strategic battle between political groups and social classes in which particular groups seek to enhance their own political openings while obstructing that of others. Democracy or rather some parts of its institutional design can offer some the opportunity to dominate and downgrade the other. Indian democracy is peculiar in the sense of being an exception to the normative regularities. Political thinkers have been sceptical about the future of democracy in India, ascribing the predictable failure of Indian democracy to the derivative Western origin of its democratic model. However the history of democracy throughout the world denotes a contingent nature of democratic growth in various parts of the world. Drawing primarily on the historical evidences from European societies, scholars of comparative politics believe that a certain degree of general economic growth was a precondition for the success of modern democracy and the success of Western democracy was ascribed to the stable industrial and capitalist tradition, whereas in post-colonial countries like India the onset of democracy was not preceded by any liberal political tradition or any stable bourgeois capitalist system. The Indian democratic experiment therefore was characterized with a lack, the lack of normative conditionalities which made the European experiment a robust one. In the Indian context the enterprise of democracy was marred by issues of caste and religious obscurantism and scholars had a hard time in defending the futural possibility of Indian democracy. But in spite of its pathologies and its dialectical aberrations, democracy in India has developed a new norm-deviant contingent model of post-colonial democracy, a model which is context-specific and which thrives on Mouffean agonism or operate within an accommodative space of conflictual maneuverings between the state and the populace. Future scholarship in this field would address further areas of research in this respect, but at present Partha Chatterjee's argument of political society does make a case for the subaltern Third World subject who strives for a different temporality of existential battle, and a Luxemburgian intervention and direct engagement with such post-colonial ontologies would definitely infuse a new theoretic agonism in this political debate.

NOTES AND REFERENCES

A. Banerjee and E. Duflo, *Poor Economics, A Radical Rethinking of the Way to Fight Global Poverty* (London: Random House, 2011).

Achin Vanaik, 'Future Perspectives for the Mainstream Indian Left', *EPW*, Vol. XLVII, No. 41, October, 13, 2012.

Arun Patnaik, 'Mass Line Revisited, Readings in Revolution and Organisation: Rosa Luxemberg and Her Critics', *Economic and Political Weekly*, Vol. 31, No. 15, 1996.

Arundhati Roy, *An Ordinary Persons Guide to Empire* (New Delhi: Penguin, 2005).

Arundhati Roy, *Broken Republic: Three Essays* (New Delhi: Penguin, 2011).

Arundhati Roy, *Field Notes on Democracy: Listening to Grasshoppers* (Canada: Haymarket Books, 2009).

Chantal Mouffe, *On the Political: Thinking in Action* (London and New York: Routledge, 2005).

Clayton Crockett, *Radical Political Theology, Religion and Politics After Liberalism* (New York: Columbia University Press, 2011).

J. Ranciere, *The Hatred of Democracy* (London: Verso, 2006).

J.B. Aristide, *Eyes of the Heart: Seeking a Path for the Poor in an Age of Globalization* (Monroe, ME: Common Courage Press, 2000).

Jayati Ghosh, 'The Emerging Left in the Emerging World', *EPW*, Vol. XLVII, No. 24, June 16, 2012.

Lasse Thomassen (ed.), *The Derrida Habermas Reader* (Chicago: University of Chicago Press, 2004).

Nirja Gopal Jayal, *Democracy in India, Themes in Politics* (New Delhi: Oxford University Press, 2012).

Partha Chatterjee, 'Classes, Capital and Indian Democracy', *Economic and Political Weekly*, November 15, 2008.

Partha Chatterjee, 'Democracy and Economic Transformation in India', *Economic and Political Weekly*, April 19, 2008.

Partha Chatterjee, *The Politics of the Governed* (Delhi: Permanent Black, 2004).

Pranab Bardhan, 'The Avoidable Tragedy of the Left in India-II', *EPW*, Vol. XLVI, No. 24, June 11, 2011.

Rosa Luxemburg, Social Democracy and Parliamentarism, Sächsische Arbeiterzeitung, June 5-6, 1904, Transcription/Markup: Dario Romeo and Brian Baggins. Online Version: Rosa Luxemburg Internet Archive (marxists.org) 2000.

Rosa Luxemburg, *The National Question, Selected Writings* (Delhi: Aakar Books, 2009).

Suhit Sen, 'The Left Rout: Patterns and Prospects', *EPW*, Vol. XLVI, No. 24, June, 11, 2011.

9

Ideas and Praxis of Socialism: The Left in West Bengal 1947-77

Ritwika Biswas

The socialist ideas which found their institutional manifestation in the formation of the Communist Party and some other left groups added a new dimension to Indian politics. This novelty lay not only in its vision of an alternative world order but in evolving a radical alternative. During colonial period while aligning with the dominant nationalist parties for a common goal of ending foreign rule, the socialist forces also alienated them by characterizing them as the indigenous agents of global mechanism of exploitation. Alternatively, they visualized 'true' liberation in establishment of economic equality and political empowerment of masses through revolution. Such ideas created tension and even a tussle in the relations of the communists with the nationalist forces.

In the post-independence period the situation became more critical. The end of British rule removed the common issue of struggle. The ideological conflict between the socialist vision of the emancipation of the masses and the bourgeois vision of the nation state came to surface. Nationalism was not merely a bourgeois construct but it also appealed to the popular imagination. This posed a serious challenge to the communists who needed to strike a balance between their radical vision of turning the existing order upside down and the Indian reality.

The role of the left in the democratic process of nation-building acquired a new dimension in the state of West Bengal, an eastern province of the country. This eastern province occupies a unique place in the political landscape of India. The truncated freedom which brought in its trail a shocking human tragedy not only of communal holocaust but also of massive displacement tended to threaten the existing structure of politics, society and economy. The rehabilitation of this huge lot of evicted people, along with other issues like growing scarcity of food, irregularities in landownership, industrial exploitation and industrial disputes invoked mass militancy and gradually disillusioned people about Congress rule. This paved the way for the intervention of the leftist forces.

Immediately after independence the Communist Party made a completely negative assessment of freedom. It denounced independence as merely a political victory with little freedom from the economic enslavement by the imperialists and their native agents. The colonial administration was dismantled, yet the Indian capitalists who were alleged to act as the native agents of foreign imperialism were said to have control over India's political and economic life. The continuation of this network of capitalist exploitation, according to the communists, made the achievement of political independence incomplete and meaningless.[1]

This bleak assessment of independence was derived from the international communist interpretation of the process of decolonization in the Third World. International guides like the Soviet Communist Party, the Communist Party in China and the Communist Party of Great Britain inspired the non-conformist attitude of the Indian communists. Their thesis argued that the process of decolonization after the Second World War did not bring any fundamental change in the former European colonies. The foreign imperialists left their native agents among the bourgeois capitalists and the self-seeking bureaucrats. The thesis suggested the building up of a people's front through the alliance of the Communist Party with other leftist forces as well as the progressive section of the bourgeoisie to destroy this evil nexus. Actually in international politics the removal of the Fascist threat nullified the justification of the Grand Alliance by the middle of the 1940s. Rather the conflict among the allied parties was intensified. The People's War paved the way to the Cold War with the sharpening of divide between the capitalist and the socialist camps. The new situation had its reflection in Asian countries, particularly in the newly liberated colonies. The expediency of the anti-colonial struggle being over the contradictions of class interests between the bourgeoisie and the proletariat came to the surface. In such a situation the idea of a popular front vis-à-vis the bourgeois establishment became a readily acceptable proposition to the Indian communists.[2]

The Communist Party subsequently built up a popular front. It was a broad-based front having members from the workers, peasants, students, youths, army, women, oppressed minorities and also some left groups like the Forward Bloc, the Socialist Party. But though broad-based, the front was a close-knit formulation. Proletarian identity was the sole criterion in selecting the front members from various social groups. For example, in the agrarian sector the party relied on agrarian labourers, sharecroppers and small peasants. The rich peasants due to their capitalist ambition were kept outside the class alliance. The party issued directives to its ranks for organizing unions in each of these fronts at provincial and district levels on the basis of election.[3,4] The nature of thrust in selecting the partners of struggle was a clear proof that the party aimed at dismantling the class character of the Indian state. Subsequently, the party adopted a policy of uncompromising militancy. In urban as well as in rural areas destruction of public property, seizure of crops, liquidation of hoarding, assault on landlords to stop eviction and to seize lands posed a serious threat to the government and its anti-people class components.[5] But this B.T. Ranadive-proposed line did not last long. Not only the state mechanism of repression created a scene of 'white terror', banned the Communist Party and made it physically impossible for the communists to continue with their disruptive activities for long but a mode of dissension also developed within the party itself. From the beginning Ranadive's programme was abhorred by some of the party members for extreme authoritarianism and reckless adventurism. The failure of the

Communist Party to mobilize sufficient mass support on such occasions like the railway strike in 1949, the decrease in the membership of the party at all fronts either due to police repression or due to purging within the party proved that neither the party organization nor the popular base of the party was powerful enough to execute a scheme for immediate revolution. Rather Ranadive's leadership itself was executed. The party took a new turn in policy making by moderating its attitude towards the class enemies. The new committee drastically revised Ranadive's guidelines in two areas: one, in selecting the partners of revolution and identifying the class enemies, two, in choosing the method of revolutionary struggle. Instead of a direct and unilateral approach to social classes the new committee tried to explicate the internal variety of these social categories and assessed their potentiality as allies on the basis of these diversities. Thus the progressive and non-monopoly sections of the bourgeoisie, the rich peasants who did not carry on feudal exploitation was considered as allies. As for the methods of revolution, the new leadership prescribed the Chinese model of guerrilla warfare at agrarian base.[6,7]

The international mentors of the Indian communists too disapproved of Ranadive's model. In an editorial of *For A Lasting Peace, For A People's Democracy*, which was the mouthpiece of the Cominform Bureau, Ranadive's policy was severely criticized as a Trotskyite adventurism.[8] As a result, the central committee of the party was reorganized with Rajeshwar Rao from the Andhra group as the new General Secretary. But the new committee, tilted towards Maoist guerrilla warfare, was branded with another form of extremism to replace the Soviet model by the Chinese model and, therefore, became unacceptable.[9] A fresh debate arose that ultimately resulted in the adoption of a new programme. The novelty of this programme lay in its flexibility to adapt to the Indian realities without diluting the revolutionary ideology of the party. It made a division between the immediate and the long-term objectives of the party. While the achievement of the complete emancipation and empowerment of the masses would be the outcome of a long-term preparation culminating into a revolution, a democratic movement could be launched on immediate but urgent issues of grievances like the insufficiency of civil rights, high prices, continuation of *zamindari* exploitation, eviction from land, retrenchment and wage-cut in factories and such populist issues.[10]

However, the idea of using the immediate issues of popular grievances and using the strength of the democratic opinion in the country to build up a mass movement opened a new avenue for the leftist forces. The revolutionary change as the ultimate objective was still the cardinal aspect of the party's political programme. But an optimistic assessment of the electoral process too was made. There were three imperatives that led the Communist Party to revise its view of the electoral process. Electoral means would offer the party a popular platform to announce its programme that the underground politics did not always provide. The neglect of the opportunities of immediate action and waiting for a distant revolution might lead the party to virtual inaction. In the absence of the communist initiative the other leftist parties might step in and capture popular leadership. On the other hand, by making a joint effort with the other leftist parties the communists could get hold of the entire leftist politics of the country. In other words, the participation in election was the strategy of survival of a party whose underground activities could not overpower the coercive apparatus of the state by mass mobilization.

The international directive approved this new turn of the Indian communists. Failing to resolve the ideological conflict the CPI deputed a commission of four members—Rajeshwar Rao, Basavapunnaiya, Ajoy Ghosh and Dange—to Moscow to discuss with the leaders of the CPSU. The Central Committee of the CPSU too set up a commission comprising Stalin, Molotov, Malenkov, Suslov, headed by Stalin, to assist the CPI in this regard. On the basis of the Soviet guideline the Politburo of the CPI in 1951 drafted a programme which consequently became the first constitution in the thirty years' history of the Indian Communist Party. In this programme the party's assessment of the Indian state was made clear. It was commented that the new state that had come into existence was essentially the same old imperialist state and the Congress government was installed in power by the British imperialists, as it was a government pledged to the protection and preservation of foreign British capital in India. It was a bourgeois-landlord state led by the big bourgeoisie, which was allying with feudal and semi-feudal landlordism and collaborating with foreign finance capital, in pursuit of the capitalist path of development. The Communist Party aimed at dismantling this state structure. This thesis was endorsed by the Soviet Communist Party.[11, 12]

The programme of creating a broad-based people's front uniting the various layers of the struggling masses on their common issues of grievance widened the party's acceptability to the people. The process of mobilization became most successful among the refugees from East Pakistan. The truncated settlement of freedom cut out for West Bengal a unique position in the political landscape of post-independent India. The large influx of refugees, who came in bulk on occasions of communal insurgencies in 1948, 1950-51, 1952, 1961-1965 but who also maintained a constant flow of migration, not only created a huge demographic pressure but raised a number of social, economic and psychological questions. The people, who migrated leaving their home and hearth, needed both material and psychological rehabilitation and for this they placed their good faith in the Congress government. The anti-communal disposition of the Congress vis-à-vis the communal holocaust conducted by the Muslim League led those uprooted people to hope for their promised land in the Congress regime in West Bengal. So the communists did not have an easy entry to the refugees who were still drawn to the nationalist image of the Congress Party.

But the actual experience of rehabilitation, which went contrary to the expectation, turned the tide towards the communists. Punjab, which was another victim of partition, had comparable problems. But there the problems could not acquire so much intensity because of such principles like the transfer of population. In 1947 the central government itself took the initiative to arrange the transfer of population in Western India. But just after a few years the Nehru government refused to repeat this action in case of the refugees from East Pakistan. Gross discrimination was alleged also in allocation of relief fund. The Government of West Bengal too failed to fulfil the aspirations of the refugees. It arranged a number of refugee camps with the provision of doles. But the measure was inadequate. Besides, what was needed was to provide them with some sort of permanent employment and residential land. But the government's effort proved to be too small and also casual to cater the need of the refugees.

All these made the situation extremely sensitive. The communists found in it a natural opportunity to mobilize the people for militancy. Initially, the Communist Party itself too was hesitant in incorporating the refugee issue in its revolutionary programme because of the dubious class character of the refugees. But the theoretical directive of the party seemed to have failed to satisfy the need of the ground level reality. Many activists found it virtually impossible to justify the emancipatory image of the party without addressing the issues of the refugees and informally attached themselves with the struggle of those suffering people. Finally, after the adoption of the strategy of democratic struggle the party wholeheartedly joined the process. The refugee issue contributed in a number of ways to the consolidation of the Communist Party as a popular force as well as a political challenge to the government. First, being disillusioned with the Congress government the refugees took self-initiative to organize their rehabilitation. They built up camp communities in each of their temporary habitats as their governing bodies and as their mouthpieces. These committees were independent of political affiliation and therefore obliged all the political parties to take step for mobilization. The Communist Party, more than anyone else, identified itself with this struggling community and mobilized popular opinion into a political movement against the Congress government both at the centre and the province. Thus it was through the mediation of the Communist Party that the economic deprivation and the social frustration of the refugees achieved a political articulation. Second, the communists could harness both the other leftist groups who also upheld the cause of the refugees and various social groups like the students, workers, peasants on a common platform to organize united movement on common interests. Thus the ideological foundation of the united front of the leftist forces that became crucial in breakdown of the Congress government in later years was laid down. Finally, in finding the solution to the refugee problem the communist idea of an alternative order emerged as a viable one.

The Communist Party conscientiously argued that by confiscating the large quantity of land, which remained concentrated in the hands of a few *zamindars*, it was possible to give shelter to those unfortunate victims of partition. The demand for the abolition of landlordism and the redistribution of land among the tillers which was central to the Communist Party's agrarian programme got further moral justification as a way to resolve the problem of rehabilitation of the refugees. The indifference of the Congress government to fulfil this demand was interpreted as the expression of the bourgeois disposition of this political regime. In other words, it was the same bourgeois and landlord classes which through the exercise of political power spread a network of exploitation over the peasants in the field and the workers in the factory that was identified as the major force in retarding the process of rehabilitation. The solution to this vexed problem of rehabilitation, according to the Communist Party, lay in dismantling the class character of the present government. Thus by incorporating the refugee issue within the corpus of the general struggle against the bourgeois system of exploitation the CPI generated a unified resistance to the Congress regime.[13,14,15]

The following decades witnessed an intensive mass mobilization by the Communist Party on a wide range of issues of economic, social and nationalist interests like the abolition of landlordism without compensation, redistribution of land among the landless peasants, betterment of the condition of the labourers in the factories, high price of foodgrains, insecure and exploitative working conditions of the teachers and government employees, rise of tram fare, release of the prisoners, rehabilitation of the refugees, transfer of the land of Berubari to

Pakistan, merger of Bengal and Bihar. All these mass struggles were directed to achieve two objectives. On the one hand, they tried to consolidate the regional identity of the people of West Bengal vis-à-vis an oppressive and a discriminating Congress government at the centre, and inspired the people to replace its provincial representative by a people's government of the left parties through electoral process. On the other hand, they were expected to impart a sort of political training and consciousness to the masses for revolutionary uprising.[16, 17]

The constitutional experiment reached its height in 1967 and 1969, when the communists along with some of their political partners as well as a breakaway group of the Congress Party (the Bangla Congress) made a united front and formed two short-lived governments in the State of West Bengal through electoral victory. During this tenure the communists, despite all constitutional limitations, adopted such radical measures like the capture of excess land of the big landholders and the distribution of that land among the landless and poor peasants as well as a pro-worker industrial policy. It is because of this radical policy that the communists not only became a threat to the opposition Congress Party but also clashed with its coalition partner the Bangla Congress and finally the coalition broke.[18,19, 20, 21, 22, 23] Thus it was clearly revealed that the communists, even while operating in a constitutional framework, envisaged a programme of nation-building, which could not be divorced from their class ideology.

This task of blending the revolutionary ideology with the constitutional praxis was not an easy one. The party faced severe internal dissensions and even suffered from a split twice, one in 1964 and the other in 1967-68. The CPI (ML), which appeared in 1967-68, made an outright rejection of electoral politics as pitfalls of revisionism and vowed to struggle against the nation-state until it dissolved its class character. But even the two other factions of the communists, i.e. the CPI and the CPI(M), which grew out of the split in 1964 and both of which adopted electoral practices, could not abandon their revolutionary ideology. On the other hand, they justified their participation in electoral politics as a means to use the constitutional instruments to provide some temporary and immediate benefits to the people, as well as to prepare the masses for a revolutionary struggle in future. Their main difference arose over their characterization of the Indian state. While the CPI appreciated the element of progressivism in a section of bourgeoisie and explored the possibility of allying with it for a national democratic revolution, the CPI(M) disqualified the economic reforms of the bourgeois-led government as well as its anti-imperialist programme in foreign policy as incomplete and illusory, and was content with no less than a people's democratic revolution. The Indo-China conflict of 1962 was a major clause in this dissension. The faction which later formed the CPI(M) was a critic of the aggressive policy of the India Government, while the old guards of the party sustaining their nationalist disposition considered the CPI(M) as enemies of the nation. The heated debate at the international level about the Soviet model of peaceful transition to socialism and the Chinese model of people's democratic revolution fuelled this controversy. Finally, both the CPI and the CPI(M) maintaining their distinction in interpreting the Indian state decided to join the united front experiment, while the CPI(M-L) started a radical phase of armed outburst.[24,25,26,27]

The situation worsened since 1972 when the Congress after a fabulous victory in an allegedly rigged election was said to have undertaken a scheme of terror and oppression to crush all sorts of communist opposition. In the face of this severe repression the communists suffered from an organizational setback and virtually suspended open political activities but survived through civil mobilization and through social and cultural means. This was rewarded in 1977 when the CPI(M) along with some of its leftist allies achieved a landslide victory in election to form the first leftist government in the state. The CPI, however, which kept its trust on the Congress government throughout the turbulent years of the 1970s completely lost its popular acceptability and suffered from an ignominious defeat in the election.[28,29,30]

The debates and contradictions at the ideological level was an integral part of the communist movement as well as communist politics. These theoretical dissensions were moulded by both international events and specific national or local necessities. Sometimes, the compulsions of the international directives clashed with the nationalist urges. These contradictions sometimes caused serious disorder in the party organization and disrupted its programme. Yet, the Communist Party could not avoid engaging with the theoretical discussions. It was a political imperative for the Communist Party to act in consonance with the course of the international communist movement. That legitimized its identity. But the adaptation to the national and regional contexts by the practical interpretations of the ideological directives was a necessity for survival. The search for a balance of these two urgencies determined the course of communism in post-colonial West Bengal. When a successful balance could be struck it could produce a radical popular outburst. When such a balance could not be effected the Communist Party had to suspend the nationalist urge for the sake of ideological affiliation. The communists tended to compensate this loss by a sincere attempt of social mobilization. Thus communism survived and flourished not merely as a political creed but as a norm of social humanism.

On the other hand, by continually referring to the revolutionary ideology as the driving force of its politics the Communist Party could create a language of class and radicalism in the democratic politics of the state. Within the constitutional framework of politics the Communist Party implanted a radical culture. The use of parliamentary instruments to promote revolutionary consciousness infused a radical spirit in parliamentary politics. The training and inspiration of the communists imbibed by the peasants, labourers, refugees and other categories of struggling masses to organize unions; to make forceful capture of land from the landlords; to launch *gherao* against the oppressive factory owners; and to undertake all such popular actions infused a spirit of militancy to democratic politics. The popular urgency to elect such a party that denied the ultimate workability of electoral politics reflected the popular acceptance of this way of politics. The history of the communist movement in West

Bengal, therefore, was a story of the adaptation of a revolutionary doctrine to a regional democracy without dissolving its revolutionary basis. And out of this experiment emerged a radical culture in the democratic politics of the state.

NOTES AND REFERENCES

1. For the Final Assault—Political Resolution of the Central Committee of the Communist Party of India, August, 1946 Collected from *Documents of the Communist Movement in India*, Vol. V, Kolkata, 1997, pp. 103-127.
2. On the Present Policy and Tasks of the Communist Party of India, January 1948—Collected from *Documents of the Communist Movement in India*, Vol. V.
3. Report on Reformist Deviation Presented by B.T. Ranadive in the Second Congress of the Communist Party of India held in Calcutta from February 28 to March 6 and Strategy and Tactics in the Struggle for People's Democratic Revolution in India: Adopted by the Politburo in December 1948, Collected from *Documents of the Communist Movement in India*, Vol. V.
4. A Circular-*Fraction o Bureau samparkey P.O.C.-r (Provincial Organizational Committee) Prastab*, Collected from S.B. Records-CPI Trade Union Activities.
5. Annual Police Report 1949, I.B. Records, West Bengal State Archives.
6. Letter of the New Central Committee of the CPI to All Party members and sympathizers, Collected from *Documents of the Communist Movement in India*, Vol. VI, Kolkata, 1997.
7. A Note on the Present Situation in Our Country prepared by Ajoy Ghosh, S.A. Dange and S.V. Ghate and circulated on September 30, 1950, Collected from *Documents of the Communist Movement in India*, Vol. VI.
8. Collected from *Documents of the Communist Movement in India*, Vol. VI (1949-1951).
9. Letter of the New Central Committee of the CPI to All Party members and sympathizers, Collected from *Documents of the Communist Movement in India*, Vol. VI.
10. A Note on the Present Situation in Our Country prepared by Ajoy Ghosh, S.A. Dange and S.V. Ghate and circulated on September 30, 1950, Collected from *Documents of the Communist Movement in India*, Vol. VI.
11. Programme of the Communist Party of India, 1951.

12. *Statement of Policy of the Communist Party of India, 1951,* Published by the Communist Party of India.
13. Anil Sinha, *Pashchimbange Udbastu Upanibesh,* Kolkata, 1995.
14. Indubaran Ganguly, *Colonysmriti* (Vol. I) (1948-1954), Ajadgarh Kolkata, 1997.
15. Tushar Sinha, *Maranjayi Sangrame Bastuhara,* Kolkata, 1999.
16. The Annual Police Report, I.B. Records Serial No. 255/1928.
17. *The Statesman, Amrita Bazar Patrika, Hindustan Standard* of the relevant years.
18. Muhammad Abdullah Rasul, *Krishak Sabhar Lakshya O Niti* (Kolkata: Pashchimbanga Pradeshik Krishaksabha, 1976).
19. *West Bengal Legislative Assembly Proceedings: Forty-Fifth Session* (June-July, 1967).
20. H.K. Konar, West Bengal UF Government's Land Reforms Programme—Policy Statement, *People's Democracy,* March 30, 1969.
21. Bishwanath Mukherjee, Paschimbanglar Khadya Samasya O Yuktafront (Sharadiya Kalantar, September 26, 1967).
22. Saroj Chakrabarti, With West Bengal Chief Ministers—Memoirs 1962 to 1977, Kolkata, 1978.
23. *Yugantar, Ganashakti, Hindustan Standard,* 1967-1969.
24. Ranen Sen, *Bharater Communist Partyr Katha (1948-1964),* Kolkata, 1992.
25. *Somnath Lahiri Rachanabali,* Vol. 4, Kolkata, 1995.
26. Jyoti Basu, *Janaganer Sange* (Vol. 2), Kolkata, 1991.
27. Jyoti Basu and Niranjan Sen, On Some Questions Concerning the Ideological Controversy Within the International Communist Movement, Collected from *Documents of the Communist Movement in India,* Vol. X A, 1964 Part I, Kolkata, 1997.
28. Sanskritik Andolan: Atit O Bartaman – Sankalan, Kolkata, 1980.
29. Samay O Sanskriti: Pashchimbanga Ganatantrik Lekhak Shilpi Sangha Rajya Committee, Kolkata, 1987.
30. *Ganashakti, Hindustan Standard,* 1972-77.

10

Interview with Manik Sarkar

Conducted by ***Subhanil Chowdhury and Gorky Chakraborty***

Q: *Let us begin by congratulating you. Your state, according to the latest statistics, has emerged with the highest rate of literacy. How could you achieve this apparently 'impossible' success?*

A: We have adopted a clear and candid attitude as regards the spread of literacy and education. We have come out with the declaration that education is the birthright of the people and everybody needs to be given the opportunity to educate himself/herself. In order to transform our attitude into action we have adopted a number of meaningful steps. We began by increasing the budgetary allocation for education which now accounts for 20% of the entire budget. This means out of every 100 rupees spent 20 rupees go for education.

Secondly, along with the increase in budgetary allocation we have given a great emphasis to child's education, beginning from the pre-primary stage. Anganwadi centres have now been transformed into schools for tinytots where children aged from 3-5 receive education. We are trying to bring as many children as possible to these pre-primary schools. And let me claim modestly, we have achieved 100% success in this sphere. The importance of the pre-primary stage is great because children can start going to primary schools only after completing the pre-primary stage. To that extent we can state that we have universalized children's education. Our calculation says that 98% of the tinytots in the state pass through this pre-primary stage while the remaining 2% are educated in private kindergartens and nurseries. Along with imparting education we are providing food to the children at the anganwadi centres. We provide books and exercise books, medical service, slippers for the feet and meals for the mother also. In fact, as the preparation ground for primary level of education these anganwadi centres are performing excellently. Now, the question is, how are these schools being run? Well, these come under the Integrated Child Development Scheme (ICDS) of the central government. Supervisors placed under child development project officers look after the centres. We also direct them from time to time. Our instruction is candid to the core. We have told them that once the child reaches 5 years, he or she would have to be admitted in Class I of the primary school. We issued this diktat three years ago; as a result all the children of the pre-primary stage are gaining admission in the primary schools. I need to mention here that the supervisors, who are government employees, have been clearly told that their career advancement would depend on the success they have achieved in bringing children to the pre-primary stage.

We also have laid great stress on infrastructure development. Let me recall the past in this context. When Nripen Chakraborty and Dasarath Deb were in the state cabinet, they announced that each square kilometre of area should have a primary school. During their days schools were few and far between. So their diktat sounded revolutionary and utopian but the process started under their leadership and today we can claim that each and every locality of this state has a primary school. The next stage was the setting up of secondary schools where children after completing their primary stage entered. At present we have around 9900 anganwadi schools and about 4800 secondary schools. These are all housed in *pakka* structures, they are served drinking water and clean sanitation facilities. The secondary schools are connected with electricity lines. As for the food that is given, it includes eggs as well as meat. As for books and *khatas*, we give these to all kids irrespective of caste and creed. As for students in Class IX to XI who come under the BPL, we give them all the textbooks they need.

All these initiatives and efforts have created a proper atmosphere and as a result we have almost attained universalization in literacy and education. One more point, we do not take any school fees from anyone. Added to this is the adoption of the campaign mode to get children admitted to schools. Every year in the month of January when the annual results are declared and the process of normal admission is completed, headmasters, representatives of the people and officers of education directorate inspect allotted regions to find out if any child is not going to the schools and also if some children are victims of child labour. These missing ones are identified and persuaded to go to the pre-primary schools. Some children who because of their age are reluctant to visit lower classes are given special coaching to cover their deficit. When they attain a required standard, they are admitted to the classes whose students are more or less the same age. We have also identified physically disabled children who find it difficult to move about. We are sending teachers to their homes.

Along with all these efforts we are also emphasizing the importance of adult literacy. The standard Indian life span for adult literacy begins from 15 years and ends in 45 years. We however, have extended 45 to 50. If someone above 50 also expresses the desire to visit adult school, we encourage him. I must state here that the entire action of child literacy and education is a great collective endeavour in which gram panchayat, town panchayat, municipalities, volunteer organizations, NGOs and government departments of education, social education and social welfare are involved. With the help of so many organizations and departments, we can ensure evening classes for the adults. Moreover, we nominate a particular school to launch motivation campaigns in a particular area. These campaigns have borne fruits—the illiterates are now gaining literacy. As a result of all these we have attained 88% literacy, according to the 2011 Census Report. You know, after attaining 88% literacy, a state can claim to be fully literate. But we have refused to accept this honour. We want the entire 100% to be literate and that is why we are now approaching the remaining 12%.

We conducted a survey and found out that 1 lakh 31 thousand men/women within the age group of 15 years to 50 years are illiterate and most of them are women and tribals. This has to be the case because when we were conducting the campaign in the tribal areas, insurgency was at its peak. It was difficult to run even a normal school. We however were determined to break this stagnation and accordingly we established 8500 teaching centres and close to 9000 volunteer teachers (VTs). We attained 95% success from these efforts. What I need to stress is that this entire education campaign was conducted with the help of the common people. We spoke to them, discussed with them and took their advice. They also tried to appreciate our efforts. In short, imparting education turned into some sort of people's movement. We have also cut down the rate of dropouts drastically. In the past, 65% of schoolgoers turned into dropouts; now the dropout rate from Class I to V is 2.9% and from I to VIII 8.5%. At this moment our rate of literacy is 94.65%. We are not complacent and are now concentrating on the remaining 5%. This remainder is our target now.

Q: *Like Education, another important Human Development Indicator is health. According to the latest statistics, Tripura has been able to bring down the child mortality rate remarkably. Efforts are being made to improve the condition of health centres and hospitals. How would you evaluate and explain this progress?*

A: Our target has been the development of human resources, and we also know that education and health are intrinsically related. In fact, these two are the two different sides of the same coin. You see our focus has been on nutrition. We have concentrated on child and mother care. While discussing education, I have said that 100% of children to the schools, along with them 85% of mothers also come to the schools, and there we attend to the health of children and mothers. We provide food to both. Sometimes mothers prefer to have uncooked food which they cook at home. To them we give what they want. We also provide folic tablets to women which would increase their iron content. These tablets are given to fulfil different needs of the mothers, which means we give the tablets twice a week as well. We also organize blood donation camps regularly. In fact, in this sphere, we have been most successful among the states in India. We have stood first in two years, consecutively. Many come to donate their blood and that is required to combat the anaemia of the women.

Before the Left Front came to power in this state, mothers used to sell their children to gain morsels of food. The fathers were without jobs and they used to leave their state with only a few returning. The families thereby got broken and fragmented. But all this is part of history, such happenings do not take place now. At present, no one dies from hunger, mothers do not sell their children and fathers don't have to venture to other states to find work. Indeed, people from other states come to Tripura to get work. But in spite of these major reversals, I am not going to claim that we have been able to eradicate the problem of malnutrition fully. There are people still suffering below the poverty line and we are attending to them.

We are trying to bring health infrastructure to grassroots. We have 1100 village panchayats in the state and around 20 wards in the city. And, our aim is to set up health centres in every ward and panchayat. We have already accomplished 75% of this mission. Wherever we have found finished buildings and big rooms, we have set up heath sub-centres in which two health workers function. They conduct the preliminary investigations and have received training for this job. When the ailment is beyond their power of examination, they take the patients to primary health centres. According to the norms of the central government, we need not have more than 60 such primary health centres (PHCs). But our target is to establish 150, out of which 100 have been already established. Construction work is progressing in 34 more proposed primary health centres. We are also increasing the bed strength of these PHCs. When the doctors think that the patients have to be examined for one to two more days they are encouraged to stay back. It goes without saying that all these facilities are provided free of cost.

Above the PHCs we have community health centres at the block level. This is the stage between PHCs and subdivisional hospitals. Frankly speaking, we need more such health centres and we are constructing them. Our aim is to have at least one community health centre in every block. We will need some time to achieve this. In short, we have fulfilled the need of primary health centres and we are at present engaged in the effort to build more community health centres as well as PHCs.

Now we come to subdivisional hospitals which are placed above the community health centres. Previously these hospitals had bed strength of 50. We have now increased this number to 100. District hospitals and tertiary hospitals function in tandem with subdivisional hospitals. We know mere construction is not enough; we need doctors, nurses and paramedical staff. In the past there was a major deficit in this sphere. In order to cover this deficit and be self-sufficient, we have established two medical colleges in the state. The regulation is very strict—those who graduate from these colleges have to serve five years in villages. If the students concerned leave the state they have to pay a hefty fine. We think that we shall reach the cent per cent appointment of doctors inside the state within the coming five years. In the past women went outside the state to receive the training of nurses. Only a few could avail themselves of this opportunity as the quotas were insufficient. But by building institutes for the nurses in the state, we have successfully encountered these deficits. Not only female nurses but also male attendants are being trained. Even the paramedical staff receives training inside the state. In other words, we are making a concerted effort to build health centres and hospitals and train doctors as well as nurses. We hope, we shall be self-sufficient in this very crucial sphere within the next five years.

Our aim is to treat the patient on the spot in his or her house. For this we need nutrition, clean drinking water and sanitation. We provide clean drinking water in all the regions. In some areas the force of the water is not up to the mark, we are trying to remove this problem. We have calculated how much water a person needs per day, for bathing, cooking and other purposes. Accordingly, we try to supply the needed quantum of water. We have also received 100% cover for sanitation. What I need to stress and re-stress in this connection is the fact that we have been receiving people's full cooperation in our work and we aim to have a flawless health infrastructure within the course of the next five years.

Q: *Identity politics has emerged as a major issue in the Indian political scene in general and in the north-east in particular. How did you and your party deal with this issue, specifically the tribal question, at the political and ideological levels?*

A: We do believe in Left politics, we do not view 'identity' from the perspective you are implying. We intend to regard this problem as one of class outlook. This however does not mean that we ignore or undermine 'identity'. In fact, we think that if we ignore the class outlook we may cause confusion or even step back to a dangerous position. The following truth in this context is unavoidable; namely, that those who are poorest in our country, they are tribals, scheduled castes, minority communities and OBCs. About 85% or 90% of those who are struggling below the poverty line belong to these disadvantaged groups. Indeed, it is this inescapable reality that has prompted us to adopt the class outlook. Hence there is a basic difference between our standpoint and the standpoint of others who propagate identity politics as a separate issue. We feel we are correct in our estimate as far as Tripura is concerned.

The tribal population here took part actively in agitations and movements associated with the spread of education and public literacy. When the Tripura tribals formed the majority in the state, they were initiated into this 'politics of education'. At the next stage, an elevation was attempted to bring them to the level of democracy. You see, both the spread of education and the nurturing of democratic attitude can only proceed if the subjects vote for a responsible political party. The tribals did not fight the king directly but at the same time struggled for full democratization. This led to the establishment of the state legislative assembly and the formation of a complete state. Once this was established slogans were raised to build a prosperous Tripura where education, health, economy, and infrastructure would flourish. There was no identity politics per se in the voicing of the above demands. I would rather describe it as a total movement which incorporated at times class struggles and at other times mass struggle. As we know, class content is always present in mass struggle and mass approach is present in class struggle. There is no point in compartmentalizing the two. It needs to be stressed strongly that the tribals of Tripura participated in this struggle with complete enthusiasm and to that extent fulfilled their historic responsibility. Even when they were a majority they voiced their demand for a separate state. They have also fought for the establishment of industry and laying of railway lines. Indeed before all this, they resisted Tripura's inclusion into Pakistan and the merger of Tripura into Assam. This, in short, is the historical background of the tribal masses of Tripura who played a very important role in the class and mass struggles. I will not deny that some elements tried to fan the issue of identity politics but they always constituted a microscopic minority. The broad base of Tripura tribals refused to go along with them. Even when some elements tried to create trouble following the declaration of Telangana as a separate state, they failed to influence the tribals, who did not extend any support to them. What is to be noted in this context is that Tripura tribals think in a modern manner and independently. They possess a modern outlook and form the backbone of the communist movement in the state. In point of fact, under the influence of the most advanced ideology, they were the first to raise the red flag in the state.

Q: *We have heard a lot about rubber plantation in the state. Does this proliferation of rubber plantation prompt tribal land displacement, that is, challenge the tribals right over their land?*

A: In our state the tribals are most eager about rubber plantation. Sometimes this creates problems. We cannot deny that rubber plays an important role in the state economy; for example, those lands which are not suitable for normal cultivation are now being used to plant rubber trees. We on our part encourage them to adopt modern technology. A rubber tree starts giving latex seven years after planting and it continues giving till it is thirty-three years old. The wood of the tree which was formerly used as firewood is now being used for other commercial purposes. The price of rubber in the international market is also lucrative, Rs 90 for one kg. We have to admit that this urge to extract more rubber has affected paddy and vegetable cultivation to some extent. We have explained to the cultivators that they should not concentrate solely on rubber. What needs to be stressed in this context is that rubber cultivation has changed the livelihood of the tribals and led to their commercial gain.

Q: *Do you think that as a result of land concentration some people will to own more land?*

A: Such a possibility is remote because the Left pressurized the central government to pass the Forest Right Act, which is now being implemented in Tripura. In our state forest area comprises more than 60% of the total landholding. This is also our problem because no one has the right to touch these special regions. In fact, problems are intermixed with benefits. For example, we have been able to distribute land and give patta to one lakh twenty thousand inhabitants. Out of the latter, only two families are non-tribal. We cannot call this land transfer in the exact sense of term. The clause is as follows: the recipient will not be able to transfer the designated land and it has to be cultivated through the generations. To put it simply, we provide patta to the father of the family; after his death the son will get it but he will not have the right to sell it and after the son's death the grandson will come to acquire it. Rubber, tea, coffee, paddy, wheat and other crops may be cultivated in these lands and along with this pisiculture as well as poultry farming can be practised. Because these landholdings have been divided in this way among one lakh twenty thousand recipients, there is no scope for land concentration. We sent a project proposal of Rs 440 cr. to improve the earning potential of these people. Well, we have not heard anything from the centre till now on our request. And we ourselves at present are providing financial incentives to improve their conditions. In short, we will not hesitate to label our programme of distribution of land as unique when one takes into consideration the population as well as the quantum of land.

Q: *We have a few questions on the tribal issue. For example, we come to the language issue on which the state government has pondered a lot and then taken steps ahead.*

A: Language, as you know, is the means to determine the

identity of a human being. Neither clothes nor attire nor food habits are dependable symptoms but language is. The Left Front government has given recognition to the language of the tribals and at present the state language is Bengali which is followed by Kokborak, the language of the tribals. Children of the adivasis learn this language till Class 8 and we are trying to move further upwards with this language. Even at the level of colleges and universities we have retained this language in the form of an optional subject.

The question of script needs to be resolved. Some would say that Kokborak should adopt the Bengali script, while others including the missionaries favour the Roman script. We are not opposing the second view. We are saying that imposition of any language, especially at the administrative level, is not correct. We need to keep this issue open and leave the choice to people and their experiences. We favour use of the Bengali script because Bengalis and tribals are moving ahead together. They are together everywhere from the market to the school, especially in the market where out of a hundred traders ninety-nine are Bengali. For less difficult communicability and exchange Bengali is needed and therefore we have opted for the latter. There is no question of imposing anything on anyone. Ultimately, daily experience will lead to the script which is needed.

Q: *In the past, the insurgency movement was quite strong in Tripura but the latest data indicate that the movement has been on the decline. This means political steps have been taken to quell identity-based insurgency. Could you tell us what steps are being taken to curb insurgency? Moreover, can the other states of India, especially those in the north-east, learn from the Tripura experience?*

A: I shall limit myself to my experience. As to whether others can learn from our experience, will be decided by others. We do not want to teach in an arrogant manner. What we should remember right at the beginning is that these insurgents are armed and to contain them the security forces have to be strong. They have to be given operational freedom as well. They should work without interference from other quarters. In our state we have told the police and central paramilitary forces 'You are at liberty to take measures and steps against the extremists but please do not be trigger happy'. In other words, those insurgents who are caught should not be killed. Rather attempts should be made to bring them to the mainstream. The other request that was made was, do not harass and bother the common innocent people while fighting and capturing the extremists. In fact, people's support is needed to curb the movement and the people should not be alienated. The common people want peace, friendly relations and healthy normal lives. Hence they should not be disturbed. These were the directives given to the paramilitary forces.

The extremists also raised ideological and political questions to which we gave ideological and political replies. Those who demanded an independent Tripura were told Tripura can get all the benefits if it remains within India. We spread this message on a campaign mode and, to be frank, we received considerable support from the tribals. We asked, 'Well, you are demanding an independent Tripura but what is your socio-political programme? We are providing education and adequate health services. We are trying to improve the infrastructure. What more can you do?' We led and spread this political-ideological campaign and approached the families whose sons and daughters had opted for terrorism. We told them to appeal to their children to reject terrorism. The insurgents, of course, said, 'We are tribals. No one bothers about our language and culture. We don't have food, homes, hospitals, roads, water, electricity, or schools. If the deprivation is so strong and many sided why should we stay with you, we shall go separate.' To this accusation our reply has been, 'We are doing our utmost to improve your living conditions. So why have you declared war against us? We want you to return to the mainstream and cooperate with us.' Thereafter we created a special package for the tribals. All these efforts and arguments have won the day and insurgency is no longer a major problem for us.

Q: *Could you elaborate on the functioning of the autonomous district councils in the state? How have these been able to promote good relations between the tribals and non-tribals?*

A: We, the Left, organized movements even during the Congress regime to form these autonomous district councils

(ADC). The Congress rejected our standpoint and claimed that formation of such councils will divide the state into two units. If that had been the case, why do we have the Sixth Schedule in the Constitution? After all, the Leftists have not created the Sixth Schedule. This was created primarily to grant autonomous administrative powers to specific ethnic groups. This, in fact, strengthens democracy and helps to remove errors. We do not intervene or interfere in the functioning of these autonomous councils. They prepare their own budgets and the money is given to them to improve the living conditions. In other words, they present the budget to us and we give them the money to build roads, to ensure water supply and electricity, to build hospitals and schools. We also want the district councils to implement this programme. We are working together holding hands, we don't regard the ADCs as something separate, nor they do regard us as aliens.

Q: *Is it correct to state that the Christian missionaries and Congress supported insurgency?*

A: Well, that has been our experience. I am keeping silent on the Christian missionaries, but our main opposition the Congress has INPT (Indigenous Nationalist Party of Tripura) as its partner. The political stand of this INPT is in no way different from the insurgents. They maintain relations as well and people know about this.

Q: *Could you elaborate on the industrialization programme and land acquisition policy of your government?*

A: At one point of time in the past we did not think at all about setting up of industries. We asked ourselves, who will come here to invest? Poverty and malnutrition even starvation was the prevailing condition. The state had nothing—neither roads nor electricity nor irrigation—it had nothing, so why should industry come here? The picture has changed and the first pre-condition of the industry, communication, is being improved. Second, we are now a power-surplus state. Thirdly, even though the quantum is not great, an internal market has developed, the standard of living has risen and the people have some purchasing power. The fourth point is we have political as well as democratic stability. All these have contributed to the creation of a favourable atmosphere. We ourselves are setting up industrial zones and we are beginning to receive responses from possible, would-be investors. In sum, when compared to a decade ago opportunities for industrialization have increased manifold in this state.

We have told private capital that if they want to set up industries, they will have to use the landbank of industrial zones. We shall offer all assistance to them. If, on the other hand, they feel that they need more land they have to search for it and acquire the land by themselves. They have to negotiate the price of land with the land owners; we on our part will enlighten them on the land status.

Q: *We shall now come back to the position of the Leftists in India. The Left have lost in Kerala and West Bengal and is beset with problems. At the same time, the parliamentary elections are approaching, what should be the policy and the role of the Left now and in the near future?*

A: There is no denying the fact that we have received a big jolt. We fared badly in the election of 2009. What is most significant is that we have lost at the state level in both West Bengal and Kerala. The defeat of the Left Front in West Bengal, which had ruled uninterruptedly for 34 years, was the greatest disaster. We were really not prepared for such an outcome in West Bengal. But this is only a bad patch or phase; this does not imply that Left politics has come to an end. We need to note one different point in this context. When we have a representative in either the parliament or assembly, he/she voices the interests of 90% of the people. But his counterpart in bourgeois parties speaks for only ten. We try to resolve burning problems by coming to the forefront; our opponents on the other hand are acquiring more votes. It is true that we have lost but we are also trying to regroup ourselves. In West Bengal the Trinamul conducted terror campaigns on the eve of panchayat elections and returned with success. No matter what the outcome is, victory or defeat, the Left are fighting.

When you cast your eyes on the multitude of problems affecting our lives, you come to realize that there is no other alternative than the Left. Shooting prices of commodities, decline of the rupee, inflation, suicide of farmers, rising unemployment, closure of factories, a situation of economic depression, deep-seated corruption—this is the state in which we are living. This is the direct result of following the neo-economic liberal policy. We are demanding a change. It has to be mentioned that BJP is also clamouring for a change but their aspiration is skin deep. They are not fighting for a far-reaching, structural transformation. Vajpeyi was replaced by Manmohan Singh but that did not bring any change. We are asking for different policies, for an alternative policy set up. We are asking for Left-democratic-secular politics which will also oppose the advance of the imperialists. We are fighting for the workers, the daily labourers, peasants, tribals, OBCs, minorities and those who are under the poverty line. We would like to reformulate the country's policies bearing their interests in view. We might need some time to come to this stage but we have no doubt in labelling this as the right approach. Indeed, genuine Left politics is the only alternative in the present context. The Congress and BJP are riding on the same boat; as a result, the actual alternative is proposed by us. I would rather not comment on the possible outcome of the 2014 elections. It is difficult to predict especially in the current situation.

Q: *One question is being raised repeatedly, what are the Left doing to block Narendra Modi?*

A: We are not concerned about the individual Narendra Modi. Rather, we are working against his politics and policies. To be candid, there is no difference between the Congress and BJP as far as economic policies are concerned. For example, take the case of the Food Security Bill. Our standpoint was: please do not make any distinction between the APL and BPL. At the last moment we modified our stand and said, 'eliminate the tax payers.' They constitute 2-3% of the population. At present, after the implementation of the bill 33% of the poor section would be left out. The question is what about their security? Second, we wanted the quantum to be raised from 25 kgs to 35 kgs for every person. This was not accepted which means 10 kgs of rice or wheat or daal would have to be bought from the market. Thus we are leaving the poor at the hands of the market. The government is also saying that they will issue foodcards if they cannot distribute actual rice and wheat. The government is saying that they would give rice and wheat at the price of Rs 3 per kg when the market is charging Rs 30. Tell me, how can food security be ensured in this situation? We, in fact, fought for 200 amendments which were not accepted. The Congress and BJP held hands together and guaranteed the smooth passage of the bill. The two parties again cooperated on the issues of the Pension Bill and Land Bill. Our demand was very simple and emphatic—the ownership of the land should be given to the actual cultivators. If this was allowed along with the granting of some more actual benefits, the unemployment problem would not have remained the same, it would have come down considerably. The economy of the country would have gone to another height. Hence my remark would be, 'For us Modi, Rahul, Manmohan represent both sides of the single coin. In order to save the country we need to change the coin.'

Q: *There is a lot of discussion on the possible nature of 21st century socialism. What is your point of view on this? Do we need to go out of the sphere of Soviet experience and concentrate on other experiences?*

A: We cannot divide socialism on the basis of centuries. Socialism does not belong to either the 20th or 21st centuries. It is based on some fundamental and essential elements. The main question is who will control the means of production. We Communists are saying that the state should be the controlling authority, whereas the capitalists would favour market. Russia has now embraced capitalism. Communism in that country broke down for several reasons and in most countries, which have walked out of the Soviet Union, capitalism has been established. Nonetheless, Russia has taken a few radical correct steps on different issues. For example, we applaud Russia's intervention in the Syrian crisis.

The discussion on 21st century socialism has emanated from the Latin American experiences. Several countries in Latin America believe in Leftist politics but their approaches are different. The Bolivarian approach, for instance, is different from the praxis implemented in other countries. At one point of time these countries—Venezuela, Brazil, Equador and Bolivia—were under the thumbrule of the United States. That phase has passed and the USA is not at all happy with the recent developments. I would definitely welcome the advance of socialism in these countries and, if needed, we can learn from their experiences. I would not label them fully socialist at this juncture. Nonetheless, they have adopted measures which have brought a new politico-economic environment which comes close to socialism. We must remember in this context that socialism has adopted different forms. The Soviet experience was unique; the Chinese experience is different from the Soviet; again Vietnam has a model of its own which is different from Cuba. In other words, the nature and type of socialism has varied from one country to another. The Indian path to socialism will also be necessarily distinctive. We have to evaluate our experiences and practices, learn from other models and try to build up an Indian form of socialism.

Q: *How do you regard the look east policy of the Indian government?*

A: Quite some years have passed since the pronouncement of this policy. It is still relevant and can turn into positive gain if the emphasis is given on infrastructure development in the north-east states. By this I imply the establishment of connectivity—road, rail, air, telecommunication—which could change the face of the north-east. In several meetings and discussions I have stressed this point of view in front of the central government. A big step forward can be taken in this regard if we build up a constructive and stable relationship with Bangladesh. According to pacts which should be signed between the two countries, India should provide water to Bangladesh and facilitate the exchange of *chitmahal*. Bangladesh should be an integral part of this connective map which will emerge in reality once the look east policy concentrates on adequate production and supply of power, forging rail links, building roads and sponsoring telecommunication. Once these are done private capital will come automatically to Tripura and other north-east states. There is no point in going to leaders of private capital asking for investment if these preconditions are not met. Even large public sector units can be set up when this crucial connectivity is effected.

11

The Democratic State and the Labour Movement

Taimur Rahman

Pakistan seems to constantly lurch from dictatorship to theocratic reaction. At best permitting only a brief rendezvous with what has euphemistically been termed "praetorian democracy". Can Pakistan's chaotic politics be understood in terms of the class struggle? How is the question of religious fundamentalism, democracy and dictatorship in Pakistan concretely connected to the class struggle? To re-examine the history of politics and state power in terms of the class struggle is the key theoretical question for the progressive movement in Pakistan. This paper will attempt to lay down a broad framework for such a re-interpretation of Pakistan's history with the limited objective of stimulating further research and scholarship in this direction.

Perhaps it is a characteristic uniquely of the historical amnesia from which the "Zia generation" suffers, or perhaps it is a product of this unique period of post-Cold War historiography, that an almost complete intellectual break from past Pakistani history totally obscures the contribution of the labour movement, not only in the development of democracy, but even in terms of their own working class interests.

Therefore, for my own generation of progressive thinkers the first and principal task consisted in recapturing the history of the labour and progressive movement in Pakistan. It consisted in rediscovering the history of the trade union movement and its connections with a left that largely operated underground or in camouflage. Moreover, it included weeding aside the liberal halo that had been spun around progressive figures and grasping the Marxist essence that guided their politics and poetry. In fact, Pakistani progressives have become so good at this camouflage that it sometimes becomes impossible for anyone to discern whether they are progressive at all.

The illusion therefore is created that Pakistan never had a vibrant progressive workers' movement and that therefore the class struggle did not play any role in the struggle for democracy. In this narrative, therefore, Pakistan was created as an "Islamic state" and its current degeneration towards terrorism as the chosen tactic for religious fundamentalists is the inevitable result of its very genetic structure as a state. The few periods of elected rule, according to this resultant narrative, could only be the result of the benevolence of the West, or the struggle within the ruling class. The historical role of the labouring population seems to simply disappear.

This entire research question is first and foremost obscured, in the opinion of this author, with the dominant and overarching liberal view that democracy is the inevitable product of capitalist development. In this framework, classes, attitudes, social structures or remnants and so on of the pre-capitalist mode of production are the principal cause of the lack of development of democracy in Pakistan. At one level, this makes sense given the history of the English, French and American revolutions — since the growth and development of the bourgeoisie led to the first forms of republican states.

However, a deeper analysis of these very republican states shows that although the bourgeoisie played a significant role in organizing the destruction of feudalism in order to clear the path for capitalist development and for their own political ascendancy (either through a revolutionary republican path or a reformist Junkers' path), nonetheless, the new bourgeois state continued to be marked by grave class, gendered, and racial restrictions. Even liberals would accept that these restrictions ran counter to the principles of bourgeois democracy. In fact, universal suffrage did not become law till the 20th century.

If market economies inherently and inexorably led to democracy then it would be impossible to explain the long periods of history of colonial rule and other forms of capitalist authoritarianism merging comfortably with capitalist accumulation. Authoritarian forms of bourgeois rule are, in fact, just as compatible with market economies as parliamentary liberal democracies. In sum, there must be an additional factor that explains the transition from authoritarian bourgeois rule to parliamentary liberal democracy?

Indeed that factor is the labour movement. In fact, it is the contention of this paper that the transition from authoritarian to parliamentary liberal democracy is the product of the growth and development of the labour movement. The classic example of a workers' movement forcing the state into male suffrage is of course the English Chartist movement. Similarly, the struggle for female suffrage was mainly supported by working class socialist parties. And in much the same way the civil liberties movements were equally tied up very closely to the progressive sections of the labour movement. Last but certainly not least, the victory of Bolshevism, the enormous international prestige of the USSR after the Second World War, the revolution in China, and the development of left-national liberation movements were key factors in the rise of welfare states in the advanced capitalist countries and the end of colonial authoritarianism in the Third World.

If one examines what is taught in universities around the world in courses that understand democratic transitions, one discovers that the impact of the labour movement on the forms and structures of state power are totally ignored. Instead, ironically the credit for these enormous changes is given not to the labour movement but to those who resisted these changes till the last.

A fairer reading of history suggests that parliamentary liberal democracy in its current form is not the inevitable product of capitalism but the result of the compromises forced upon capital by the labour movement. Contrariwise, the absence of a vibrant progressive labour movement that is able to force representatives of capital to a class-compromise will more likely result in authoritarian bourgeois states. Last but not least, the unwillingness of the ruling class to compromise with the labour movement produces the most ruthless form of bourgeois authoritarianism, namely fascism.

Bourgeoisie as the New Aristocracy

When the bourgeoisie was an oppressed class it struggled for a republic—a state ruled by the people—since it was part of the people. However, in the era of late capitalism, it is no longer part of the people but has taken the position of the old aristocracy. It has no incentive any more to open up the state to public participation. On the contrary, it would much rather do entirely without democracy. Ruling classes have always fought against democracy, even while appropriating its form.

Social leadership and control over the working people is the only remaining political incentive for the bourgeoisie to uphold democracy. Such a need can easily be fulfilled with a facade. But even this illusion itself is only necessary when the working people are organized enough to actually contest or at least challenge political power at a meaningful level.

There should be no doubt that bourgeois parliamentary democracy serves capital. It maintains and even masks class exploitation. It is, in its essence, a democracy by the rich, for the rich, and of the rich.Yet, parliamentary liberal democracy gives workers much greater freedom in which to organize the class struggle. The rights of representation, association, assembly, speech, and so on, are vital freedoms for the development of the class struggle. Moreover, if a socialist state, called the dictatorship of the proletariat by Marx, is to be understood as nothing other than the extension of the principle of democracy into all spheres of political and economic life, then the struggle for democratic reforms, even within the political and ideological confines of the capitalist state or ideology, nonetheless, accelerate the class struggle and train the working class in the principles and ethics of democracy.

Hence, it may not be unreasonable to conclude at the very general and at the very abstract level that in the context of late capitalism it is not the bourgeoisie but the working class that is principally served and interested in the development of democracy. In others words, it is the workers who want and need democracy more than the bourgeoisie. Democracy, though appropriated by the bourgeoisie in its parliamentary manifestation, is inevitably always principally the need of the poor, the oppressed, and the downtrodden.

To conclude, a democratic state for the rich, by the rich, of the rich is still better than an authoritarian state by the rich, for the rich, and of the rich. The latter of course is very much still the norm in the vast majority of capitalist countries in the world.

Limitations and Qualifications

Thus far we have been speaking about classes in class struggles as binary opposites. These assumptions work well within the context of nation-states. However, in more complex societies where the articulation of the several modes of production interacts with multiple nationalities transformed often making the transition to capitalism under colonial or neo-colonial imperatives are incredibly complex social formations. To begin with, in such societies there may not be one ruling class accosted by one working class but several ruling classes in contestation with several different types of working classes. Moreover, all these permutations of classes are further divided by national differences. Add to this the complexity brought about by the influence of imperialism pursuing not merely economic but also geo-strategic interests and one can only conclude that trans-historical generalizations about such complex social formations become nearly impossible. Furthermore, as with nearly every proposition in the social sciences, there may be other historically contingent phenomenon specific to individual countries that mitigate the relationship between the labour movement and the development of a bourgeois democratic state.

Having made these qualifications and recognizing the limitations of a singular developed capitalist nation-state as a model for neo-colonial multinational states that exist on the social formation of the articulation of several modes of production, let us nonetheless consider whether the model can help us to understand democratic development in Pakistan. In other words, let us examine whether we can posit a relationship between the development of democracy and the labour movements of Pakistan.

Agrarian Class Relations in Pakistan

Arguably the first fact that needs to be grasped are the immense and rapid changes in the structure of classes that have been developing in Pakistan since Partition. The pace-scale of these changes escalating the objective basis of the class struggle cannot be underestimated. In addition to the inevitable operations of the market economy that lead to the concentration of capital, state policy itself was ironically designed to concentrate capital and inadvertently escalate class contradictions. In agriculture, the elite farmer strategy of the Green Revolution rapidly led to a sharp rise in landlessness and the escalation of class differences. The GINI coefficient for land distribution was touching nearly 0.6 points. Its decline in 1972 is mainly the impact of an effort by landlords to under-report their land holdings by transferring them into the name of dependents in order to evade land reforms. But as one can see the last agricultural census reported that GINI coefficient for land inequality in 2000 goes all the way back up to the same position it was at in 1962.

Table 1: Index of Inequality in Land Distribution, 1960, 1972, 1980, 1990, 2000

Year	*Inequality in Cultivated Area*	*Inequality in Irrigated Area*
1960	0.5992	0.5926
1972	0.4215	0.3841
1980	0.4867	0.4433
1990	0.568	0.562
2000	0.609	0.599

Source: Haq (2007: 1018).

Figure 1: Index of Inequality in Land Distribution, 1960, 1972, 1980, 1990, 2000

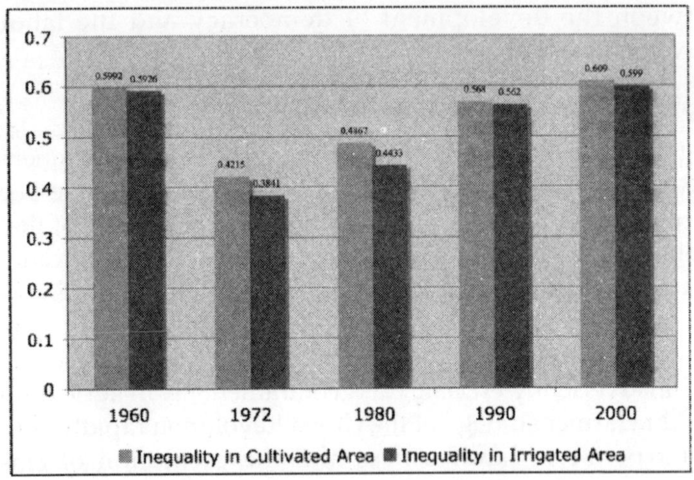

Source: Haq (2007: 1018).

Similarly, Table 2 and Figure 2, compiled from five agricultural censuses, demonstrate that owner-farms are replacing tenant farms both in terms of area and in terms of the number of farms.

Table 2: Number and Acreage of Farms by Tenure Classification, 1960-2000 (%)

Year	*Owner Farms*		*Owner-Cum Tenant Farms*		*Tenant Farms*		*Avg. size (acres)*
	Farms	*Acreage*	*Farms*	*Acreage*	*Farms*	*Acreage*	
1960	41.0	36.0	17.0	23.0	42.0	39.0	10.1
1972	42.0	40.0	24.0	31.0	34.0	30.0	13.0
1980	55.0	52.0	19.0	26.0	26.0	22.0	11.6
1990	68.8	64.9	12.3	19.0	18.7	16.1	9.4
2000	77.6	73.3	8.4	14.5	14.0	12.1	7.6

Source: Agricultural Censuses of 1960, 1972, 1980, 1990, and 2000.

Figure 2: Tenure Classification of Farms

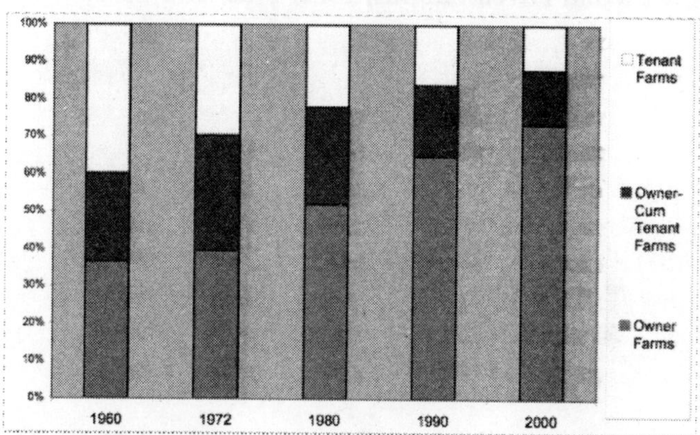

Source: Compiled from the Agricultural Censuses of 1960, 1972, 1980, 1990, and 2000.

These changes in landholding and tenure patterns have resulted in a dramatic rise in the use of casual wage-labour (see Table 3 and Figure 3).

Table 3: Pattern of Agricultural Workers by Type of Labour

Type of Labour	*1960*	*1972*	*1980*	*1990*
% family workers per family (above age 10)	N.A	55	60	29
% of all farms reporting casual labour	N.A	30	45	50
% of farms reporting permanent hired labour	6	7	4	2

Source: Agricultural Workers (2008).
Note: Data on family and casual labour was not collected by the Agricultural Census of 1960.

The 'percentage of family workers per family (above age 10)' means the percentage of family members above the age of 10 that are working on their own farms on a whole or part-time basis.

Figure 3: Percentage of Farms Reporting Permanent and Casual Hired Labour, 1972, 1980, and 1990.

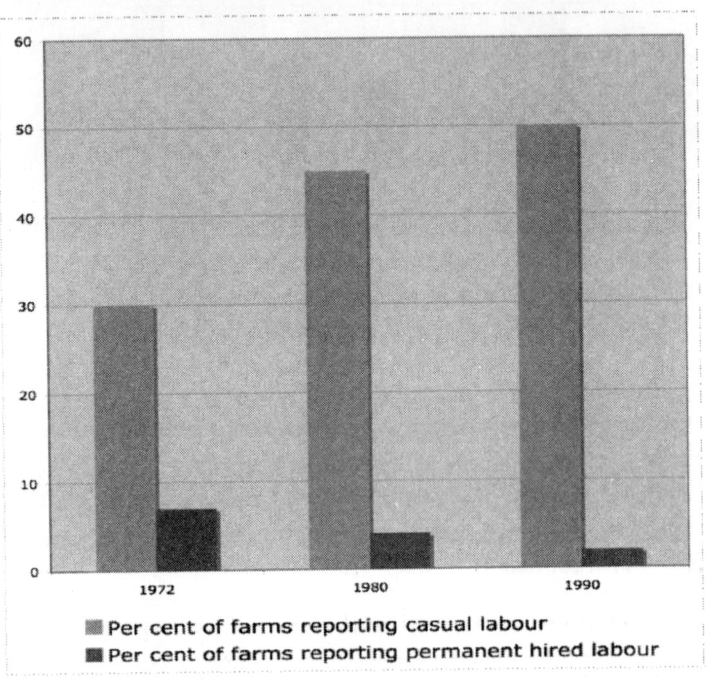

Source: Agricultural Workers (2008).

The Development of the Industrial Proletariat

The capitalist development of the 1950s and 1960s created, for the first time, an industrial proletariat on a large scale. In 1948, the country had scarcely 1,000 factories registered with the government. By the end of the Ayub era, this number had reached just under 6,000 factories. It climbed slowly through the 1970s, 1980s, and 1990s, reaching over 10,000 factories by 2000.

Figure 4: Number of Registered, Working and Reporting Factories in West Pakistan

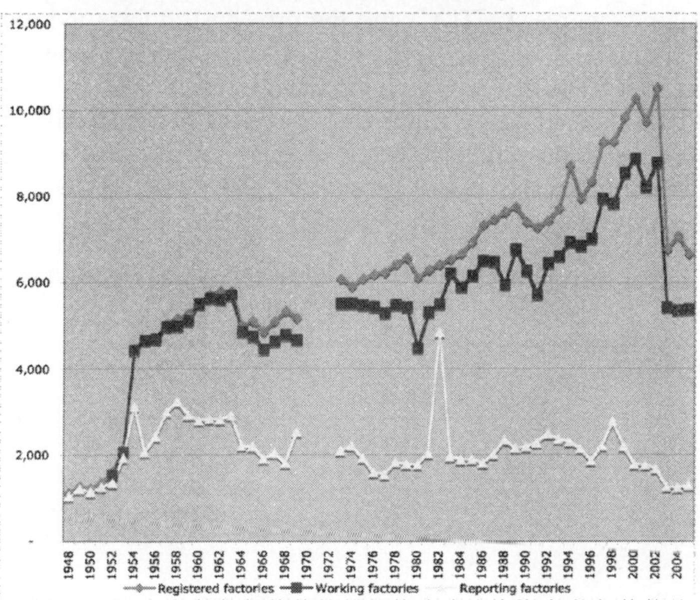

Source: *Pakistan Statistical Yearbook (1948-2007).*

Note: 'Registered factories' are all the factories registered with the government. 'Working factories' are those factories that are known to be operational. 'Reporting factories' are those that have provided up-to-date information, about labour conditions, to the government. The drop in registered factories after 2002 represent dramatic changes as a consequence of the Industrial Relations Ordinance 2002.

Nonetheless, we see from the Labour Force Survey of 2007, the dramatic transformation in the structure of employment and classes.

Table 4: Allocation of Labour Force 2007

Category	*Approximate Numbers (million)*	*Percentage of Total Labour Force*
Agricultural	22	44
Non-Agricultural	28	56
Informal	20.5	41
Formal sector	7.5	15
Total Labour Force	50 million	100%

Source: *Labour Force Survey* (2008: 2).

There was only a very small organised labour movement in Pakistan. Two unions—the communist-led All India Trade Union Congress (AITUC) and the pro-Muslim League Indian Federation of Labour (IFL)—had strong support among the unionized workers of the region that became Pakistan. Nearly 90 per cent of these organized workers in West Pakistan belonged to the public railways; unions were also strong in the Karachi Electric Supply Corporation, the Karachi Port Trust, and several cement plants in Karachi.

Table 5: Union Membership in Selected Areas on the Eve of Partition, 1946

Organization	*Bengal*		*Sindh and Punjab*	
	Unions	*Membership*	*Unions*	*Membership*
AITUC	112	139,000	32	20,000
IFL	641	106,000	23	95,000
Total	153	245,000	55	115,000

Source: Shaheed (2007: 84)[1]

Figure 5 shows the dramatic rise of trade unions after 1970. However, the problem with compiling figures related to the trade unions is that a number of larger unions represented workers in both East and West Pakistan. Figure 5, therefore, contains the total registered trade unions in East and West Pakistan before 1971 and the total registered trade unions in only West Pakistan after 1971. The vertical line in Figure 5 represents this division—its purpose is to illustrate the explosion in the number of trade unions after 1971. From approximately 1000-1500 unions before 1971, the figure rose to nearly 8,000 unions in a matter of a few years. Figure 5 shows that the number of unions remained at this level till the 1990s. Since the 1990s, the trade union movement has been losing its drive and members (also see Amjad, 2001; Kutty, 2004a, 2004b; Qadir, 2003).

Figure 5: Total Registered Trade Unions

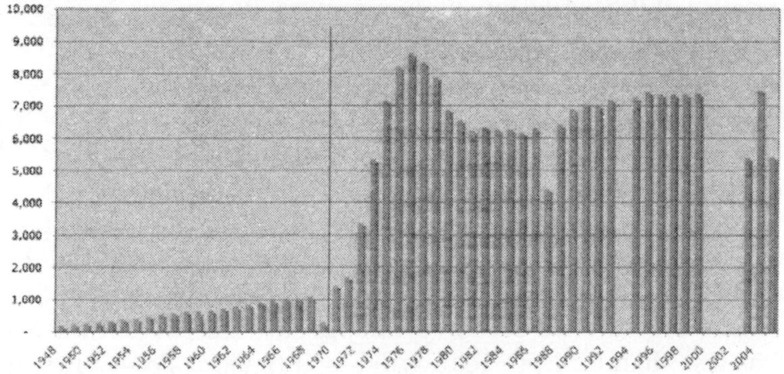

Source: *Pakistan Statistical Yearbook (1948-2007).*
Note: The figures before the vertical line are for East and West Pakistan. The figures after the vertical line are only for West Pakistan. Data for 1993, 2000, 2001, and 2002 are not available.

Data on the total membership of registered unions shows that union membership rose steadily after 1962. The vast majority of organized workers were from East Pakistan (where the unions were stronger). Despite the enormous loss of numbers after the creation of Bangladesh, total membership of reporting unions in West Pakistan continued to rise, and remained at a relatively high level till 2001 (see Figure 6).

Figure 6: Total Membership of Reporting Unions, 1948 to 2004

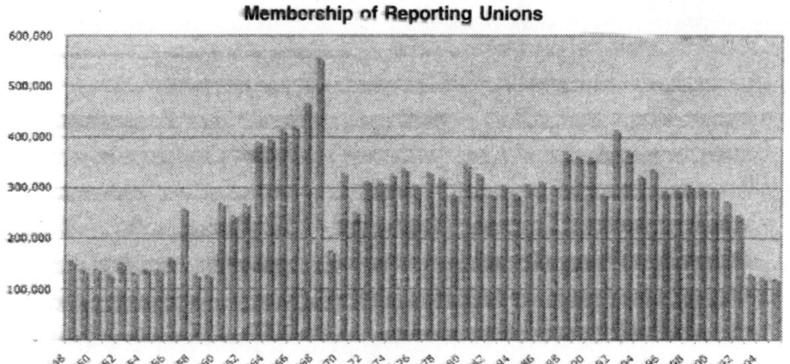

Source: *Pakistan Statistical Yearbook (1948-2007).*
Note: The figures before 1971 are for East and West Pakistan. The figures after 1971 are only for West Pakistan.

The main increase in numbers, after 1962, came about because of the explosion of unions among the textile workers.[2] The unionized labour movement, nonetheless, never represented more than a small percentage of the overall labour force in the country. At their high point, in terms of absolute numbers of members, the unions organized about 415,000 workers in 1992; that is, about 1.2 per cent of the overall labour force—of 35 million—of that year. By 2005, the membership of unions had declined to about 120,000 workers. Given that the estimated labour force of Pakistan was about 50 million that year, the organized section of the labour force, consequently, was less than 0.24 per cent of the total (Labour Force Survey, 2005-06: 2). If we exclude all agricultural workers from the equation—about 44 per cent of the labour force—then, the unions managed to organize just above 2 per cent of the non-agricultural labour force. By 2005, this proportion had fallen to 0.4 per cent of the non-agricultural labour force.

The Turning Point

This development of the working class and the global ideological changes of the late 1960s came together to form a popular Left wing working class movement in Pakistan. Spontaneous student and working class protests, in 1968, sparked a nationwide movement against the Ayub dictatorship. The high point in the development of the working class movement was in this period of the anti-Ayub movement and the period immediately following his overthrow. This is clearly visible when one examines the data on industrial disputes. The figure demonstrates the rise of labour activity, which has not been seen before, or since, in the brief history of Pakistan.

The figure below only demonstrates one section of the mobilization of the working people. But it clearly indicates the kind of activity in other sections of the working people. From the peasantry to the urban petty-bourgeoisie.From national minorities on the fringes of capitalist accumulation to the heart of the Green Revolution. This was nothing other than a broad based class revolt, confused and chaotic as all revolts are, against the establishment.

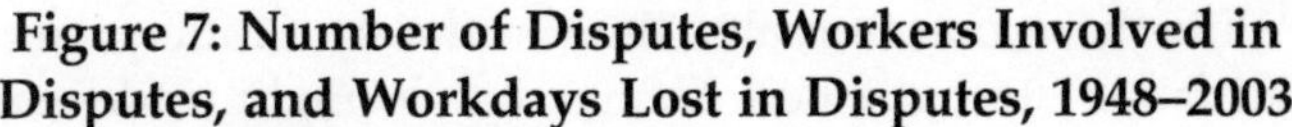

Figure 7: Number of Disputes, Workers Involved in Disputes, and Workdays Lost in Disputes, 1948–2003

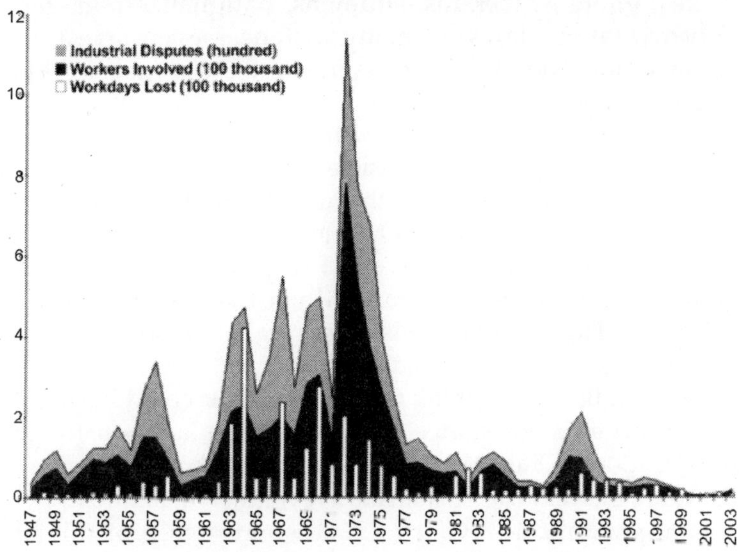

Source: Candland (2007: 43).

This incredible period in Pakistan's history marks a turning point not only for the working masses but more importantly for the ruling class itself. It is the point where various sections of the ruling classes of Pakistan recoils from all secular and democratic development and turns to the Islamic fundamentalist military dictatorship in order to subdue the working masses.

The state subsidized industrialists of Pakistan were always partial to a civil military dictatorship. They had benefited to an unimaginable extent under Ayub. They had no mass constituency in Pakistan's political constituencies and hence could not have won elections either directly or through their representatives. The minority biradari structures were typically developed in a very insular manner that made them averse to mass politics. Finally, they could never have competed in terms of man-power with the far more entrenched landed classes of Pakistan. For them a civil military bureaucratic partnership was the ideal political setup.

With these mass revolts, their anti-democratic prejudices were further strengthened. Democracy brought trade unions, strikes, gheraos, lock-ins, sitdowns, nationalizations, land reforms, labour laws, in many instances even arrest and humiliation. Overall, democracy made the common working person "rebellious".

Like labour agitation everywhere else in the world, there could have been one of two possible outcomes. Either an attempt by the ruling classes to crush the movement, which invariably leads everywhere to fascism.Or an attempt to compromise with workers, which would have led to parliamentary liberal democracy in a welfare state. Much like the agitation of Gramsci's Turin workers this labour agitation convinced the ruling classes that they could crush it.

It is an illusion to think that there was or could have been any bourgeois resistance to Zia-ul-Haq's agenda for the Islamization of Pakistan. On the contrary, the bourgeoisie of Pakistan, the very class that made a revolution in France in 1789, was adamantly in favour of state sponsorship of military religious fundamentalist dictatorship. Provided this fascistic cancer, which was so useful to crush rebellious workers, did not creep into their own homes or impact the process of capital accumulation. Fundamentalism and dictatorship for the masses, modernity and Westernization for the elite.Opium and jails for the masses, Aitchison and boardrooms for the elite.

This inevitably led to a further social divide between the privileged and the working people. With the two sections of society moving in such polar ideological directions (one by force, the other by choice)—now public space could no longer be shared. Cinemas, parks, coffee houses, universities, schools, restaurants, every geographic space in Pakistani urban life underwent a dramatic transformation in less than a decade (see Asad Sayeed). Now it was not merely wealth but even more importantly a new cultural division that made the free and easy intermingling of classes impossible. For how could the riotous rebellious masses who were being force-fed conservatism be exposed to the life, luxury, wealth, and liberalism of the rich and famous. The only solution was the complete social division of all public space.

And as Pakistan's urban elites turned away from public spaces, the entire intelligentsia followed in its wake. To quote some examples from my own city, it was no longer the railway workshops, the Pak-Tea Houses, the tea stalls in Anarkali bazaar, the open air theatres of Lawrence Gardens, the Kot Lakh paths of Pakistan that would be meeting places of intellectuals —whether progressive or not. The locus of debate became private schools, universities, colleges. As the entire intelligentsia moved away from public spaces, the progressive intelligentsia of Pakistan gravitated spontaneously in the same direction. Foreign funding of "civil society" helped, perhaps even inadvertently, catalyze this transformation. This overaching class phenomenon created the most important break between the progressive intelligentsia and the labour movement that is at the heart of the weakness of the Pakistani Left today.

On the other end, it laid the foundation for the rise of Islamic fundamentalism that we see in Pakistan today. In the Left we often ascribe this mainly to the influence of imperialism. And of course 40 billion dollars worth of funding could only have imbalanced the natural evolution of classes in Pakistan and Afghanistan. But to ascribe this to imperialism alone would be to forget that it was the Pakistani ruling class that wanted and supported fundamentalism even before the Afghan revolution of 1978. They used it as a blackshirts equivalent in relation to the struggle against Bengali nationalism. They continued using it as fascist shock-troopers against the labour movement. And they used it to conduct proxy wars in the neighbourhood and beyond.

Conclusion

To conclude, the views that capitalism will inevitably spread democracy in Pakistan; that the bourgeoisie must inevitably struggle for a liberal parliamentary system — its failure to do so is merely because it is not yet fully aware of its historical role or true class interests; that imperialist funding for jihad is *solely* responsible for the rise of Islamic extremism; that the doctrine of "strategic depth" is the main reason for the rise of Islamic militancy and so on are held by many off and on. All these views are designed to exculpate the Pakistan bourgeoisie's consistent opposition to democracy in Pakistan. They are designed to mislead the intelligentsia into the blind alley of thinking that capitalism is not the problem. Perhaps, it is more reasonable to recognize that the specific articulation of capitalism in Pakistan is not only entirely compatible with authoritarianism but in fact is a rock solid foundation for it.

NOTES AND REFERENCES

1. After Partition, the AITUC renamed itself the Pakistan Trade Union Federation (PTUF), with Mirza Ibrahim as its president. Its main strength lay with the railway and textile workers in Punjab. In West Pakistan, the Indian Federation of Labour (IFL) changed its name to the Pakistan Federation of Labour (PFL), with M.A. Khan as its president. The PFL claimed a membership of 50,000 workers in 22 affiliated unions (Keddie, 1957: 580). At the same time, unions in East Pakistan united to form the East Pakistan Trade Union Federation (EPTUF), under the leadership of Dr. M.A. Malik. In 1950, PFL and EPTUF merged to form the All-Pakistan Confederation of Labour (APCOL), with strong ties to the ruling Muslim League. APCOL was affiliated with the International Confederation of Free Trade Unions (ICFTU), and the government openly encouraged the dominance of this union. Dr. M.A. Malik, the president of APCOL, became the Minister of Labour in 1950 and later an ambassador to Sweden.
2. Railway workers were the largest proportion of organized labour in the 1950s. For instance, in 1952, railway workers made up half of the entire unionized working class. After the development of the textile industry, their share in the organized working class movement shrank and the role of the textile unions in private enterprises became moreover prominent.

Agricultural Census 2000 (2003). Agricultural Census Organization, Government of Pakistan. Retrieved from http://www.statpak.gov.pk/depts/aco/publications/agricultural_census2000/agricultural_census2000.pdf.

A. Sayeed (June 1990), The Emergence of a New Breed of Entrepreneurs under Zia, *Herald*.

Agricultural Workers (2008). Retrieved from http://www.statpak.gov.pk/depts/aco/publications/agricultural_workers/Agri_work.html

C. Candland (2007), "Workers' Organizations in Pakistan: Why No Role in Formal Politics", *Critical Asian Studies,* Vol. 39, No. 1, pp. 35-57.

Labour Force Survey (2008), Retrieved from http://www.statpak.gov.pk/depts/fbs/publications/lfs2006_07/lfs2006_07.html

Pakistan Statistical Yearbook (1948–2007). Federal Bureau of Statistics, Government of Pakistan.

R. Haq (2007), "Land Inequality by Mode of Irrigation in Pakistan, 1990-2000", *The Pakistan Development Review,* Vol. 46, No. 4, pp. 1011-1022.

Z. Shaheed (2007), *The Labour Movement in Pakistan: Organization and Leadership in Karachi in the 1970s,* Oxford University Press.

12

Pakistan: Transition to Democracy and Challenges Before the Left

Mathew Joseph C.

Elections in Pakistan always evoked mixed reactions in the international community. The political system in Pakistan dominated by the military rarely allowed free and fair elections to take place in the country. However, the 2013 elections in Pakistan differed from the usual pattern. It was a historic event in more than one way. Till it happened the international community was not sure that it would happen. There was a strong belief that the all-powerful Pakistan army using one pretext or the other would sabotage it. Also there was a fear that the religious extremists who were opposing the elections would disrupt the process through organized violence throughout the length and breadth of the country. Despite all these apprehensions elections took place more or less smoothly with 55.02 per cent voters casting their votes.[1] The voter turn out in this election was much above that of the previous election conducted in 2008.[2] The voting percentage in the 2008 elections was 44.23 per cent. See Ibid.

This was a clear indication of voters' increased interest in the democratic process.

The election results have not produced many surprises. As expected the Pakistan Muslim League (Nawaz)"—PML (N)—led by Nawaz Sharif secured a comfortable majority. The anti-incumbency wave affected the performance of the Pakistan People's Party (PPP) and its main ally the Awami National Party (ANP). The important aspect of this election was the massive showing of Imran Khan and his party, the Pakistan Tehreek-e-Insaf (PTI). The PTI emerged as the third largest political party in the National Assembly apart from becoming the single largest party in the Provincial Assembly of Khyber-Pakhtunkhwa. The anti-American and anti-Western posturing of the PTI helped it to secure the position of the third largest party in the National Assembly.[3] The religious parties performed badly in this election. They could cumulatively secure only five per cent of the votes polled. The main religious parties, the Jamiat Ulema-e-Islam—Fazl (JUI-F) and the Jamaat-e-Islami (JI) got 2.09 per cent and 1.1 per cent votes respectively.[4]

The PTI's entry into the national political mainstream in a big way made the 2013 elections very significant. This heralded a change in the accepted pattern of the electoral politics in Pakistan. In the period between the military regimes of Gen. Zia ul-Haq and Gen. Pervez Musharraf (1988-1999), the electoral politics revolved around the personalities of Benazir Bhutto and Nawaz Sharif and their political parties. The Islamic parties and the provincial parties including the Muttahida Quami Mahaz (MQM) used to join either of them for power depending upon the political circumstances. In the 2008 elections also one could see this trend in which the PPP and the PML (N) dominated the political landscape with the PPP playing the role of the left of centre party and the PML (N) the role of the right of centre party. This pattern has undergone a change in the 2013 elections when the PTI emerged as a third pillar in the electoral politics of Pakistan.

Imran Khan and the PTI were present in Pakistan politics for quite some time. However, this time only the PTI could capture the imagination of certain sections of people. In the run up to the elections, Imran Khan was presented as a Messiah who could cure all the problems Pakistan faces. Certainly it was a propaganda blitzkrieg in which other political parties failed to match. Imran Khan's image as an untested leader helped him in a big way to campaign as an answer to all the ills Pakistan experienced at this point of time. The PTI campaign in the social media helped the party to spread its message among the young voters very effectively.[5] In the social media campaign the PTI was far ahead of other political parties.

Apart from this he got the support of the army and other groups who are opposed to the kind of politics which the mainstream parties used to play over the years. This section included the cyber savvy new generation of urban young people who harbour a sort of antipathy towards "politics" as such. For this section Imran Khan and his brand of politics was a welcome change and they accepted it as such. These sections were behind the PTI's massive rallies in Lahore and other urban centres. Undoubtedly, Imran Khan's high voltage election campaign mobilized this seemingly apolitical and anti-political crowd to the polling stations. The improved polling percentage was an evidence of that.

In the spectrum of electoral politics in Pakistan, Imran Khan and the PTI represented the rightist position. In earlier times this space was occupied by the Islamic parties. Owing to Imran's new avatar as a beardless Mullah, the Islamic parties suffered a lot in the national as well as provincial elections. Islamic parties traditionally champion the anti-American sentiment, however this time that space had to be divided between them and the PTI. The PTI successfully marginalized the religious parties in their traditional strongholds. The PTI's impressive showing in Khyber-Pakhtunkhwa is due to the anti-Drone and anti-American rhetoric unleashed by Imran Khan and his supporters for quite some time.

Though the PPP could not perform well in the elections, one cannot write it off completely and underrate its contribution towards the continuance of the democratic process in Pakistan. During the five-year rule of the PPP-led coalition (2008-2013) there were many occasions when the government could have collapsed following the pressure exerted by the vested interests and circumstances like the capture and killing of Osama bin Laden in 2011. The PPP under the guidance of its leader and President Asif Ali Zardari, displayed utmost tact and flexibility so that all these instances were managed well in a manner that strengthened the government vis-à-vis the army and other deeply entrenched vested interests.

The then opposition PML (N) and its leader and current Prime Minister Nawaz Sharif should be credited for this as well.

In the last five years, on no occasion did the opposition function in a manner that could precipitate a political crisis in the country. It seems both the PPP and the PML (N) have entered into a tacit understanding whereby the re-entry of the army into active politics is prevented. They differed on many occasions and criticized each other vehemently, but never crossed the mutually accepted threshold of criticism against each other. This mutual realization and the resultant acceptance of each other by both the parties helped to improve the civil-military relations in favour of the former. This was certainly a change of course of the usual ways of politics in Pakistan.

During the period of democratic interlude (1988-1999), both parties used the army and bureaucracy against each other. Both Benazir Bhutto and Nawaz Sharif though elected as prime ministers twice could not complete their term. The political instability and the weakness of the civilian political establishment vis-à-vis the army and the bureaucracy were mainly caused by this behaviour of the PPP and the PML (N). It seems they have learned their lessons well and do not want to repeat them again. This shows a certain level of increased political maturity among the political class of Pakistan.[6]

The need of the hour in Pakistan is the consolidation of democracy and institutionalization of democratic practices at various levels. That is the only way through which the culture of authoritarianism nurtured and perpetuated by the army and the feudal classes can be pushed out of the political sphere of Pakistan. The main political parties have come to that consensus. This will progressively reduce the manoeuvring capability of the army and other vested interests in the political realm. Also an important task is to fight the forces of extremism. The extremist forces in Pakistan are of two types: one section is sectarian in nature and the other is targeting the state and minorities. The former category includes sectarian organizations like the Lashkar-e-Jhangvi and the latter category includes Tehreek-e-Taliban Pakistan (TTP) and others linked to the Al-Qaida network.

The army is responsible for the creation of most of the extremist organizations as the army hoped that they would be useful in their strategic calculations inside and outside Pakistan. They were very useful for the army in its moves in Afghanistan and Jammu and Kashmir. The Pakistani army always wanted these extremist forces to be used in its strategic adventures in the region. According to Kazi Anwarul Masud, "... the Pakistan Army and its intelligence services have retained ties with the militants and Taliban sympathizers as a hedge against abandonment by the US in the event of a Pakistan-India conflict."[7]

However, the extremists have a different agenda. They want to transform Pakistan into an Islamic state and use it as a springboard to Islamize the region and beyond. The agendas of both the army and the extremists are in that way going in different directions. From the extremists' side the alliance with the army is only tactical. The extremists would work with the army only to secure their own benefits. The army could not foresee this opportunistic thrust and now the time has come for the army to deal with the extremist forces. By now the extremist forces have developed enough capability to undermine the hegemony of the army. The TTP violence in and around the Federally Administered Tribal Areas (FATA) and the way the army has dealt with it is ample proof of that.[8]

In the specific political context of Pakistan the fight against religious extremists cannot be reduced to an affair between the army and the extremists. The political parties and various civil society actors have to play a crucial role in that. Rather they should be the main actors in the fight against religious extremism. But the mainstream political parties are reluctant to take on the extremists politically and ideologically. The overarching political discourse in the country is anchored around Islam and its opposition to the Western civilization. The Islamic parties and their feeder organizations dominate in this discourse. None of the mainstream political parties have the capability to engage with that.

It is interesting to note that the Islamic parties and their frontal organizations do not have much electoral presence. However, their street power and capacity to determine the tone of political discourse in the country is quite emphatic. They along with the extremist elements largely shape the political discourse in Pakistan.[9] According to their point of view, secularism is a Western concept and hence it is not acceptable for a Muslim majority country like Pakistan which came into being in the name of Islam. Owing to this strident anti-secular position the mainstream secular parties avoid political and ideological confrontation with the Islamic parties. This ostrich like approach is not good for the secular mainstream parties and for the future of the country.

If the secular mainstream political parties are not able to break the hegemonic ideological consensus established particularly after the Islamization drive of Gen. Zia it would be very difficult to broaden and deepen the process of democratization in the country. It cannot be achieved through counterinsurgency operations against the religious extremists. Unless and until the forces of extremism and authoritarianism are opposed politically and ideologically, a forward movement of democratization in Pakistan would be really difficult. This political and ideological opposition to religious extremism and authoritarianism has to come from an Islamic standpoint. Then only will it be effective. The mainstream political parties are not in a position to do that. This can only be possible from a "left" standpoint.

What is that "left" standpoint? Are there any genuine left organizations to articulate that? These pertinent questions would lead to an interesting aspect of Pakistan's politics. It is widely believed that parties like the PPP and ANP represent the left in Pakistan. In the popular imagination these parties are considered to be the genuine left parties in the peculiar context of Pakistan. Certainly they represent the left of centre political opinion in the electoral political spectrum. At one time these organizations also represented the marginalized sections in the politics of Pakistan. The political self of these parties changed considerably after that. Now they are part and parcel of the neo-liberal regime in Pakistan. It would be very difficult to distinguish them from other parties yet they carry the aura of their earlier left political self.

This does not mean that no other "left" parties and groups

are present in contemporary Pakistan. At the grassroots level one can find many "left"-oriented individuals and groups working. The left political groups anchored around Marxism-Leninism have traditionally occupied marginal political space in Pakistan. The absence of a relatively strong working class, absence of a tradition of indigenous academic Marxist discourse and writings and the repression of the army-dominated establishment supported by imperialism were the main reasons responsible for this situation.

The Communist Party of India (CPI) was very active in the Punjab before Partition. However, the majority of its cadre from Punjab was either Hindu or Sikh. Owing to various reasons the CPI could not spread its influence among the Muslim masses. Hence the "Muslim cadres of the CPI were instructed to join the [Muslim] League to organize a Left pressure group within it, and to support its "progressive" elements...."[10] When Partition took place the Hindu and Sikh cadres of the CPI migrated to India,[11] leaving the few number of Muslim Communists there in Pakistan.

The CPI supported the movement for Pakistan on the basis of the principle of national self-determination of nationalities.[12] When Pakistan was formed Communists were not present in adequate numbers to make any impact in the politics of the newly born country. Hence the CPI deputed its Muslim cadres to go to Pakistan and set up the party structure there. Sajjad Sahir from Lucknow was made the General Secretary of the Communist Party of Pakistan (CPP) in 1948.[13]

In the wake of Partition, the Hindus and Sikhs of West Pakistan moved to India while a sizeable Hindu population remained in East Pakistan. After the exit of Hindus and Sikhs, the state establishment and the religious extremists started targeting the leftists of which the Communists represented the most visible and vocal segment. Ishtiaq Ahmad describes the state's attitude towards the Communists as follows:

> ... in independent Pakistan, hostility towards communism became a centrepiece of state ideology. The battery of religious rhetoric that, during the election campaign, was directed at Hindus and Sikhs was now turned against leftists, and class struggle was

> denounced as inimical to Muslim brotherhood and solidarity... A popular discourse drawing on notions of an Islamic order and an Islamic state began to be churned out by Muslim *ulema* (clerics). Quite simply, the argument that came to characterize the discussion on the ideological foundations of Pakistan was that since it was an Islamic state, therefore, there was no place for atheistic ideologies in such a polity.[14]

The hostility towards the Communists shown by both the state and the religious extremists never deterred them from pushing forth their politics. The formation of trade unions and their strikes under the Communist leadership further increased the hostility towards the Communists. The demands of the CPP such as "Pakistan's withdrawal from the British Commonwealth; discontinuation of dependence on imperialism; confiscation of foreign economic interests; and nationalization of key industries and their placement under the collective ownership of workers"[15] were not acceptable to the ruling elite of Pakistan. This led to a severe repression of the Communists. The imperialist support for the purging of Communists made the situation more complicated. As a result of these the CPP General Secretary Sajjad Sahir and his comrades were implicated in the Rawalpindi Conspiracy Case in 1951 along with Major General Akbar Khan[16] and consequently the CPP was banned in July 1954.[17]

After the ban of the CPP, the Communists formed the Azad Pakistan Party (APP) which merged together later with other left groups to form the National Awami Party (NAP) in 1957.[18]

The NAP was a party which talked about reforms rather than revolutionary transformation. In other words it was a moderate reformist party. This posturing of the NAP may be due to the possibility of severe repression under the military regime of Gen. Ayub Khan. The Sino-Soviet split and their ideological rivalry appeared in the early 1960s and this was also reflected in the programme of the NAP. The ideological differences within the party in the context of the Sino-Soviet rift led to the formation of two factions favouring the Soviet Union and China respectively. The faction led by Wali Khan took a pro-Moscow stand, while the faction led by Maulana

Bhashani took a pro-Beijing stand. In 1968, a faction of the pro-Moscow NAP came out of it and formed the Mazdoor Kisan Party (MKP) in Peshawar.[19]

The MKP tried to organize peasants in the province of Khyber Pakhtunkhwa. The MKP led a militant peasant movement at Hashtnagar in Charsaddah district of Khyber Pakhtunkhwa.[20] The leaders of the movement tried to organize the peasant resistance there in the model of China and Vietnam.[21] This movement was happening along with the Naxalbari Movement in India. Like the Naxalbari Movement, the Hashtnagar Movement in Pakistan was heavily influenced by Maoist ideas. Under the leadership of Afzal Bangash of the MKP, the Hashtnagar area was freed from the control of landlords.[22] However the movement could not expand to other parts of Pakistan. The lack of objective conditions for the spread of a militant movement was largely responsible for the confinement of the peasant movement in and around Hashtnagar.

The aftermath of the 1965 War with India opened new opportunities for the left in Pakistan. The discontent against Gen. Ayub Khan which was brewing for some time erupted in 1968.[23]

However, the left could not benefit much from this. Zulfikar Ali Bhutto and his newly formed PPP made maximum benefit out of it. In the atmosphere of anti-establishment feeling that prevailed at that time the Communists and other left-minded people flocked towards the PPP. After the break-up of united Pakistan, the PPP came to power in West Pakistan which retained the name of the country. However, the socialist pretensions of Bhutto were exposed in no time. This led the leftists to leave the PPP and form small autonomous groups.[24]

The military regime of Gen. Zia-ul-Haq (1977-1988) was no different from the regime of Gen. Ayub as far as the left groups are concerned. Under Gen. Zia's regime the leftists were targeted along with liberal democrats, secular modernists and feminists. The Islamization drive of Gen. Zia's regime pushed the leftists further to the margins of Pakistani politics due to their beliefs in "un-Islamic" socialism, secularism and atheism. According to Farooq Sulehria the "1980s were years of resistance against the dictatorship. The proletariat offered heroic resistance and an unprecedented fight back."[25] The collapse of the USSR and the liberalization of Pakistan economy resulted in the shrinking of political space for the left. The left groups in Pakistan lost their vigour in the 1990s following the ideological turmoil which affected the left thinking all over the world and the consequent stagnation as well as lack of direction visible in the left politics in Pakistan.

The weakness of the left in Pakistan helped the ruling class to implement their agenda without much of a real opposition. The liberals and social democrats in Pakistan have been co-opted within the system over a period of time. The marginality of the left in Pakistan has emboldened the ruling class to behave in a completely authoritarian fashion. "For some left activists, the current state of the state is a direct corollary of the disappearance of left wing politics from the public sphere, which leaves the field wide open for rightist religious extremism and pro-market social conservatism."[26]

The first decade of this century witnessed efforts in the regrouping of the scattered left groups in Pakistan. This decade also witnessed an awakening of left forces all over the world by which reinvented themselves in their specific national contexts. In this phase many peasant struggles and the struggles of slum dwellers took place in Pakistan with the active support of the left groups.[27]

The experiences of these struggles were consolidated in the merger of three main left political parties in Pakistan, namely the Awami Party Pakistan (APP), the Labour Party Pakistan (LPP) and the Workers' Party Pakistan (WPP) to form the Awami Workers' Party (AWP) in November 2012.[28]

The formation of the AWP is mainly influenced and informed by the evolution of the "New Left" in Latin America and elsewhere. The ideological flexibility visible in the utterances of the leadership of the AWP is an example of that. The AWP has identified the unity of the left forces in Pakistan, has engineered efforts to consolidate the gains of the democratic experience, worked for the creation and expansion of mass organizations, addressed the issue of national question which is evident in the struggle in Balochistan and fought against the twin evils of religious fundamentalism and imperialism. The AWP is aware that "... socialism for the 21st century had to step outside the traditional bounds set by Leninism, Maoism and Trotskysm."[29] The leaders of this "New Left" are realistic enough to understand the weakness of the left politics in Pakistan and expect certain results in a decade or so.

The transition to democracy has created space for all shades of political opinion to express their views in the public realm. The secular parties and the Islamic parties are using this opportunity to their advantage. According to Pervez Hoodbhoy, "The Left needs to know that there is not a chance in a million of capturing state power in the foreseeable future... Therefore the Left must pick its fights, and not try to fight everyone at the same time."[30] The left parties, which include the AWP and other left parties, and groups, though not very influential are aware of this and are trying to make use of the openness provided by the democratic atmosphere in Pakistan to expand their politics. The main challenge before the left in Pakistan is to make a distinct space for itself in the political landscape and influence government policies for the benefit of the marginalized sections and minorities. For this the left parties have to strive hard and break the hegemony of the elite consensus at this point of time.

The growth and strengthening of left politics in Pakistan is linked to the stabilization of the democratic process. The left parties in Pakistan have rightly identified this fact. Expanding the arena of democracy is therefore the primary political task of left parties in Pakistan. This can only be achieved by consistent ideological and political struggles in the civil society.

NOTES AND REFERENCES

1. This figure is as per the announcement made by the Election Commission of Pakistan (ECP). See *The Express Tribune* (Internet Edition), May 21, 2013, URL: http://tribune.com.pk/story/552368/pakistan-elections-2013-total-voter-turnout-55/ (accessed on November 4, 2013).
2. The voting percentage in the 2008 election was 44.23 per cent.

See Ibid.

3. For an interesting account of 2013 elections see Mohammad Hanif, "Pakistan Elections: How Nawaz Sharif Beat Imran Khan and What Happens Next", *The Guardian* (London), 13 May 2013, URL: http://www.theguardian.com/world/2013/May/13/pakistan-elections-nawaz-sharif-imran-khan (accessed on November 4, 2013).
4. "Religious Parties Not Well-received This Election", *Pakistan Today* (Internet Edition), May 17, 2013, URL: http://www.pakistantoday.com.pk/2013/05/religious-parties-not-well-received-this-election/ (November 4, 2013).
5. See Sameen Hassan, "The Social Media and Elections 2013", published in his blog *The Way I See It!* On May 27, 2013, URL: http://sameenhassan.wordpress.com/2013/05/27/social-media-elections-2013/ (accessed on November 4, 2013).
6. Babar Ayaz, *What's Wrong with Pakistan?* (New Delhi: Hay House India, 2013), p. 15.
7. Kazi Anwarul Masud, "A Critical View of the Political Developments in Pakistan", *Criterion Quarterly*, Vol. 4, No.1, November 20, 2012, URL: http://www.criterion-quarterly.com/a-critical-view-of-the-political-developments-in-pakistan/ (accessed on November 6, 2013).
8. For details see Shuja Nawaz, *FATA-A Most Dangerous Place: Meeting the Challenge of Militancy and Terror in the Federally Administered Tribal Areas of Pakistan* Washington DC: Centre for Strategic and International Studies (CSIS), 2009), URL: http://csis.org/files/media/csis/pubs/081218_nawaz_fata_web.pdf (accessed on November 6, 2013).
9. Stephen P. Cohen, *The Future of Pakistan* (Washington DC: The Brookings Institution, 2011), p. 141.
10. Sadia Toor, *The State of Islam: Culture and Cold War Politics in Pakistan* (London: Pluto Press, 2001), p. 16.
11. See "Left Politics in Pakistan", *Dawn* (Internet Edition), March 16, 2010, URL: http://dawn.com/news/843289/left-politics-in-pakistan (accessed on November 10, 2013).
12. See G. Adhikari, "National Unity Now!", *People's War* (n p), August 8, 1942 in T.G. Jacob (ed.), *National Question in India: CPI Documents 1942-47* (New Delhi: Odyssey Press, 1988), pp. 16-28. Also see G. Adhikari, "Pakistan and National Unity" in G. Adhikari (ed.), *Pakistan and National Unity: The Communist Solution* (Bombay: People's Publishing House, 1943) cited here from T.G. Jacob (ed.), *National Question in India: CPI Documents*

1942-47 (New Delhi: Odyssey Press, 1988), pp. 33-71.
13. Donald M. Busky, *Communism in History and Theory: Asia, Africa, and the Americas* (Westport: Praeger Publishers, 2002), p. 61.
14. Ishtiaq Ahmad, "The Rise and Fall of the Left and Maoist Movements in Pakistan", *India Quarterly* (New Delhi), Vol. 66, No. 3, September 2010, p. 253.
15. Ibid.
16. Hassan Abbas, *Pakistan's Drift into Extremism: Allah, the Army and America's War on Terror* (New York: M.E. Sharpe, Inc, 2005), p. 27.
17. Christopher Candland, *Labour, Democratization and Development in India and Pakistan* (New York: Routledge, 2007), p. 50.
18. Khursheed Kamal Azeez, *Party Politics in Pakistan, 1947-1958* (Lahore: Sang-e-Meel Publications, 2007), p. 111.
19. Ahmad, "The Rise and Fall of the Left and Maoist Movements in Pakistan", p. 261.
20. For details see "Afzal Bangash Speaks: Class Struggle, Not a Tribal War", *Pakistan Forum*, Vol.2, No.9/10, June-July 1972, pp. 14-18., URL: http://www.jstor.org/discover/10.2307/2569038?uid=3738256&uid=2&uid=4&sid=21103472532223 (accessed on November 10, 2013).
21. Ibid.
22. See Saadia Toor, "The Neo-liberal Security State" in Madiha R. Tahir, Qalander Bux Memon and Vijay Prashad (eds.), *Dispatches from Pakistan* (New Delhi: LeftWord Books, 2012), p. 54.
23. For details see Lal Khan, *Pakistan's Other Story: 1968-9 Revolution* (Delhi: Aakar Books, 2009).
24. Ibid., pp. 286-292.
25. Farooq Sulehria, "The Left in Pakistan: A Brief History", *Links – International Journal of Socialist Renewal*, URL: http://links.org.au/node/170 (accessed on November 13, 2013).
26. Sarah Humayun, "Left in Pakistan–1: Political Alternative", *The News* (Karachi), September 22, 2013, URL: http://jang.com.pk/thenews/sep2013-weekly/nos-22-09-2013/poll.htm#1 (accessed on November 13, 2013).
27. Among these various struggles the struggle of the farmers in Okara farms in Punjab, managed by the Pakistan military is very significant. In the Okara farms, the farmers protested against the military regarding its strategy to evict the farmers from the farms which they were cultivating for years. This heroic struggle of the Okara farmers happened in the beginning of this century and it was led by the left-oriented umbrella organization the

Anjuman-I Mazarin-I Punjab (AMP). For details see Toor, "The Neoliberal Security State", pp. 38-65.

28. "Awami Workers Party: Interim Leaders Elected for New Left Party", *The Express Tribune* (Lahore), November 12, 2012, URL: http://tribune.com.pk/story/464255/awami-workers-party-interim-leaders-elected-for-new-left-party/(accessed on November 13, 2013).
29. Ibid. For a detailed discussion on the AWP's political views see Aasim Sajjad Akthar, "21st Century Socialism in Pakistan?", *Economic and Political Weekly* (Mumbai), Vol. 47, No. 45, November 10, 2002, pp. 27-29.
30. Pervez Hoodbhoy, "Can the Left Become Relevant to Islamic Pakistan?", *New Politics* (New York), Vol. XIII, No. 1, Summer 2010, URL: http://newpol.org/content/can-left-become-relevant-islamic-pakistan (accessed on November 13, 2013).

13

Left in Bangladesh: Past and Present

Badruddin Umar

A leftist may be defined as one who is opposed to feudal remnants, comprador bourgeoisie and imperialism. Leftists in this sense almost entirely belong to the communist movement. Formally outside the communist movement there may be persons or groups who are inclined to the left, but while being so they are necessarily friendly towards the communist movement in a general way and gravitate towards it. From Fidel Castro and his revolutionary group to Maulana Abdul Hamid Khan Bhasani of East Bengal are relevant examples. Thus any one opposed to and inimical to the communist movement is excluded by definition as a leftist and invariably belongs to the rightist camp. This is for the simple reason that the communists are ideologically and organizationally the most consistent and effective forces against feudalism, comprador bourgeoisie and imperialism and opposition to the communist movement inevitably leads any one or any group towards the forces of reaction.

The communist movement in Russia, though led mostly by those from the middle class, was based on the working class. In China it was based on the peasantry. But in India it was led by men from the middle class and was at the same time based on the middle class. In the late 1930s and 40s of the 20th century the Communist Party of India organized working class trade unions and peasant associations and some of the movements led by them were powerful and effective, but they did not constitute the base for the communist movement in the sense the working class in Russia and the peasants in China did. This difference went a long way in shaping the character of the leadership of the Indian CP as well as the movements led by it.

There was another factor which differentiated the Indian CP from that of Russia and China. In India the parliamentary system of politics introduced by the British and practised by the Indian bourgeoisie had a profound influence on the communists and the communist movement. This was the reason why in India the working class and the peasant movement organized by the CP remained tied to constitutional politics and the electoral system could not acquire a truly revolutionary character as it did in Russia and China. There is no scope for elaborating this point here, but it must not escape our notice that so far revolutions have not taken place in any country of the British Commonwealth.

There was a third factor which influenced the character of the CPI. Unlike in Russia or China, a very large number of leaders and workers of various terrorist organizations like the Onushilon, Jugantar and others joined the CPI in the late 1930s and 40s. It was the time when communist movement in India began to take shape and be organized on a large scale. The CP came to be led by many former terrorists. They had forsaken their terrorist ideas and practices, but most of them could not overcome their sense of alienation from the people which characterized their earlier mode of thinking. The terrorists wanted to change the society, but they had no programme to take the people along with them. They were well- meaning, but they thought that they could achieve their objective in isolation from the people as their liberators. This goes a long way to explain why terrorist thinking came to influence and determine the line of political struggle in India. In fact, in India the political line for sometime moved like a pendulum from one side to another, from parliamentary practice to terrorism, and finally came to be divided on a national scale on that basis. The division in the international communist movement also contributed to this development. Both parliamentary practice and terrorism in the name of revolutionary action strengthened the middle class base of the communist movement and created conditions for the liquidation of its communist character.

The state of the communist parties in Bangladesh and the character of their leadership cannot be understood without a reference to the communist movement and communist leadership in pre-independence India, because the Communist Party in East Bengal was formed out of it and was led by the same people belonging to the middle class. The communist party of East Pakistan (EPCP) held a party conference in Kolkata in 1956. There they decided to carry its political work through the Awami League which was then the biggest political party in East Bengal. They decided to pursue this tactical line because they had difficulties in communicating with the people directly. Most of the CP members and leaders at that time were from Hindu families. They thought that it would be more effective if they could work through Muslims. For this reason Abdullah Rasul and Mansur Habibullah were sent to East Bengal. Abdullah Rasul did not stay for long. Mansur Habibullah was arrested in 1949 and externed from East Bengal after the language movement. Pursuing the same policy they first formed the Gonotantric Dal (Democratic Party). But the Gonotantric Dal could not make any headway. Then they decided to work through the Awami League.

What is surprising is that they did not try to organize the working people, the peasants and workers. The old peasant organization and the trade unions were liquidated after the collapse of the Ranadive line in 1950. The Student Federation also ceased to be a functioning organization.But the EPCP had no plan to reorganize them. Instead, they decided to work among the people, the people at the grassroots, through the Awami League. Their fraternity with the Awami League did not last long. It ended in early 1957 at the Kagmari conference of the Awami League after their confrontation with the latter on the question of the Pakistan-American military pact signed in 1954. Being opposed by Suhrawardy and his followers, the impractical attempt of the communists to force the Awami League to change its pro-imperialist foreign policy failed. But the communists did not learn the proper lesson from this. They did not realize that it was not possible to coerce a bourgeois petty-bourgeois political party to change its class character. So they came out of the Awami League and formed another petty-bourgeois party called the National Awami Party (NAP) in 1957.

The communists were in a much better position in the NAP and held leading positions in it. It emerged as an anti-imperialist and anti-feudal democratic organization. Peasant and trade union organizations were formed at the initiative of Maulana Bhashani and came to be largely controlled by the communists. But communist leadership did not mean leadership of the CP. The efforts of the communists were crucial in organizing these mass and class organizations, but its political benefit went to the NAP and its president Bhashani. The peasant and trade union organizations were formally associate organizations of the NAP and were politically tied to it. The NAP, in spite of its declaration of allegiance to socialism, remained a petty-bourgeois party. As such it influenced the activities of the peasant, trade union and student organizations. The communists had no way of preventing this development. On the contrary, they too began to be more bourgeois in character, and in the process whatever communist character they had eroded considerably. Thus, while trying to develop NAP as a socialist party, the communists themselves began to imbibe all sorts of petty-bourgeois values and in spite of all their revolutionary clap-trap the party largely lost whatever communist character it previously had. This change was clearly visible after the communists left the NAP. They did not realize what harm was already done to their own character and their ideological perception. They failed to realize that a basic rightward trend already developed in their party. This process continued after the split in the international communist movement and through the fractured development of the new parties.

The CP in East Pakistan was further alienated from the broad masses of the people, the workers and the peasants, in the changed circumstances. As has been said earlier, the leadership of EPCP was not only middle class but the vast majority of leaders and workers came from Hindu families. Apart from being middle class, as Hindus, they felt isolated from the people, the vast majority of whom were Muslims who were under the spell of Pakistan. After the partition of the country the CP led peasant movements in certain areas of East Bengal, but those areas were all inhabited mostly by non-Muslims, Santals, Hajangs and such others. After the collapse of those movements, the CP had no peasant orgaizations. The idea of organizing peasants and workers were virtually abandoned by the CP after 1950 and they decided to reach the people through petty bourgeois political parties organized and led mostly by Muslims. With this object in view they first took the initiative in organizing the Gonotantri Dal and then decided to work also through the Awami League.

These are very important and decisive factors which determined the character of the CP, its leaders and members in general. In spite of all declarations of working class leadership and revolution, the EPCP was basically a party of the middle class like its parent organization, the Communist Party of India. On the eve of the war of independence, the pro-Chinese parties followed the Naxalbari line formulated by Charu Majumdar, which in spite of its declared pro-peasant character had no real mass base in the countryside and quickly degenerated into terrorism.

There is no scope for a detailed account of what happened to the CPs in 1971, but it has to be stated briefly. The pro-Russian EPCP endorsed the Awami League line without any reservation and thereby virtually liquidated whatever remained of their so-called communist character. As a follow up of this development they formally liquidated the CPB and merged with the Bangladesh Krishak Sramik Awami League (BAKSAL) formed by Sheikh Mujibur Rahman in 1975 and formally became a part of the ruling class. The pro-Chinese Communist parties which were called EPCP (ML), opposed the Awami League line and described the fight between the Awami League and the Pakistan military government as a fight between two dogs. Being wholly divorced from the realities of the existing political situation in 1971, they were completely alienated from the people. Their line was doomed and it liquidated their position as communist parties. Each of these parties was split during the course of the war, and in spite of their nominal existence became politically irrelevant. After 1971, Sheikh Mujibur Rahman hunted down his political opponents like the Jatiya Samajtantric Dal, a breakaway section of the Awami League, and particularly the leaders and workers of the pro-Chinese CPs and their sympathizers and killed thousands of them. The Rakkhi Bahini, a para military force, formed by him, had its camps throughout Bangladesh and it arrested and then tortured and physically liquidated them.

The ruling Awami League was a party of lawyers, jute brokers, other kinds of middlemen, small traders, primary and secondary school teachers, insurance agents, unemployed youth, etc who were divorced from production, After seizing state power, instead of acquiring wealth through production, they began to plunder existing wealth. In order to extend their area of plunder, they nationalized industries, commercial houses, banks, etc in the name of socialism. In addition to this, thousands of opportunities were created for the Bengalis to build their careers and acquire wealth. In the absence of any left and democratic political process, the entire youth in Bangladesh began to avail themselves of every opportunity at hand to build their careers and fortunes and it shaped their mindset. From that time onwards, for them there was no looking back. It became a part of their culture.

This turned out to be the most serious impediment to a new left political development. The CPB which merged with Sheikh Mujib's BAKSAL was revived when Ziaur Rahman lifted the ban on political parties. But emerging from the womb of a fascist party like BAKSAL it had no communist character. It is still the largest of the so-called left parties in Bangladesh, but being still ideologically tied to the Awami League it is impotent as a leftist political force. The pro-Chinese parties split into several groups and tried to reorganize themselves after 1971. But, being theoretically bankrupt, they were incapable to formulate any concrete and workable line for a new political development. Consequently, they became parties or groups of no consequence.

After the establishment of Bangladesh, the contradictions which intervened in the growth and development of the revolutionary communist movement in India and East Pakistan were resolved or became inconsequential. Communal, linguistic, racial and regional contradictions which acted as impediments were virtually removed. What survived was the class contradiction. In such a situation it was natural to expect that class contradictions would rapidly develop. The youth and the common people were expected to join the socialist movement actively and in large numbers. But that did not happen. As has been said above, unprecedented opportunities opened up before the old and new generations of people and in the absence of any mentionable left or communist movement, personal careerism became the order of the day. Bangladesh came to be ruled by a regime which began to expand and consolidate a new middle class basically through all conceivable ways of plunder, corruption and deception and it created a social and cultural climate in which any revolutionary development became utterly impossible. It created habits and attitudes of the new middle class which made them indifferent, and even hostile, to the interests of the broad masses of the people, the peasants and workers. In the old days revolutionary ideas used to attract a significant section of students and the youth. But the state of the society in Bangladesh became such that the new generation was not at all inclined towards socialist and revolutionary ideas and not interested in organizing any movement for a radical social change. On the contrary, for promoting their self-interest they developed a kind of commitment for maintaining the status quo. This has not changed even after 42 years of the independence of Bangladesh.

It, however, cannot be said that the students and the youth in Bangladesh are indifferent or apathetic to politics. Reactionary political parties like the Awami League, the BNP and the Jamat-e-Islami have their large student and youth organizations. They dominate the educational institutions and rule the streets. It is quite consistent with the general condition of the new society in Bangladesh in which pursuit of self-interest has become the summum bonum of the new generation. Vested interests have been created for them and they have developed a stake in middle class politics. Thus the leaders and leading workers of student and youth organizations of the parties in power not only get large sums of money form their parent organizations, but are also allowed to make money by manipulating government and university tenders. Collecting money as chanda or contribution from commercial establishments and rich people is a major source of their acquiring money. These are nothing but forces of plunder let loose in the political field by the ruling class. Here mention has been made of student and youth politics of the middle class because the leaders and workers of student and youth organizations of the traditional left are also drawn from the middle class and are influenced by them.

One other factor must be mentioned here. In addition to domestic intelligence operations, Bangladesh has now become a field of various international intelligence agency operations. In addition to this, there are foreign-financed non-government organizations (NGOs), some of which organize intelligence operations in addition to their overt activities. Students, youth and other people active in political, cultural and other areas are not wanting who are connected with them. These intelligence operators infiltrate more in the leftist than in the rightist organizations. I have described here very briefly not the condition of the left movement, but that of the left itself, because this is the most important aspect of the present situation. If we properly understand the character and condition of the left, then the virtual absence of any effective leftist movement and the character of some minor movements led by them will become quite evident. It is not surprising that today, the left in Bangladesh has practically no workers and peasant organizations worth the name and their student and youth organizations are unworkable political instruments for any kind of revolutionary movement. They all operate within the framework of bourgeois politics.

It, however, would not be proper to say that the entire new generation is totally indifferent to the condition of the people and are unwilling to do anything for them. There are some who try to help exploited, oppressed and distressed people in their individual capacity. There are others who, in small groups, organize some kind of charitable activities. But in spite of their good intentions their efforts are basically non-political and do not contribute in any way to develop democratic and socialist political organizations and movements without which it is not possible to effectively strengthen any struggle for social change.

At the end it must be mentioned that in the situation obtaining in Bangladesh, as has been described above, there exist very small Communist organizations which operate outside the framework of ruling class politics. In the face of an indifferent people, a hostile bourgeois intelligentsia and press and a fascist ruling class, they are struggling hard. But in spite of great possibilities, their influence on the general political situation is still insignificant. It is, therefore, no exaggeration to say that the left as a political force has long been ineffective in Bangladesh. What is known as left, particularly the traditional left, may be described as left of the ruling class.

14

Democracy and Statecraft in a Neo-liberal World: Narratives and Counter-narratives in Bangladesh

Meghna Guhathakurta

Bangladesh is at a critical juncture. Many seem to think it is on the verge of becoming a middle-income country and celebrate that idea. Others are wary of what such a development can mean for the millions of people still struggling to achieve minimal standards of living in a world being rapidly encroached by subtle and not so subtle forms of corporatism. The notion of democracy and rights are also being negotiated in the national and international arena by neo-liberal forms of state power. My paper offers a critical commentary of such trends perceived as it is from Left scholarship.

Introduction: Social Transformation in Bangladesh

Agriculture was once the basis of the socio-economic structure of Bangladesh. But in the last forty years, this rain-fed agriculture subsystem has been undergoing transformation. Rice was a staple crop which was cultivated three times a year in the Aus, Aman and Boro season. The Aman season during the monsoon season was the most cultivated with the highest production. In the Boro season when rice was grown in during the dry winter season was only grown in low lying areas. But in recent decades the technology of High Yielding Variety rice combined with the supply of irrigation through deep and shallow tube wells jointly owned by farmers of an area brought together through government and NGO interventions have worked to make this the highest producing rice season transforming Bangladesh from a basket case of the 1970s to an economy that is self-sufficient in food.

But on the other hand, we see a discerning trend in the decrease of agricultural households. According to government figures of 2008 the gross numbers of agricultural farms have increased but the percentage of households depending on agriculture had decreased. For example, in 1983/84 the percentages of agricultural farms were 72.70%, in 1996 that decreased to 66.18% and in 2008 it became 56.74%. In the same vein we see a parallel decreasing trend in the rural households dependent on income from agriculture. In 1983/84 they constituted 69.7%, in 1996, they became 35.90% and in 2008 they decreased to 34.90%. The percentage of landless in 2008 was seen to be 12.84% which in 1996 was 10.18% and in 1983/84 was 8.67%. (BBS, 2007) What these figures demonstrate is that although the Bangladesh economy is still to a large extent agriculture-based, the trend is on the decrease. The reason for this could be the demographic pressure and the division and fragmentation of farm land, which is causing landlessness and a greater rate of migration to the cities. (Guhathakurta, 2013).

Migration has not been limited to the cities too. From its very beginning the Bangladesh state had selected manpower export as one of the prime mechanisms in which to address its population pressure. Currently Bangladesh is one of the main migrant sending countries in the world using both official formal channels and unofficial channels. In the year 2012, the official figures for migration came to 0.50 million and in that same year the official earnings from remittances sent back through migrants amounted to 10.9 billion dollars, in other words constituting about one-fourth of the total export earnings of Bangladesh.

The impact of this phenomenon on society, and politics on the country and outside has been tremendous. Most of the money invested from this earning has been put into real estate and the construction business. As a result, shopping malls have mushroomed and the cityscape has been changing drastically.

On the other hand, as a result of the increasing primacy of the non-agricultural sector in the economy, there has been an increasing interest in education that would provide an alternate means to livelihood. From 1980 to 2009, women's literacy rate has increased to 30% and male literacy has increased to 21%. Women's entry into the urban workforce has also shot up given the mushrooming rise and consolidation of the RMG industries. Linked with extension of basic education the proliferation of technology affectionately and politically coined as Digital Bangladesh has enabled the linkage of the rural and urban the national and international at a rate that was hitherto unprecedented (Guhathakurta, 2013).

All this has had the impact of long-term effects in the social formation. A new rising middle class whose base is small capital and trade, are not limited to urban sites but also cover rural areas is emerging. It is this trend that is giving way to a strong domestic market which was absent in the time of Bangladesh's independence. But before we talk about Bangladesh it would be pertinent to review some of the trends that is impacting Bangladesh from the global perspective.

Political Economy

The New Global Horizon

In recent years a major economic crisis—characterized as the "Global Economic Crisis" has impacted many parts of the world especially those suspect to the ups and down of finance capital. It has shaken the global economic power in general but has shifted the global economic power structure in favour of Asia. The factors responsible for this were that Asian economies are characterized by "high savings and investment levels, considered to be key elements for sustaining higher economic growth, high growth in private sector driven domestic demand which has made these countries attractive destinations for FDI; strong balance of payments positions characterized by high level of reserves and sustainable level of current account balances, stronger fiscal positions with adequate space to respond to the crisis without giving rise to medium and long-term sustainability issues. But Bangladesh's position in this all Asia perspective needs to be viewed from the time of its incorporation onto the global economic order as a peripheral economy. (Mansur and Islam, 2010)

The Global Neo-liberal Paradigm

Bangladesh has been entrenched into the global political order ever since its inception, but in the late 1980s with the growth of the neo-liberal order and the pressure of privatization, economic transformations were also taking place within Bangladesh. Neo liberal regimes upheld the minimalist state syndrome, although for certain south-east Asian states like Malaysia and Singapore, where strong authoritarian regimes held sway but stable conditions and high growth rates gave rise to the phenomenon known as the New Tigers. There have been more doubts than debate as to whether Bangladesh would ever be able to follow that model, as despite the periods of military backed government which had come to power in the 42 years of Bangladesh's independence, none had been able to bring about that stability, and yet as we look at the future scenario of Bangladesh, it is according to many on the verge of becoming a middle-income country.

Bangladesh's experience with other Asian countries has been better than expected. It was hit by the crisis, but at a later stage than expected. More than 80% of Bangladesh's exports are destined to the EU and the USA, both of which were severely impacted by the crisis. It's narrow export base comprising mostly of textile products also made Bangladesh's economy vulnerable to the crisis. Both unit price and volume of textile exports to both destinations declined significantly, but continued strong demand, supported by strong inflow of migrant workers' remittances (which was used to provide stimulus packages for export and agricultural sectors) helped sustain the domestic economy despite sluggish export demands. Among the key macro-economic policies adopted were to boost agricultural output, support the export sector suffering from power shortages, and providing inputs to diversify export destinations. (Mansur and Islam, 2010).

From the perspective of the Left the above developments indicate the extent that the respectable growth rate of 5.5-6% that economists so boasted about was sustained predominantly by the hard labour of workers both migrants and national as well as the effort of agricultural workers and farmers. It is time therefore to have a look at what has been happening in these spheres that has been able or unable to impact Left discourse. The current debate on primitive accumulation provides us with an ideal entry point.

The Left Discourse—Addressing New Realities

Demystifying and Contextualizing the Classical Discourse

In the classical Marxist discourse primitive accumulation "entailed taking land, say, enclosing it, and expelling a resident population to create a landless proletariat, and then releasing the land into the privatized mainstream of capital accumulation". More recently David Harvey's adaptation and redeployment of Marx's notion of 'primitive accumulation'—under the heading of 'accumulation by dispossession' (Harvey, 2003)—has reignited interest in the concept among geographers and others (Glassman, 2006). The main thrust of their thesis is that primitive accumulation not only creates 'the conditions for capitalism' at its historic origin, but also renews the conditions of its expansion over time. Viewed in this perspective, it is an ongoing process which is integrally related to the expansionary dynamic of capitalist development. On the one hand, primitive accumulation is logically prior to capitalist production; on the other, it both precedes and follows the expansion of capitalist production in historical time (Adnan, 2013).

In this form primitive accumulation as accumulation has been applied to both the global north as well as the post-colonial south with implications for understanding contemporary neo-liberal globalization and the political struggles it generates.

In the post-colonial south the mechanism of primitive accumulation is distinctively different from expanded reproduction and centralization of capital. The difference is specified in terms of the nature and purpose of the accumulative process, rather than the specific forms and institutional mechanisms involved, i.e. whether market or non-market, or non-economic coercive or voluntary mechanisms. In other words, the 'transformation of social property relations constitutes the real primitive accumulation, providing the prior basis which compel economic agents to behave in specific ways characteristic of capitalist production (Adnan, 2013). For example, if land grabbing is to be considered as an instance of primitive accumulation then it should feed into the expansionary dynamic of capitalist production and not merely be seen as a means of extracting (pre-capitalist ground) rent or, as well as the basis of traditional social status and political power among the peasantry. Mechanism of primitive accumulation in short must make available resources in forms of property that can be potentially deployed in capitalist production, i.e. as capital and labour power.

Having said that one must then focus on the processes of forming a proletariat that Marx had originally forecast but which has been revisited by many neo-Marxists. They have seen primitive accumulation to be useful for capitalists and many have said that they discourage them from intentionally promoting full proletarianization (Wallerstein, 1979: 277–78, 290). Glassman suggest that the contours of class struggle are indeterminate and in this way primitive accumulation remains a fixture within capitalist development. Workers may struggle, as Wallerstein suggests, to gain employment aswage laborers, as well as to gain access to the forms of social expenditure that have oftenaccompanied full proletarianization. "But there is also a long historyof workers resisting their full proletarianization —primarily because of the loss of independence entailed and the undesirabilityof working conditions in the waged jobs availableto workers removed from agriculture, petty commodity production, and the like. Given these complexities, the process of proletarianization seems much more a contingent outcome of specific class struggles than a predetermined trajectory of capitalist development. Forces exist that both accelerate and retard proletarianization, and neither kind of force is the exclusive preserve of one or another social group" (Glassman, 2006).

A further complexity works when the arena of social reproduction is perceived as integrated into formal processes of capitalist accumulation. For example, activities such as research and development, publicly funded training and education of workers, gendered and racialized household labour are considered to be connected to capitalist property relations, a terrain that has been termed as the 'social factory' (Tronti, 1973). This is particularly relevant to feminist analyses of gendered labour of social reproduction and ways in which household labour and subsistence production have made possible the accumulation of capital in the cash economy. Some scholars such as Maria Mies have gone even further to conclude that patriarchal control of women's bodies that engenders division of labour is an instance of primitive accumulation. All this obviously has implications for the organization of class struggles and perspectives from the left in Bangladesh. I shall draw some examples from Bangladesh which illustrate what has been thus far theoretically narrated.

Structural Transformation in Rural Areas: Changes in Traditional Agriculture

First, we will look at the changes arising in the agrarian system where a capitalist form is emerging through market forces, both national and international. Second, we will look at trends where although differentiation of classes emerges in areas of shrimp farming, albeit in a nuanced way.

In Bangladesh, especially in the rural areas, land is considered as the key determinant of poverty, inequality and livelihoods. Poverty mapping studies strongly suggested that poverty is densely concentrated among these rural households who do not have access to productive assets such as land, water and common resources. As the ICARRD Declaration rightly pointed out food insecurity, hunger and rural poverty often result from the imbalances in the present process of development which hinders access to land, natural resources and livelihood assets in a sustainable manner. In Bangladesh, about 67% of total households are marginal and landless, a major portion of these households' livelihood depends on land leasing and sharecropping thus viability and sustainability of these families are very often threatened by the land owners. There has been a significant change in land leasing practices since the 1990s that is evident from the following Table:

S. No.	*Land Leasing System*	*% of Land Leased*	
		In 1997	*In 2007*
1	Sharecropping (one-half system)	60	10
2	Sharecropping (two-third system)	5	10
3.	Collateral leasing system	10	5
4	Contract leasing system	15	45
5	Cash leasing system	10	30

Source: Selim Raihan, Sohani Fatehin and Iftekharul Haque, 2009. *Field Study in Rangpur*

The above study documented a notable and significant change in land leasing patterns in greater Rangpur region of Bangladesh. Data revealed that sharecropping has reduced drastically with the emergence of other dominant patterns of leasing, i.e. contract leasing and cash leasing system. Rapid population growth, introduction of cash crop cultivation, land owners' migration to cities, and most importantly rise in prices of agricultural produces contributed in reshaping the dominant land-leasing system, especially the sharecropping practice that prevailed over centuries. Market forces replaced a great part of the localized practice and capitalist mode of production that emerged strongly in agriculture. In the"Contract System" of leasing, the cultivator agrees with the landowner to pay a fixed amount of the produce after harvesting. The rest of the produce is kept by the cultivator. So, the more a cultivator produces, the more he/she can keep for themselves. According to the cultivators, this system provides them enough incentive to invest heavily in increasing production. To the farmers, this is a superior system compared to one-half sharecropping system. In this system, farmers can produce rice as high as 20 maunds (40 kg per maund) per bigha (25 decimal) and they need to pay the landowners around 5-6 maunds of rice. In the contract system, the amount of produce to be paid differs heavily depending on the type of crop and the fertility of the land. The amount to be paid is fixed through a competitive system where the landowners ask a pool of cultivators how much of the produce they want to pay and the highest bidder is awarded the right to cultivate. However, under this system, since the landowner does not contribute in investment, the risk of crop failure is entirely borne by the cultivator. In case of significantly lower production for climatic hazards like cyclones or excessive rain, the cultivator tries to renegotiate the amount of produce to be paid but mostly fail to do so. However, in case of full damage by flood, the contract system becomes invalid.

On the other hand, the "Cash Lease System" is basically a monetary transformation of the contract system and is widely practised in cash crops like potatoes, maize, spices and vegetables. In the beginning, landowners provided land to the vegetable cultivators under the contract system but soon the landowners found that the price of vegetables fluctuates too much and they were not getting the desired amount of money by selling their share of vegetables. So, some landowners started to ask cultivators to pay a fixed amount of money rather than a fixed amount of produce. Eventually, some cultivators agreed and the cash lease system emerged. Soon, most of the landowners embraced this cash lease practice to reduce their risk. Another key reason for the emergence of cash lease system is the migration of landowners to distant cities. It is painstaking for these landowners to visit villages during harvesting, collect their amount of produce and sell it to the local market. So, they have shifted swiftly to the cash lease system. Earlier, under the contract system the cultivators had to pay the agreed amount produce after harvesting the crop, but in the cash lease system cultivators have to pay cash first and then they get the permission to cultivate. This shift in time of payment has a significant implication. Earlier the small farmers could take land under the contract system and could pay the agreed amount after harvesting the crop, but now they cannot take the same land as they do not have the money to pay before starting cultivation. Thus medium and large farmers have been replacing the small cultivators with the emergence of the cash lease system. There are two types of cash lease system: yearly and seasonal. The landowners who lives in distant cities prefer the yearly system, while those who live in villages or close distances practise the seasonal system. (Ali, 2013) As per estimate of 2007, landowners of Rangpur, landowners, on an average, charged Taka 3,000 per 25 decimals of land for two consecutive crops: potato and maize (7 months). However, yearly (for 12 months) the cash lease price was found as Taka 4,500. Share of of land lease market by the landowners, absentee landowners and other professions were 60%, 10% and 30% respectively in 1997. But in 2007, contribution to the land lease market by the landowners, absentee landowners and other professions were found as 30%, 40% and 30% respectively. Contribution to land lease market by the absentee landowners have increased significantly. Share of different categories of farmers in using different land leasing systems may be seen from the following Table:

Categories of Farmers	*Leasing System (%)*		*Sharecropping System (%)*		*Collateral System*
	Contract	*Cash*	*One-half*	*Two-third*	
Landless Farmers	10	2	80	30	-
Small Farmers	65	18	20	60	-
Medium Farmers	20	40	-	10	40
Large Farmers	5	40	-	-	60

Source: Selim Raihan, Sohani Fatehin and Iftekharul Haque, 2009. *Field Study in Rangpur.*

The types of crops preferred by the farmers under different leasing systems are also important. Under the contract lease system, the most preferred crop grown by the farmers is rice while potatoes, maize, vegetables and spices are the most preferred crops grown in land taken under the cash lease system.

Land leasing system in other parts of the country has certainly undergone significant changes too and such changes need to be identified and assessed. In the absence of implementation of land leasing law as well as ineffectiveness of the relevant law for the sharecroppers, the absentee land owners either limit the scope of land leasing to the marginal and small farmers or very often create tenure-related insecurity for informal tenants/sharecroppers. Moreover, indiscriminate land acquisition by the state have led to conversion of fertile agricultural and forest land (80 hectares/day) not only for public utilities, but also for commercial and real estate purposes, thereby threatening the food and livelihood security of poor farmers. Last but not the least, there is growing feminization of Bangladesh agriculture due to male migration, widowhood, etc which in the absence of secure land rights of women, affect agricultural productivity growth.

Marginal and small farm households who constitute 67% of the total farm households share only 36.30% of total cultivated land and the remaining 63.37% of land is owned by the 6.18% of medium and large farm households. There are 1686,354 acres of government Khas land of which only 11.5% distributed among the landless HHs while the rest are occupied by the rich and powerful (Barkat et al., 2000).

Structural Transformation in Rural Areas: Shrimp Farming

Thus far what has been described above pertains to traditional agricultural practices. We will now look at an area which has been introduced through policy guidelines informed through neo-liberal paradigms of export-oriented agricultural manufacture, i.e. the saline water shrimp farming industry which is the second largest foreign currency earner of Bangladesh. The advent of shrimp cultivation has served to link Bangladesh with the global economy and in doing so it has resulted in the disarticulation of a subsistence peasant economy at a pace hitherto unanticipated.

The south-western region of Bangladesh consists of the southern lowlands of the current districts of Bagerhat, Khulna and Satkhira. It is a coastal area constituted by fresh waters of the innumerable rivers and distributaries, which end up in the saline waters of the Bay of Bengal. It is a region, which house part of the world's largest mangrove forests, the Sundarbans. According to the Gazette of 1978 the area covered by the Sundarbans were recorded as 2,316 square miles. This tidal plain with mangrove forests is the most complex ecosystem with the highest biological productivity in the world. The intricate intertwining of the environment and people's lives and livelihood is a noticeable feature in this region or rather it was till the influence of the mono-culture of shrimp cultivation began to disarticulate this organic link between people and environment.

One of the first evidence of the change and transformations taking place is to be found in the pattern of land usage. The change in land use in an area traditionally rich in agriculture and fishing has important and serious repercussions for lives and livelihood. This change is part and parcel of the structural transformation taking place in both production and production relations in the area. (Guhathakurta, 2008).

Capitalism means labour as commodity. But according to Wallerstein, in an era of agricultural capitalism, wage labour is only one of the modes in which labour is recruited and recompensed in the labour market. Slavery, coerced cash-crop production, sharecropping, and tenancy are all alternative modes. Thus with the growth of the shrimp industry we notice features such as the diversion of productive land into shrimp farms. Along with it is seen the consequent release of farm labour either into trade or activities subsidizing shrimp farming, e.g catching shrimp fries, transportation of shrimp fries, or where feasible rearing of cattle and poultry. All these activities are relevant in the mapping out of the structural transformations taking place in the area as a consequence of the shrimp industry.

Structural transformation is evident in changing class hierarchies within the region. For example, during and after the Partition of 1947, the area was mostly Hindu-dominated with the Hindu zamindars controlling the lion's share of the landholding. It was also an area, which had yielded a great variety of crops along with the staple rice and where the adjunct Sundarban forests and the intertwining of the multitudinal rivers provided employment opportunities of a wide variety. Hence a stratified system of caste-specific hierarchies was also predominant which evolved round particular occupations, for example, *kolus* (those who ground oil from mustard seeds), *rishis*, (trading in leather and leather products), *moualis* and *bawalis* (thriving from the forests) and weavers and fishermen.

The injection of the cash economy is eroding traditional caste boundaries such as these and in certain cases a certain upward mobility among the poor can be noticed. For example, those who catch fries mention they can get 50 to 60 taka per day for an average catch. This is ready cash in hand, while as day labourers, cash payment would be uncertain and their payment would partially be in kind, e.g. one meal a day.

But there is another side to the picture. Not everyone is benefiting from these transformations. Many among the poor still hold onto their lands and are used to tilling the land. They somehow do not possess the aptitude to do any other kind of work. They are the ones who feel intimidated by the changes taking place. They also feel that the shrimp industry is aggravating the difference between the rich and the poor.

Thus we see that structural changes are taking place in two ways. First, those landowners who are benefiting from a windfall gain in profits reaped from leasing their land to shrimp farms. This is turning a class of hardworking farmers into a rural-based intermediate class. However, they admit that there is a certain degree of risk involved since the payments promised may not be as forthcoming from the *gher*(shrimp farm) owner if a virus affects the crop. Second, it is also creating a class of poor who are not left with any other alternative work except to work for the industry through collecting and selling fries or work in the farms or leasing their lands to them. Environmental degradation has succeeded in displacing agricultural and agriculture-related work and activities like rearing of cattle and poultry. It has also proletariatized a class who previously could depend on the economy of a stable agricultural household. Now everything is bought and sold in the market. There is no stock of rice available for handouts in the lean season any more. Two features characterize the emergence of this class of poor labourers no longer dependent on the land. First, the daily payment in cash for their annual catch or work is a welcome change from the delaying tactics of their former landholding masters. Second, the change in the relations of production has brought about a certain starkness in the confrontation between the rich and the poor. Many of the older norms of society *shomaj,* which used to bind together a village society no longer exists.

Thus class relations are more prone to violence and the poor find themselves defenceless against the representatives of a predatory state bent on pocketing the lion's share of profit from the industry.

Transformation in Gender Relations: Feminization of the Proletariat

Women workers in post-colonial societies occupy a specific social location in the international division of labour, which illuminates and explains crucial features of the capitalist processes of exploitation and domination. (Alexander and Mohanty, 1997) These are features of the social world which are usually obfuscated or mystified in discourses about progress and development, e.g. creation of jobs for the poor, women's economic and social advancement. Interconnections between gender, and ethnicity and the ideologies of work locate women in particular exploitative contexts. It is easy to see from the field how contemporary global capitalism positions women workers in ways which effectively both reproduces and transforms locally specific hierarchies. Maria Mies in her seminal work on the *Lace Makers of Narsapur* (Mies, 1982) studied Indian housewives who were producing lace for the world market. She points out that ideologies of seclusion and the domestication of women are clearly sexual, drawing as they do on the masculine and feminine notion of protectionism and property. They are also heterosexual ideologies based on the normative definitions of women as wives, sisters and mothers—always in relation to conjugal marriage and the family. Domestication works into the capitalist mould through the persistence and legitimacy of the ideology of the housewife, which defines women in terms of their place within the home, conjugal marriage and heterosexuality. It defines women as non-workers and consequently trivializes women's labour. Their definition as housewives makes possible the definition of men as breadwinners. Here class and gender proletarianization through the development of capitalist relations of production, and the integration of women into the world market is possible because of the history and transformation of indigenous caste/class and sexual ideologies. What this means is that although production for the world market may throw open opport unities for women to enter the market as wage labourers, capitalism may very well work with the patriarchal culture of the region to devalue women's work in the market and simultaneously extol ideologies of domestication. Hence instead of a classical case of capitalism freeing women's labour, we see the onset of a capitalist patriarchal culture which eulogizes the domestic sphere and hence creates resistance to ultimate polarization.

In a situation where subsistence economy based on household production and consumption is undergoing structural transformation, it is women who have to confront the dual scourges of capitalist exploitation and patriarchal hegemony in their struggle to adapt to changing realities.

In a research on indigenous Chakma women from the Chittagong Hill Tracts who are being increasingly drawn into the labour force in the Export Processing Zones, some of the relevant points which emerge in relation to ongoing processes of structural formation stated above are the following:

1. The main reasons for indigenous women migrating to mainstream employment sectors are poverty, lack of jobs in tune with their educational qualifications in rural areas, restless and insecure law and order situation especially in the case of the Chittagong Hill Tracts, the advantages of better logistical and infrastructure in the urban sector operating as pull factors and also changing gender relations in the country in general that open up space for equitable contribution of women and men in the economy.
2. Indigenous women rely a lot on support networks, e.g. family and community networks, places of worship and informal savings committees.
3. Despite the challenges they face, indigenous women feel empowered in certain respects. They could accumulate modest savings for themselves, they could invest in land and economic enterprises back home, sometimes even in the urban sector, e.g. in share markets, they could support dependents in the family,

they gained important decision-making roles in family matters, and they enjoyed the appreciation of their contribution from family and community back home.

4. It was noted that though the main driving force behind indigenous women coming to work in the cities was poverty of their natal household and lack of opportunities, a few came to seek out their fortune and be independent. Many mentioned the respect they earned when they became providers of the family they left behind and how that gave them satisfaction and more importantly they also mentioned how gender relations were gradually changing in both their natal communities as well as in general whereby a working woman could gain a certain amount of respect, something that was not so evident in the first generation of the women's labour force in the urban sector. This may very well implicate the changing gender relations brought about by a complex of factors such as increase of income generation opportunities for women in both the private and development sectors, propagation of and rise in women's education, and the effects of a women's struggle in the Bangladesh polity that is finally getting recognition at home and abroad. (Guhathakurta and Ali, 2010)

Hence we see that though some positive trends may be emerging for women's opportunities in newly defined work areas, albeit with a cost, few women seem to be considering this to be a permanent feature in their lives yet. Most dream of settling back into their home districts with enough to provide for their families, natal or post-conjugal. Even as they are driven to find work in the cities, they reinvest in family networks: educating younger siblings, providing for care of the elderly, or even building social capital through familial and religious networks.

Hence the fact is that these women are not undergoing the classical eviction from structures of production as Marx predicted for the proletariat, but is being used by the capitalist mode as an extension of social reproduction! This is made possible by engaging that complexity of relations that transverse both patriarchal and capitalist forces in post-colonial society.

What does it have to say about the nature of organizing labour or engaging democratic practices in current Left discourse in Bangladesh. What can constitute an effective counter-narrative to this dominant discourse?

Democratic Practice

Formal democratic practice is not at its very best in current Bangladesh. After a two-third majority lead by Awami League and its allies in the 9th Parliament, amidst frequent and continuous walk out by the main opposition the Bangladesh Nationalist Party (BNP) it was not unexpected that they could not come to an agreement on the modus operandi of the 10th national parliamentary elections. The Awami League in its 15th Amendment brought about changes like the scrapping of the Caretaker Government clause, so that elections would be held with the incumbent government in power and by the Election Commission. The Opposition alliance refused to abide by this and called for a series of strikes and blockades which created nationwide unrest. The BNP led alliance also called for boycotting of elections.This combined with the war crimes trials, which put most leaders of Jamaat-e-Islam, the largest ally of the BNP's led alliance into jail charged with crimes against humanity, led to violent elections in January 2014 One hundred and fifty-three seats in the elections went uncontested and the Awami League candidate came to power automatically. The remaining seats ,were contested by the Jatiyo Party and independents. Although the elections were criticized by many international and national observers, it was considered necessary to fill the vacuum which would have resulted if the elections did not take place as scheduled. Bangladesh has now a sitting 10th Parliament where the Awami League controls two-thirds majority, the Jatiyo Party is the main opposition with 34 seats and BNP is out of Parliament after 33 years.

Faced with a weak opposition many seem to dread (and not illogically) growing authoritarianism on the part of the incumbent government. But interestingly the current alliance which is considered progressive compared to more right wing parties such as the BNP-Jamaat alliance, also has two important Left parties (Workers' Party and Jatiyitabadi Shomajtantrik Dol) in government inclusive of ministerial posts. It is a wonder how a state that is coming more and more in control of a growing capitalist class with entrenched interests in accelerating the pace of capitalist development and welcoming neo-liberal trends in the economy can also accommodate left parties in its wings. The answer is simple. Such a state recognizes the challenges of depending on the remittances of migrant workers and the sweat of workers, small farmers and agricultural workers to fuel the economy and feed the teeming millions and is not equipped to face total alienation from these classes. There are of course additional challenges of facing religious fundamentalism and terrorism from extreme right wing quarters as well.

But the Left in power has not been completely helpless in getting their agenda across either. In the last Parliament they helped to pass a Bill recognizing the rights of agricultural workers and specifically women workers. According to the ILO framework, one of the issues is that very often women in families work small farm/agriculture end up working for nothing because they are the daughter/wife/sister. They do not get money, goods or property in return. In rice production in Bangladesh there are about 23 steps from the seed to the production of paddy or rice. And out of these 23 steps 17 steps were done by the women. In current practice all 23 steps are done by the women. Hence there was a need for all to recognize the value of their labour. Women who did this agricultural work started to demand recognition.

The demand was articulated and actualized through an alliance consisting of different peasants' associations, Communist Party, Jatiyobadi Shomajtantrik Dal (JSD), Workers' Party. The proposed labour law covered not only women but men as well, and hence it was to the general interest of all to support the demand advocacy strategy consisted of forming a cell of 25 members in each area, which bargained with the farmers who are the employers of peasants. A nationwide advocacy campaign and lobbying was launched. Finally the labour law was amended in 2013.

Another law is already being drafted and has been submitted to the Labour Department and the Ministry of Agriculture. This process is being led by the alliance called 'Krishi Sromik Odhikar Moncho' (Rights of the Peasants Workers Rights Alliance).

Outside formal politics however contestation of state power is being generated by conventional and radical trade union politics. Recent disasters such as the Rana Plaza incident has foregrounded the plight of workers in the area but has not been addressed to the extent of punishing the culprits.

Broader and more context-based movements are also taking place such as the movement led by the *'National Committee to Protect Oil, Gas, Mineral Resources, Power and Ports (NCPOGMPP)* successfully against open pit mining in Fulbari and currently against the installation of a 1320MW coal fired power plant in the world heritage site of the Sundarbans, the largest mangrove forest in the world.

Future Directions

It is not my intention here to narrate the dynamics of each movement that is taking place in Bangladesh. Rather I would like to conclude that when one looks at future directions of Bangladesh society in the more immediate range, we cannot foresee the blossoming of either the idyllic 'Sonar Bangla' (the nationalist imaginary of the Bangladesh state) or a Proletariat Bangladesh. In a land scarce country there is little expectation of gaining land for the landless, hence the focus on education becomes the demand of the day, as also the desperate need for a foundational consensus that would provide stability for small business and young professionals in a rapidly changing world. Hence the symbol of 1971, is the only thing that seems to bring a broad-based national platform (urban, small town and rural) of upcoming generations together and gives them an identity. It would be interesting to see when the dynamics of proletarianization does set in how the symbol of the Liberation War would be re-negotiated among the potential players, i.e.

as an ideology of national consensus supported by the state or as the ideology of the people. It is then that the actual counter-narrative to the neo-liberal paradigm will begin to take shape in the understanding and in the practice of the Left.

NOTES AND REFERENCES

A. Barkat, S. Zaman and S. Raihan (2000), *Distribution and Retention of Khas Land in Bangladesh* (Dhaka: Human Development Research Centre).

Ahsan F. Mansur and Ifty Islam (2010), The Global Crisis, Rise of Asia and Policy Challenges, (2012), *The Financial Express*, December 14, reprinted in Sadiq Ahmed (ed.) *Bangladesh Growth Strategies, Trade and Regional Cooperation* (Dhaka: Policy Research Institute).

Bangladesh Bureau of Statistics (BBS) (2007), Dhaka, *Statistical Yearbook of Bangladesh*, Government of Bangladesh.

David Harvey (2003), *The New Imperialism* (Oxford: Oxford University Press).

Immanuel Wallerstein (1979), *The Capitalist World Economy* (Cambridge: Cambridge University Press).

Jim Glassman (2006), Primitive Accumulation, Accummulation by Dispossession, Accummulation by 'Extra-economic' Means, in *Progress in Human Geography*, 30, 5, (2006) pp. 608-625.

M. Tronti (1973), *Social capital*. Telos 17, 98–121.

M.J. Alexander and Chandra Talpade Mohanty (eds.) (1997), *Feminist Genealogies, Colonial Legacies, Democratic Futures* (London: Routledge).

Maria Mies (1982), *The Lace Makers of Narsapur: Indian Housewives Produce for the World Market* (London: Zed Press).

Md. Korban Ali (2013), *Internal Paper* (Dhaka: Research Initiatives, Bangladesh)

Meghna Guhathakurta (2013), *Bangladeshey Shamajik Shangskritik Rupantor (Social and Cultural Transformation in Bangladesh)*, paper presented at Bangla Academy, Ekushey Bou Mela, February 3. Dhaka.

Meghna Guhathakurta (2008), Globalization, Class and Gender Relations: The Shrimp Industry in Southwestern Bangladesh in *Development: Issue on Gender and Fisheries* Vol. 51, No. 2–June.

Meghna Guhathakurta and Md. Korban Ali (2010), *Employment of Indigenous Women in the Urban Sector* (Dhaka: Research Initiatives, Bangladesh).

Selim Raihan, Sohani Fatehin and Iftekharul Haque, (2009), *Access to Land and Other Natural Resources by the Rural Poor: The Case of Bangladesh.*

Shapan Adnan (2013), Land Grabs and Primitive Accumulation in Deltaic Bangladesh: Interactions between Neoliberal Globalization, State Interventions, Power Relations and Peasant Resistance, *The Journal of Peasant Studies*, 40:1, 87-128.

15

The Role of the Left in Bangladesh's Democracy: Challenges and Prospects

Srimanti Sarkar

Introduction

The modern democracies have rendered the party system as an indispensable factor in every political society. Undeniable is the fact that party politics have become a universal phenomenon and this is evident from the ever growing concern for the ways in which political leaders, social groups and political parties strive to achieve political power. Therefore it becomes a necessity to study them carefully in order to critically understand the functioning of the polity. While doing so one has to consider the fact that in most of the South Asian countries the party system does not have a linear path of evolution or development. Their long and shared historical legacies play a significant role in the making of their political systems. Varying and intermittent spells of democracy and authoritarianism engulf many of the nations as a result of which party systems also develop in a manner uncommon to each other and common features are thus not clearly identifiable as are found in many of the Western democracies.[1] But despite their speckled characteristics they continue to be the vital conditions of modern political processes as their emergence and functioning presuppose a necessary degree of social development, political consciousness, and popular desire for democracy. Therefore, considering the several factors that illustrate the varied functioning of the party system such as the nature of social composition, economic divisions, religious and ethnic affiliations, cultural diversities and political differences over matters of internal and external policy of the state and so on—one needs to carefully evaluate their role.

In Bangladesh also a viable form of party system prevails. Like many other South Asian countries, here political parties have not evolved from within the legislatures as in some of the Western countries nor have they followed Maurice Duverger's theorization of the formulation of the party systems within parliament[2]. Instead, political parties have come into existence following the hands of the nationalist leaders who steered the nation out from the colonial yoke then through the struggle for national liberation and subsequently from the problems of highly unstable political developments in the aftermath of political independence. Bangladesh's political scene has been tumultuous ever since the country's inception. Periods of democratic rule have been interrupted by military coups, martial law, and states of emergency. In the midst of this confusing scene, there are five major political forces that operate significantly in the country[3]. At the foremost is the ruling AL party which has now transformed into a centre/centre-left political party after its birth as a socialist organization under the founding leadership of Sheikh Mujibur Rahman. The main opposition is led by the Bangladesh Nationalist Party (BNP) and its allies which form the right-of-centre to conservative grouping in Bangladesh. To the extreme right or left, lies another set of political groups which although not supported by a large fraction of the populace, is typified by having very dedicated followers. To the extreme right is a group of parties, including Jamaat-e-Islami and Islami Oikyo Jote, who calls for an increased role for Islam in public life. To the left lies an array of splinter groups including the pro-Soviet Communist Party of Bangladesh (CPB), factions of the Jatiyo Samajtantrik Dal (JSD), the Workers' Party and other socialist groups who advocate revolutionary changes in the society but do not comprise of a unified whole. Finally the fifth major party is the Jatiyo Party (JP) party founded by ex-military ruler General Ershad, which though ideologically not too different from the AL or the BNP supports Islamization of Bangladesh and operates independently.[4]

In this context the current essay will focus on the role of the Left in Bangladesh polity which in spite of their considerably long political existence fails to emerge as a viable political force. Thus a brief evolutionary background of the Left since the time of independence will be laid in the first section to understand their contextual existence in the country. This will lead us to critically evaluate their position in the present political scenario with due consideration of the important challenges that they face in the second section. Furthermore, by addressing some of the significant socio-economic and political factors such as the class dynamics, global economic and electoral trend some crucial pointers are intended to be identified to assess their credibility and relevance in Bangladesh politics. Through the following three sections of the essay a careful probe into the characteristic features of the Left in Bangladeshi democracy will be thus attempted.

Evolution and Position of the Left in Bangladesh

The Left in Bangladesh has a long and strong legacy dating back to the time of the country's struggle for independence or even before that. But it was the Liberation War of 1971 that sowed the seeds for unifying the much diversified political forces of the country. Ideologically the Left was belligerent which got integrated by the nationalist agenda of independence. They joined together with the other political forces of the country and primarily the AL, to overthrow the twenty-three years of exploitative rule of West Pakistan. During the time of the independence the primary task of the Left was to build popular consciousness and to propagate unity among the masses against the Pakistani forces. This nationalist agenda was complemented by their struggle against the imperialist forces of the world in general. It was the Leftists who felt the need for uniting and organizing the people from even the lower rung of the society like the working class, peasants, and labourer class—to harness the support for national unity and freedom from the international community. Thus organizing the volunteers, training the freedom fighters and ordered propaganda were a means of their functioning at that time. They played an invincible role in popularizing their national toil along with the AL[5]. But immediately after the independence in 1971, a large number of party supporters left the country and went to India. Around 6000 party supporters, leaders and members settled in the adjoining states of West Bengal, Tripura and Meghalaya as a result of which the integrated strength of the party suffered a major halt. They faced the primary challenge of re-organizing themselves into a coherent force thereafter. However, the agenda of the Left in Bangladesh should not be considered as only vital during the nationalist struggle. They continued to function as a potent force in post-independent Bangladesh in lieu of their broader vision to develop a free space for economic and administrative advancement of the country. They provided a model in front of the nascent state that was not built exclusively upon nationalist ideals but also from the perspective of the toiling masses, so that a non-exploitative and free society can be fashioned. It was this mass appeal and the inclusive vision of uniting the downtrodden of the society into the mainstream that signified the role of the Communist Party in Bangladesh. The Left thus earned its credibility by stressing this aspect of the then Bangladeshi society that was not strongly sought by even the most popular AL party during its early days of nation building.[6]

However, today the political Left in Bangladesh, represented both by a number of socialist as well as communist parties, is numerically small and significantly divided by internal dissensions. These differences are deep and evolutionary. The Left was marked by a discernible division between the Maoist and Stalinist currents since long time back. Likewise the Communist Party of East Pakistan (Bangladesh since 1971); which was the primary Leftist political force in the country and which drew much of its historical legacy from the Communist Party of India (CPI); was divided between a pro-Moscow wing and a pro-Beijing wing. While the former was considered as one of the main unifiers of popular support and strength for the liberation struggle, belonging to the neighbouring Indo-Soviet socialist camp and as the propagator of worldwide communist revolution, peace, independence and democracy; the later was considered as pro-Pakistan in its overtures supported by the imperialist and reactionary powers like the United States and China.[7] This internal divisions in their ideology resulted into two radically opposed positions of the communist party during the war of liberation in 1971. The Communist Party of Bangladesh (CPB), which was pro-Moscow ideologically, supported the war of liberation and avowed for the establishment of socialism in Bangladesh along the parliamentary road. This orientation led it to associate more closely with the AL which emerged as the dominant power immediately after the war of liberation.

The pro-Beijing wing on the other hand, following the Maoist position was opposed to the partition of Pakistan and did not support the war of liberation. It radically advocated total revolution based on the Maoist model and considered the Bangladesh liberation movement as an 'unfinished revolution'. This group was comprised of the various Leftist underground parties who rejected Mujib's socialism as a 'petty-bourgeois' ideology and subsequently discarding it wanted to establish a socialist state in Bangladesh inspired by the Chinese revolution[8]. One of the most significant radical militia leaders of this thread was Siraj Sikder who led the East Bengal's Workers Movement (EBWM) since January 1968 and later formed the Purbo Bangla Sarbohara Party (PBSP- East Bengal Proletarian party) on January 3, 1971. The Sarbahara Party actively joined hands with the Mukti Bahini (Liberation Army) to fight against Pakistan in the liberation war. But when Sheikh Mujibur Rahman formed his own militia, namely the Mujib Bahini (Mujib's Army) sidelining the Leftists within the guerrilla army, the Sharbahara Party got dissociated from the mainstream. It did not accept the liberation and instead envisaged to replace the 'petty-bourgeois puppet government' with a revolutionary socialist system. Their subsequent threats and militant activities against the newly formed government led to the growing chaos that brought Mujib down finally in 1975. But this strand faced a significant impediment with the decline of Maoist ideology in

China and rendered the Bangladeshi revolutionaries without major ideological support from abroad.[9]

Today the Left wing underground militias function primarily in the rural areas. Having no coherent ideology their doctrines often act against the interests of the communists, secularists and the women like that of the Islamists. They often emerge as 'village arbitrators' with their monopolization of the traditional village arbitration institution named *Salish* and are heavily criminalized. Thus being stigmatized as 'outlaws' by the law-enforcing agencies they now struggle incessantly for their own survival.[10] The Purba Banglar Communist Party (PBCP) is another such Maoist splinter organizations in Bangladesh that has a revolutionary agenda of capturing state power through armed struggle. Drawing its inspiration from the Chinese revolution it believes in the rise of China to pave the ways for the realization of their goals. Nevertheless, the PBCP cadres have been reportedly involved in acts of murder, robbery, extortion, land grabbing and abduction for ransom and have significantly spread their influence in the south-western regions of Bangladesh, bordering the Indian State of West Bengal and the north-east.[11] The other party, namely the Purbo Bangla Sarbohara Party (PBSP) that was founded by Siraj Sikder has been reorganizing itself as an underground force with its new generation cadres forming the Maoist Unity Group (MUG). It aims at confronting the state forces and developing the 'People's War', that had been foreseen by Sikder, through active militarization. However not all factions of the PBSP endorse this mission and contrarily believes in engaging in open politics by adopting a more moderate stance.

Under the successive military dictatorships in the later parts of the 1970s and 1980s, the difficulties of the Leftist, revolutionary and radical parties accentuated further reinforcing tendencies towards their continued divisions. After Sheikh Mujibur Rahman's assassination in 1975 the CPB faced enormous repression in the hands of the rightist military rule. The party leaders of the center and the district levels were indiscriminately arrested during this time and in October 1977 the CPB was declared banned. However, in 1978 the ban on the party was withdrawn and its leaders were released thereafter which the CPB participated in the general elections of 1978. But due to their consistent poor performance in terms of acquiring parliamentary seats, the CPB along with the other Leftist parties were forced into supporting roles within alliances with the major opposition parties. In the first and second general elections of 1973 and 1979 they could not capture a single parliamentary seat.[12] Subsequently the CPB joined the 15-party alliance led by AL in 1983 against the military rule of Hussain Muhammad Ershad and played a vital role in the movement to oust Ershad in 1990. But with the collapse of the Soviet socialism in 1991 the CPB faced another great ideological crisis. The party leaders got further divided into two camps. One favored the abolition of the CPB and its replacement by a new platform on democratic line, while the other favoured maintaining the party in its original form. This conflict grew to be acute in 1993 when the two opposing groups arranged separate convention in Dhaka. The Marxist-Leninist group in their convention held on June 15, 1993; however resolved for the independent existence of the Communist Party in Bangladesh, and had their new central executive committee formed with Shahidullah Chowdhury as president and Mujahidul Islam Selim as General Secretary.[13]

A more significant socialist party in the late 1980s was the Jatiyo Samajtantrik Dal (National Socialist Party- JSD). This party began operating in 1972 after the defection of radical elements from the AL. It organized an armed opposition to Sheikh Mujibur Rahman's regime in the mid-1970s and became very influential among the military dictators during the late 1970s. It formed its action wing namely the Jatiyo Sramik Jote (National Workers Alliance) with the help of which it gained popularity in the labour unions and earned some success in parliamentary elections. But by the 1980s, it also got split into a number of factions with different strategies. One wing, headed by A.S.M. Abdur Rab undertook policy measures that were almost indistinguishable from those of the Jatiyo Party of General Ershad. It cooperated with Ershad's government, praised his martial law rule, supported the move to include the armed forces in district councils and the denationalization bill of June 1987, and participated in the parliaments elected in 1986 and 1988. Another faction, was led by Shajahar Siraj, came to be known as the Jatiyo Samajtantrik Dal (Siraj). It participated in the 1986 Parliament but consistently voted against the government, calling for "unity of left democratic forces." Still another faction, namely the Jatiyo Samajtantrik Dal (Inu), headed by Hasan Huq Inu, refused to cooperate with the government and became part of a highly visible five-party alliance along with the Sramik Krishak Samajbadi Dal, (Workers and Peasants' Socialist Party); the Bangladesh Samajtantrik Dal (Bangladesh Socialist Party) which was again comprised of two factions; and the Workers' Party. The Jatiyo Samajtantrik Dal (Inu) operated a radical student front called the Jatiyo Chhatro Samaj (National Students' Society).[14]

Thus what we see of the political Left in Bangladesh is that, it had been ridden by factionalism since the time of the country's inception and further fragmented into innumerable sections afterwards, rendering it much more diversified and weaker. While the inability of the political Left to draw a consensus among themselves drifted them away from capturing power at the centre; the active presence of the Left wing militant groups in the countryside poses a serious threat to Bangladesh's national security on the other hand[15]. Presently there are about two dozen Leftist political parties in Bangladesh, out of which only few are visibly active in terms of meetings, rallies and protests. Most of them restrict themselves to statements and press notes in the media and that too the others restrict themselves to insignificant ceremonial activities. In a way, many of these parties exist in name alone—with ineffectual leaders at their head and seemingly non-existent workers. They function primarily as prerogative to the ruling AL or the BNP as their singular parliamentary performances has been unfortunate. For instance, in the December 2008 parliamentary elections the JSD won 3 seats and the Workers' Party won 2 seats contesting under the AL symbol of the boat. But while contesting in the same election under the JSD's own symbol (a flaming torch), its two other candidates failed miserably, as did the two other candidates contesting for the Workers' Party. The other Left parties—including the CPB, National Awami Party (NAP), Bangladesh Samajtantrik Dal (BSD), Gonotantri Party and Biplobi Workers Party—collectively floated 118 candidates in the national polls, but secured a combined total of less than 110,000 votes[16]. Such pitiful results only re-emphasize the continuing weakness of Bangladesh's Left parties among the people triggering the interest to identify some of the possible factors that led to this plight of the Left in Bangladesh.

Factors Affecting the Role of the Left

The Left in Bangladesh today is perhaps faced with the recurring question of: Why are they so persistently fragmented and disjointed? One of the primary reasons behind the disunity of the Left as identified by many of the analysts is that a general sense of mistrust prevails amongst the parties themselves which prevents their emergence as a unified front keeping their potential supporters away. Beginning with the ideological dilemma that had been stated before, they continue to remain diffused in their guiding motive even today. The inner-party functioning certainly contributes to the general sense of scepticism. The General-Secretary of the Biplobi Workers' Party, Saiful Haque; and the leader of the CPB, Mujaheedul Islam Selim stated that "many Left leaders today are unwilling to make the necessary sacrifices or take risks in the present political context. Such leaders are too ready to compromise with the 'capitalist values' in their eagerness to become MPs or ministers" as against the guiding principles of socialism. Other commentators, call the Left in Bangladesh as 'dominantly pro-Indian', and dictated by the political discourse of the US-led 'war on terror'. They say that many leaders simply parrot US foreign-policy terms such as 'fundamentalism' and 'Islamism'[17] thereby tanning their own credibility. Capitalism and increased consumerism thus plays a vital role here in disillusioning the Left from their socialist goals and secondly the long hankering for political power acts as another factor that leads the Left to associate diversely for sheer calculated benefit. About two dozen Left political parties today consider themselves as 'hardcore' communists. But careful analysis will show that only—the CPB,

BSD (Khalequzzaman), (Lt.) Nirmal Sen, NAP (Muzaffar), Badaruddin Umar and a few others—have remained faithful to Left ideology, despite splits and rifts along the way. The others merely act like opportunists with a Left facade.

Secondly, another factor preventing the unification of the Left is the lack their own class analysis. The basic condition for the formation of a united Left front is the maintenance of a separate and distinct organizational identity with a certain unity of purpose, unity of approach and goals[18]. The Bangladesh polity underwent through subsequent bouts of civilian, military and democratic rules. But each of them tends to protect the same class interests more or less in order to sustain their regime's legitimacy. Thus within the given class framework the interests of the various social groups such as the industrial, financial, trading class, the bureaucracy, intellectuals, political elites, etc are more or less similarly meted out. This has rendered the Left with lesser choice to cultivate a separate class allegiance of their own. As a result of which they are widely found to associate with the other political forces. The Left and right forces in Bangladesh are both from the middle classes and in this respect the Left fails as they cannot readily de-class themselves, and thus at the same time cannot uphold the aspirations of the people. They remain in a fluxed position gravitating towards the right on one hand, whereas opposing the rightist revolutionary and democratic forces on the other.

However, there is another significant dimension to this class aspect in Bangladesh. The socio-political practice in Bangladesh largely resembles that of a 'spoils system' where a significant degree of cultural degeneration has occurred. Social activist and theorist Badruddin Umar terms this as 'cultural poverty of the ruling classes'. He states that "the role of the intellectuals and cultural workers as social prop of the propertied ruling class is common to all societies which are divided into classes"—and Bangladeshi experience is no exception to this[19]. They get aligned to the various political parties and become their prerogative and pay allegiance to them for political benefits. This group includes the writers, teachers, performing artists like actors, singers and so on who are different from the mere party cadres adding an exceptional flavour to the dominant rule. Bangladeshi intellectuals also reflect very authentically all the basic features of the ruling classes including their cultural poverty. Many of the Leftist political leaders and activists also fall into this category of intellectuals. In post independent Bangladesh the CPB led by Moni Singh in the absence of political line distinct from the AL, worked as its cultural wing. Even today, most of the Leftists support the ruling AL party although they refrain from defying the principles of the ruling political parties overtly. What we find is a gradual co-option of the Leftists with the ruling parties leading to the gradual suppression of the individual worth of the former.[20] On the whole, the absence of a coherent class interest acts as the primary impediment for the Left unification which is all the more heightened by the camaraderie of the intellectual class in the society.

Thirdly, the Leftist parties lack in forming effective organization due to their non-inclusiveness. Apart from some of the above mentioned Left parties which are comparatively well-organized; there are two other types of parties which belong to the Left. One that is radical Left which indulges in terrorist activities and is virtually alienated from the people; and the other that is neither election-oriented nor inclined to terrorism. The former have no clearly defined social bases or dominant ideological commitments and hence fails to organize properly the working masses and direct them towards specific political targets. They are rootless reactionary political forces as opposed to the earlier mentioned Left parties which fail to initiate, direct and organize political movements in the interest of the working people. However, it is in the second type of Leftist political groups in whom one may find great socio-political possibilities. These are moderate groups that work in the interest of the workers, peasants and all kinds of the working people following a clearly defined ideological basis and at a more grassroots level. Many such sporadic groups are even found to be working for the cause of indigenous people of the Chittagong Hill Tracks (CHT) and other tribal areas. Given the significance of such works capable of delivering outstanding results in social justice, (especially in the troubled peripheries of the state like the CHT), it is important to harness their potentials. The goal of much aspired democratic revolution and socialism can only be achieved if these groups are co-opted within the mainstream Left orbit. When these several strands work separately they provide a diffracted picture of the Left altogether. It is thus important to re-think about re-organizing the myriad Leftist political forces who although work unnoticeably at the deep societal levels fail to mark a line in the eyes of the national populace.

Relevance and Significance of the Left in Present Bangladesh

However, in the final analysis it will be unwise to say that the Left has obliterated completely from the orbit of politics in Bangladesh or they have lost all their relevance and significance. It is the Left, after all, that is most vocal in protests about vital national issues such as oil, gas, seaports, and the Phulbari coalmine or even the recent Shahbag Movement. In the recent mass uprising that triggered around the trials of the war criminals of the liberation struggle at Shahbag in Dhaka, one finds an active role of the various Left wing political parties. Apart from the ruling AL the Left political parties and their student wings which joined the rally, raised active protest slogans at the Gana Jagoran Manch and led the people's movement were the Worker's Party of Bangladesh, Communist Party of Bangladesh (CPB), Jatiya Samajtantrik Dal (JSD), Bangladesh Samajtantrik Dal (BSD) and Ganotantrik Bam Morcha.[21] Such protests that already have or are yet to have a deep mark on the masses may be considered as a positive step indicating the required actions for broadening and reviving the scope and vitality of the Left.

Furthermore, in the recent political context of the country—where the state is literally ripped apart by the 'secularist' and the 'fundamentalist' forces and violent street politics—the role of the Left can be re-envisaged. Since February 2013, in Bangladesh the Shahbag Uprising had stirred the nation by severe violence perpetrated by the fundamentalist groups like the Jamat-e-Islami and the Hefazat-e-Islami who resorted to violent protest against the trials of the war criminals of 1971 genocide. This has become even more a serious issue as the BNP had openly stood by the sides of the Islamic radicals. As a counter force the secularist forces led by the AL and her allies raised the four fold demand for capital punishment for Abdul Quader Mollah and other war criminals. However since no steps were beyond the meticulous calculations of winning the electoral seats in the forthcoming tenth *Jatiya Sangsad* elections one has to consider the inherent nuances. The onslaught of Islamic fundamentalism and perplexing rivalry between the BNP and the AL has created a vitiated political landscape where one can evidently witnesses an uptight national population anemic and apathetic to the entire state of political affairs. The common people at large accord seemingly less trust in either of the two major political parties but fails to envisage the future beyond them. It is in this context one might have located the significant role of the Left as a viable alternative in the national politics. Ever since the democratic transition of the state in the 1990s, only the BNP and the AL had been systematically alternating their political power at the centre with no scope of any other opposition. The Left with their continuous movement against the extreme rightist forces should have used this scope to mark a strong ground in the wake of challenging communalism. But although the recent democratic uprising of Shahbag—which is significantly one of its own kind in the history of Bangladesh—hinted upon a decisive role of the Left as a potent political force; the political reality after the tenth *Jatiya Sangsad* elections held on January 5, 2014 reflected a picture of missed opportunity. Contesting under the AL's electoral symbol of "Boat" to win their respective seats the Workers' Party (WP, Menon) acquired only 6 or 2 per cent seats whereas the Jatiya Samajtantrik Dal (JSD, Inu) managed 5 or 2 per cent seats reducing the hope of the revival of the unified Left in Bangladesh at its lowest[22]. It would have been noteworthy if the dichotomy between secular nationalism and religious fundamentalism that exists in Bangladesh had given way to a politics of Left versus the non-Left instigating in return a fresh impetus to the democracy that has been cherished in the country.

Last, but not the least with the onset of globalization and the collapse of the Soviet Union there has been a significant upsurge of capitalism and consumerism all over the world. The impact of the same can be observed in Bangladesh. Bangladesh like many other Third World countries of South Asia quite un-astonishingly balances her tradition with modernity in keeping with the modern times. While on one hand, one can find some of the most advanced city structures staring from lavish apartments to huge shopping complexes (Vasundhara City); one may likewise find the old city delights like the famous colourful rickshaws of Dhaka honking all over the city nooks and crevasses putting the city traffic at loggerheads. As the numerous outlets of BFC (Best Fried Chicken), Pizza Hut and several other expensive restaurants hail eloquently the banner of global consumerism; it feels equally defeating to find the outsized number of beggars on the city roads. All these readily reflect the growing influence of capitalism and the presence of wide social disparity in the present Bangladeshi society like in many other nations of South Asia. The ill-effects of heightened capitalism may be perhaps further understood in the context of the greatest industrial catastrophe that occurred in the recent past. The collapse of the illegally constructed nine-storied Rana Plaza complex in April 2013, claiming lives of over a thousand garment factory workers (one of the biggest industrial debacle in Bangladesh's history) reveals the high exploitation level that prevails in the Ready Made Garments (RMG) sector—which is the most significant economic sector of Bangladesh. The plight of the garment factory workers, and reports about their poor working conditions and wages published after the incident and the subsequent sanctions by the Western investors for maintaining safety standards and necessary labour conditions signifies the social need of the Bangladeshi society[23]. The tragedy of the Rana Plaza immediately after the Shahbag Movement signifies another pointer that show reluctantly the ever engulfing consumerism and capitalism are been handled by the state. It is here, the Leftists could have capitalized their ideological role as effective promoters of socialism fulfilling the lacunae of the existing government widening their credibility and relevance in the Bangladeshi society.

Conclusion

All together it may be stated that the Left in Bangladesh are indeed a significant political force that has been functioning since ages. But the gradual unfolding of the state operations has rendered them weak, fragmented and thus powerless. So much so, that in spite of their consistent presence in the social and political ambit of the polity they are most often considered as redundant. However in the global context of today one may locate the possibilities of their renewed importance. The Bangladeshi polity which is essentially a transitioning Third World state is riddled by the numerous obstacles on its way towards development and progress. Likewise, we can experience the various good as well as ill effects of modernity and antiquity. Globalization and capitalism with its emphasis on market driven economy is one such necessary evil that entangles the state into its cob-web at a greater social cost. Similarly, the inherent class structure of the society prevents the formation of a coherent alternative force whilst the Frankenstein of religious fanaticism in the name of 'Islam' consistently beset the harmony of the state. All these factors are mutually inter-related to one another in the leeway and create a complete flux in the body politics of Bangladesh altogether. But it is this impasse that one may consider as the most opportune moment to re-envisage the role of the Left in Bangladesh; that hold the immense possibilities to infuse the much needed impet us to its state of democracy.

NOTES AND REFERENCES

1. Peter R. deSouza, Suhas Palshikar, Yogendra Yadav, 'Surveying South Asia', *Journal of Democracy*, Vol. 19, No. 1, 2008.
2. Randhir B. Jain, 'Implementing Party Reforms in South Asia: Challenges and Strategies', *Party Reforms in South Asia*, 17.12.01/ 6.2.02, <http://www.ndi.org/files/1331_th_partyreform.pdf>as retrieved on July 20, 2013.
3. Joyeeta Bhattacharjee, 'Bangladesh: Political Trends and Key Players', *Strategic Trends: South Asia Series*, Observer Research Foundation, Vol. 1, Issue 2, November 2011.
4. '*Virtual Bangladesh: Bangladesh Politics*', <http://www.virtual

bangladesh.com/bd_politics.html> as retrieved on July 27, 2013.

5. Talukdar Maniruzzaman, *Bampanthi Rajneeti o Bnagladesher Obbhudoy*, Bangla Academy, Dhaka, 2007, pp. 17-24.
6. Moni Singh, 'Mukti Youdhe Communist Party' in Mesbah Kamal (ed.) *Bangladesher Swadhinata Youddhe Bampanthider Bhumika*, Ganaprakashani and Samaj Chetana Publishers, Dhaka, 2001, pp. 177-179.
7. Ibid., p. 176.
8. A.M.M. Quamruzzaman, *The Militia Ideology in Bangladesh*, <http://ssrn.com/abstract=1569796> retrieved on 13.07.2013.
9. Danielle Sabai, 'The left and social movement struggles in Bangladesh', *International Viewpoint*, IV 442, November 9, 2011. <http://internationalviewpoint.org/spip.php?article2372> as retrieved on July 18, 2013.
10. A.M.M. Quamruzzaman, *The Militia Ideology in Bangladesh*; <http://ssrn.com/abstract=1569796> retrieved on July 13, 2013, p. 31.
11. South Asia Terrorist Portal, *Terrorist and Extremist Groups-Bangladesh*, <http://www.satp.org/satporgtp/countries/bangladesh/terroristoutfits/PBCP.htm> retrieved on August 25, 2013.
12. A.S.M. Samsul Arefin, *Bangladesher Nirbachan 1970-200*, Bangladesh Research and Publications, Dhaka, Bangladesh, 2003, p. 27.
13. Official website of The Communist Party of Bangladesh, <http://www.cpbbd.org/#con> as retrieved on August 5, 2013.
14. James Heitzman and Robert Worden (eds.), *Bangladesh: A Country Study*, Washington: GPO for the Library of Congress, 1989. <http://www.countrystudies.us/bangladesh/99.htm> as retrieved on July 7, 2013.
15. Ishfaq Ilahi, 'Bangladesh Defence Budget 2008-09: An analysis',*The Daily Star*, July 5, 2008, available at http://www.thedailystar. net/pf_story.php?nid=44241, accessed 05.04.2013.
16. Anwar Parvez Halim, 'No Left in Bangladesh', *Himal South Asian*, July 2009,<http://www.himalmag.com/component/content/article/564-no-left-in-bangladesh.html> as retrieved on July 16, 2013.
17. Ibid.
18. Badruddin Umar, 'Problems of Left Unity in Bangladesh', *Economic and Political Weekly*, July 21, 1990, p. 1576.
19. Badruddin Umar, 'Bangladesh: Intellectuals, Culture and Ruling

Class', *Economic and Political Weekly*, May 15, 1999, pp. 1175-6.

20. Badruddin Umar, 'Circular Movement of Bangladesh Politics', *Economic and Political Weekly*, August 8, 1987, pp. 1336-7.
21. Samir Kumar Das, 'Democracy's Three Ripples: Reflections on the State of Democracy in India's Neighbourhood', *World Focus*, 403, July 2013, p. 7.
22. Mahfuz Anam, 'An Ornamental Sangsad?', *The Daily Star*, March 10, 2014, <http://www.thedailystar.net/editor-s-pick/an-ornamental-sangsad-9195> as retrieved on March 10, 2014.
23. Sarah Butler, 'Retailers Urged to Take Bangladesh Safety Deal Further', *The Guardian*, July 28, 2013, <http://www.theguardian.com/world/2013/jul/28/retailers-bangladesh-safety-deal-further> as retrieved on August 17, 2013.

16

The Nepal Constituent Assembly Experiment: Process, Successes, Failures and Lessons

Srinivasan Ramani

Nepal went through a series of tumultuous political events from 2001 to the present. It transited from being a Constitutional monarchy to periods of return of absolute monarchy from 2001 to 2005. Various mass protest movements, in particular, the powerful Jan Andolan II in 2006 eventually paved the way for the end of the monarchy and the declaration of a republic. This momentous development coincided with the end of a long-standing civil war between the Nepali state and the Nepali Maoists (between 1996 and 2005) that was made possible by a Comprehensive Peace Agreement(CPA) between the political actors including mainstream parties and the Maoists in 2006. Republicanism emerged as the main demand in the Jan Andolan II as civil society actors, and republicans from the mainstream as well as the Maoist parties participated in massive street demonstrations demanding restoration of dissolved Parliament and fresh Constituent Assembly(CA) elections. The setting up of a popularly elected Constituent Assembly was one of the chief agreements signed in the CPA in 2006. This paved the way for CA elections held as a part first past the post system-part Proportional Representation system polls in 2008. The CA despite immense work done by it was unable to draft a Constitution as the second elections to the CA were concluded in 2013 recently.

We discuss the successes and the failures of the Constituent Assembly process, the factors responsible for them and what lessons does this experiment in democratization in Nepal entail for us.

The Chief Political Actors in Nepal

In order to do the above, we would require understanding the political story that led to the CA formation; who were the actors involved; their class/sectional basis and motivations. There were clearly three sets of actors—three in the "mainstream", two in the "radical outstream" and external actors (international forces).

The "mainstream political actors included the following:

- The Nepali Congress which was primarily supported by the incipient and rudimentary Nepali bourgeoisie and which had a social democratic basis and mindset since its inception nearly five decades ago. The party was in power in 2002 when parliament was dissolved by the monarch leading to pro-democracy agitations.
- The Communist Party of Nepal (Unified-Marxist-Leninist) or the UML, which had been formed in the early 1970s in Nepal and was inspired by the Naxalite revolution in India. The party had gradually shifted to parliamentary politics following a number of upheavals, mergers and had adopted parliamentary democracy as its credo in order to build socialism in the 1990s. The party has a strong cadre base that had extensive patronage networks both in government as well as in the humongous NGO sector in Nepal.
- The monarchy which had lost its absolute status following the 1990 Constitution but which still retained control over the then Royal Nepali Army. The assassination of King Birendra and his immediate family had seen the succession by his brother Gyanendra, who for a brief period between 2002 and 2005 restored the pre-1990 era of absolute rule. Partially this was justified by the monarch in order to take on the Maoist insurgency directly subverting the

elected democratic process involving mainstream political parties. Partially, this was also an attempt to restore the pre-1990 situation wherein the monarch had near absolute powers and to overturn the post-1990 era of "constitutional democracy" with only some crucial powers being vested with the monarchy.

The "outstream" actors during the transition from monarchy to a republic included:

- A radical outstream which constituted of the United Communist Party of Nepal (Maoist). The party led a decade long Maoist insurgency from 1996 onwards and was successful in occupying close to two thirds of Nepal's hinterland, particularly strong in the western and mid-western hilly areas and in the east. The UCPN(Maoist) had emerged historically from a left base representing landless peasants, Janajati groups, among others. The party had its roots in the "Fourth Convention" party prominent in the 1970s. The party had successfully combined an emphasis on ethnic recognition of Nepal's marginalized identities, armed struggle, area domination, creation of base areas and Nepali nationalism to emerge as a leading political actor in the 2000s. In the areas where the Maoists were strong, they enjoyed a "multi-class" support base that included support from the petty bourgeoisie, middle classes beyond the landless peasants and Janajatis.
- Others in the outstream were the Madhesi parties which included the more upper caste landed gentry based Terai Madhesi Loktantrik Party and the newly formed Madhesi Janadhikar Forum (with a generic Other Backward Classes base) which articulated the demand for a new autonomous province within the Terai region called the "Madhes". These parties had grown in significance following a series of social upsurges that coincided with the demand for CA elections and the peace process beginning from 2005.

Essentially led by landed sections, the bureaucratic elite and the middle classes of the Terai region, the Madhesi parties had also been radicalised by Maoist support for the demand of ethnically determined federal restructuring of Nepal. Significant class differences at the same time created an antagonistic relationship against the Maoists in the run up to the CA.

The external actors included:

- The Indian establishment comprising the security apparatus, the external affairs ministry (and the embassy) apart from some political actors. The Indian establishment is very much involved in Nepal and is motivated by two contradictory impulses. One is governed by geopolitics, treating Nepal as an outpost of Indian security. This impulse has largely determined Indian outlook towards the Maoist insurgency and support for the twin pillars of constitutional monarchy and parliamentary democracy in Nepal. The other impulse is one that is keen on regaining an involved nature of intervention in Nepal as a means of securing India's near-neighbourhood and is therefore cognisant of democratic Nepali public opinion.
- The US Embassy played a major role in arming and guiding the the Nepali Congress government led by Sher Bahadur Deuba and later the monarchy to take punitive action against the Maoists. This was in line with their "anti-terrorism" and general intolerance towards radical leftism post 9/11/2001.
- Chinese foreign policy in Nepal has generally confined itself to security interests related to Tibet. Geopolitical competition with India has been another minor aspect of Chinese policy as China also supplied monarchy with military aid during its phase of absolute rule.
- Other western actors include West European and

northern European donor communities which were actively involved in aid, developmental projects and also in the democratization process post 2001.

The Demand for the CA and Proclamation of the Republic

Following the suspension of the democratic process, dismissal of the elected government led by the Nepali Congress and the dissolution of Parliament by the monarchy in 2002, massive street protests took place in Nepal, particularly in the Kathmandu valley. Differences between the Palace and the mainstream polity emerged following failures in realizing a ceasefire agreement with the Maoists, as the palace again dismissed an appointed government (led by royalists) in 2004. This set the stage for cooperation between the various forces in the mainstream polity and raised the possibility of cooperation between them and the "radical outstream" represented by the Maoists.

This possibility could have been realized without the intervention of external actors such as India, which was particularly alienated by the monarch's decision to take absolute power in a coup in February 2005. The Indian establishment, wary about growing international influence in Nepal, including the provision of massive US aid in military supplies, sought to reverse its policy supporting the monarchy. They were egged on by members of the security and foreign policy establishment in doing so. The presence of Left in India in the governance arrangement—the left parties were then supporting the United Progressive Alliance government from the outside—also enabled the possibility of talks between the seven party alliance and the Maoists facilitated by India.

Following these manouevres, the mainstream political parties formed a Seven Party Alliance (SPA) in 2005 which was tacitly supported by the Indian establishment. They agreed to a 12 point understanding with the Maoists in November 2005. Joint protests organised by the civil society, the Maoists and the SPA led to the monarch giving up power and the restoration of elected government (dismissed in 2002). In many ways, the conjuncture bringing together disparate political forces and the tacit facilitation of the process by the Indian establishment resulted in the monarch's decision to hand over power back to the elected government.

The monarch's role in bringing back absolute rule, the manner of his succession which was made possible due to a brutal assassination of the erstwhile monarch Birendra and his family, allegedly by Birendra's son Dipendra, led to a steep fall of popularity and legitimacy of the institution of monarchy among the Nepali people. Combined with the Maoists' sudden strident opposition to monarchy and the getting together of the mainstream political parties against the monarchy, a wave of support for republicanism swept Nepal and made it possible for the nearly 2000-year-old monarchy to come to an end in Nepal.

After coming to power, the G.P. Koirala-led government immediately sought UN assistance in ending civil war, and soon a Comprehensive Peace Accord was signed in 2006 between Maoists and the SPA government that paved way for the end of the decade and a half long civil war, the promulgation of an interim constitution and national government and most importantly, the realization of a Constituent Assembly. Through the aegis of CPA, the Maoists and the seven party alliance announced an interim Constitution to precede Constituent Assembly elections that was to be held in the near future. The accord also spoke about a ceasefire and the handing over of the weapons held by the Maoists to a UN monitoring agency and confinement of the "Maoist army" into various cantonments; a proposal to "integrate" and "rehabilitate" these combatants among others.

The demand for a CA was primarily made by the Maoists who were dissatisfied with the Constitution that was written in 1990 following Jan-Andolan I. In sum, the Maoists played a major role in the transition from monarchy to republic, and they were key actors in the realization of a popularly elected Constituent Assembly. These and other reasons—effective work in "base areas" in the rural countryside—resulted in the Maoists achieving the lead position after CA elections, emerging as the single largest party.

The Madhesis and the "State Restructuring" Demand

Even as this announcement of the CPA was made, a new eruption of protests occurred in the plain regions of southern parts of Nepal. The plains' dwellers—the "Madhesis"—led by an hitherto unknown group named the Madhesi Janadhikar Forum (Madhesi People's Rights Forum or the MJF) rose in opposition to the seven party—Maoist alliance demanding regional autonomy and non-discrimination. More than the intensity of the protests, what surprised observers was the anger against the Maoists themselves, who had conceived their struggle during the people's war phase to not only overthrow state power led by their mainstream political opponents—whom they termed class enemies—but also to overcome the inherent discrimination and disenfranchisement of various marginalized groups in the country.

The Maoists in 2000 had also established the Madhesi National Liberation Front (MNLF) in 2000 which voiced among other demands, proportional representation for Madhesis in state institutions, distribution of citizenship certificates, use of Maithili, Bhojpuri and Awadhi as local official languages, revolutionary land reform among others.

Yet just as the peace process brought the Maoists 'into the mainstream' and a comprehensive agreement was brought into place to stop hostilities, the Madhesis had 'broken away' from the Maoists, despite the latter's insistence on "state restructuring" and radical views on reorientation of the state and recognition and distribution of power to linguistic and ethnic minorities in the country. The differences could be narrowed down to two issues – a) the Maoists were less inclined to support the Madhesis' demand for an autonomous and united "Madhes" province encompassing the entirety of the plains. In the Maoists' conception of a federal model (to be described later), the multiple linguistic identities from within the Terai had to be provided separate federal units. This was resented by the Madhesi parties. b) The Maoists were sceptical of the Madhesi parties' role and saw them as adversaries in their 'class-struggle'. The Madhesi parties' leadership was dominated by land owning sections of the plains, in the Maoists' view, and for the latter, comprehensive land reform in the plains was an important measure for economic upliftment in the region. Also, the Madhesis were clearly in loggerheads with the Maoists' anti-India positioning and rhetoric.

These issues saw the break of the Maoist-Madhesis' alliance, resulting in armed attacks and anarchy in the region in the aftermath of the peace agreement between the seven party alliance and the Maoists. Later the SPA-Maoist alliance incorporated the demands of the Madhesis to add the issue of federalism to the interim Constitution and by the time elections were held for the Constituent Assembly, the Madhesis had grown into a major electoral force (the MJF and the Terai Madhesi Loktantrik Party finished fourth and fifth among the electoral victors after the Maoists, the Nepali Congress and the UML).

Soon the Madhesis, after the formation of the Constituent Assembly became a "buffer force", making an integral section of the various governments that came to power, led either by the Maoists or the NC/UML. In other words, the Madhesis had no longer been a marginal force to be co-opted by the mainstream political parties. With the rise of the Maoists, the Madhesi political parties had also become a major political force, mirroring the rise of the regional parties in neighbouring India. The demand for federalization of Nepal, that brought the Madhesi political parties into positions of power, therefore became a core and important issue to be resolved through the CA deliberations. Over the course of the CA deliberations for nearly four years, there was significant progress in talks about the future federalisation of the country, but this issue—surprisingly—became the reason for the breakdown of the CA as the political parties were unable to come to a consensus on "state restructuring".

Post-CA Developments

Following elections to the Constituent Assembly, the Maoists in Nepal emerged as surprise winners, securing 220 of the 601 CA seats in the part-First-Past-the-Post and part-Proportional Representation electoral system. It had emerged as the single largest party—defying expectations by relegating the Nepali Congress and the UML to the second and third positions respectively—even as a new Madhesi party—the Madhesi Janadhikar Forum (Madhesi Peoples' Rights Forum) ended up as the fourth largest party following the elections. While the Maoists did much better than what many believed could be possible—in particular the Indian establishment—their party could not secure an absolute majority and coalitions were made to be inevitable. The best course of action that would have eased the process of writing the Constitution in the Constituent Assembly would have been the formation of an all-party national government with atleast the four major parties participating in it based on cooperation and consensus. Yet, consensus was always lacking immediately after the CA results as ideological and sharp political differences prevented cooperation. The earlier bonhomie between the seven party alliance (since then dissolved) and the Maoists following the peace accord was not to last any further. In any case, contradictions with the Maoists and the Madhesis had already emerged in the course of the run up to the elections as well as explained before.

The fraying consensus after the elections led to the formation of a new alliance with the Maoists-UML-Madhesis coming together against the Nepali Congress to form the first government following the CA elections as Maoist chairman Pushpa Kumar Dahal (Prachanda) became prime minister. As soon as the CA was commenced, the assembly declared Nepal as a constitutional republic in its very first setting, extinguishing the 240-year-old Shah dynasty led monarchy in a historic decision. Except for four members of the CA, belonging to the Rashtriya Prajatantra Party (RPP) factions, the rest of the members of the CA voted unanimously to declare Nepal a secular republic.

It was evident that post-the CA elections, there were two unresolved "contradictions" despite the near unanimity among the main political actors on the need for the abolition of the monarchy—

1) The question of integration/rehabilitation of the

Maoist "Peoples' Liberation Army" and indeed, the completion of the peace process through an end to the decade long conflict

2) The "state restructuring" issue that had flared up in the course of the Jan Andolans

These two issues—on which the main actors, the Maoists, the UML, the Nepali Congress and the Madhesi parties had varied positions—ensured that a consensus government was never going to be possible. This in turn also affected the Constitution writing process, which was given an ambitious deadline of two years in the interim Constitution.

The first iteration of government formation post the CA elections saw the Maoists—by virtue of their strength of being the single largest party—aligning with the UML and the Madhesis to form the government. The ascension to power by the Maoists and certain steps taken by the Maoist leaders in power, were not welcomed by the Indian establishment. There were internal differences within the establishment as to whether this was a sound strategy to "deal" with the Maoists during the events leading to the CPA. There was also an underestimation in the Indian establishment about the strength of the Maoists and Indian embassy officials had not expected that the Maoists would emerge as the single largest party in the CA elections.

India's Distrust of the Maoists

Some of the actions by the Maoists after coming to power—in its seeking to establish direct (democratic) control over the Nepali army by virtue of leading the government, enunciation of a policy of equidistance between China and India (evoking memories of the "Zone of Peace" proposal earlier in the 1970s) —did not go too well with the Indian establishment. The security related sections of the Indian establishment had intricate linkages with the Nepali Army—the Indians continue to supply Nepal with essential defence equipment. As part of a tripartite agreement between India, Nepal and Britain, the former continued to recruit Nepali citizens (Gurkhas) into the Indian Army's Gorkha Regiment; several Nepal Army senior officials were trained in military colleges in India and so on. Seen in this light, it is understandable as to why the Indian establishment did not "endorse" the Nepali Maoist chairman Prachanda's decision as prime minister to remove the Army chief General Rupmankad Katawal from his post—a decision that precipitated the fall of the Maoist-led government after coalition and opposition parties opposed the move made by the Maoist prime minister.

The diplomatic cables from the Kathmandu embassy of the United States—leaked by the whistleblower website Wikileaks —point to deep discomfort in the Indian establishment about the Maoists' moves to establish what they called, "civilian supremacy" and their maneuvers leading to taking forward the steps in the peace process. After the government was formed, the Indian establishment, while cautiously studying the moves made by the Maoist led government, also understood that the Maoists in government would adopt a moderating path that will not lead Nepal away from its "special relationship" with India. Even on the issue of "civilian supremacy", the Indian ambassador had conveyed to his American counterpart over parleys that the Indian establishment was in favour of the effort to bring the army under civilian control (see http://cablegatesearch.wikileaks.org/cable.php?id=09KATHMANDU320), but had not endorsed the manner in which the Maoist supremo was seeking to establish the chain of command in the Army.

Soon, within a year of the Maoists in government, the Indian establishment had taken a position of antipathy towards the Maoists, "alarmed" in its view that the Maoists were going too far in trying to restructure the army, in the manner the serving chief of army staff was sought to be removed. This "antipathy" resulted in the Indian establishment micromanaging and supporting a new anti-Maoist coalition that came to power once the Maoists resigned from power, seeking to garner public support on the issue of "civilian supremacy".

The ascension of a new coalition to power in May 2009, including the Nepali Congress, the UML and a breakaway section of the Madhesi Janadhikar Forum along with other minor parties certainly had the support of the Indian establishment. It was clear that the Indian establishment was seeking to isolate the Maoists from the mainstream after the few years of bonhomie were short-lived. The former Prime Minister Madhav Kumar Nepal—who had ironically lost in the 2008 CA elections—became the prime minister again after this new coalition came to power. With the single largest party, the UCPN(Maoist) isolated and the peace process hanging in the balance with issues related to integration/rehabilitation of the Maoist combatants unresolved, no progress on Constitution writing could be made even as the deadline for the completion of the Constitution was nearing.

Internal differences within the Nepali Congress and the UML also came to the fore as this was an unstable coalition which soon collapsed in June 2010. The resulting instability ensured that there was no government with repeated elections in the CA resulting in stalemates before the formation of another UML led government, this time having the prime minister as UML Chairman Jhalanath Khanal in February 2011. The inherent instability in the political process due to the isolation of the Maoists was somewhat rectified after the UML Chairman came to power, with the Maoists' support.

The Indian establishment finally changed tack and reversed its policy of supporting the isolation of the Maoists and instead sought to take a hands-off approach to the political processes in Nepal while reiterating support to the Constitution writing process. It was no coincidence that the change in tack happened with the appointment of a new ambassador to Nepal in August 2011, and also saw the return of the Maoists to power and a final—but messy—conclusion to the peace process with an agreement between the Maoists and the Nepali Congress, the UML and the Madhesi parties. It is another matter, that the Maoists themselves split, as the hardline faction left the party to call themselves the CPN(Maoist) (the undivided party was the Unified Communist Party of Nepal (Maoist)—UCPN (Maoist)) and despite the resolution of the peace process, no agreement was possible on the other main issue of state restructuring, as conservative positions in the mainstream political parties saw yet another political polarization. This time, at one end were those who favoured a "ethnicity/nationality based" restructuring of the Nepali states—the UCPN(Maoist) and the Madhesi parties—and at the other end were the Nepali Congress and the UML. Interestingly, the Indian establishment had indicated support to the federal initiative.[1] This polarization prevented the completion of the Constitution writing process and the CA was declared "dissolved" by Maoist Prime Minister Baburam Bhattarai in May 2012.

Successes of the CA

The first iteration of the CA might have failed but the thematic committees that deliberated various issues in the CA managed to come up with provisional features of a progressive and democratic Constitution which could have laid the superstructure of a future socialist Nepal. As Shyam Shrestha (2014) points out,

> ..due to the efforts in the CA, the highly centralised and unitary state of Nepal had been in principle transformed into a federal state. ...
>
> Many features of the Constitution in the making had a decisive socialist character and inclusive nature about them. The right to proportional, social inclusion of women, dalits, ethnic minorities, Madhesi communities, oppressed groups, workers, the poor farmers in state structures and institutions had been ensured as a form of social justice in the Interim Constitution (IC) promulgated in November 2006.This special right had been unanimously agreed to be included in the new draft Constitution as well.
>
> The rights to employment, free secondary school education, free basic health services, food, social security for children, elderly people, widows and the destitute had been ensured as the fundamental right of every citizen in the IC and the new draft Constitution as well. Besides these rights, the right to access to proper accommodation and right to free higher education for dalits and people below the poverty line had also been added in the new constitutional draft proposed by committees in the first CA. With these, Nepal had been transformed into a benevolent social democratic state.
>
> The declaration of the reinstated Nepali Parliament on reserving 33% of seats for women in all the state mechanisms in 2006 was also a landmark event in the history of women's inclusion

> in Nepal. Three additional important rights for Nepali women had been guaranteed in the Interim Constitution: namely, the equal right of daughters and sons to ancestral property; the right of every child to get citizenship in the name of the mother as well (children who have no father and who were born out of wedlock); and, the right to reproduction and reproductive health....
>
> The initial draft of the new Constitution had also given Madhesis, Janajatis and Muslims the right of inclusion in all the state organs at all levels and its leadership on the basis of proportional representation. The highly marginalised and endangered communities would obtain special protection rights as well.

These were no mean achievements for a poor, unequal and stratified society.

Reasons for the Failures in Concluding the CA Process

As explained above, the non-resolution of the "state restructuring" issue was a major stumbling block in the promulgation of a new Constitution. The two parties, the NC and the UML seemed most vociferous in preventing a deal on the "state restructuring" issue. But a closer look at the developments leading to the dissolution of the CA-1 suggests that a resolution on the issue wasn't too far away as was made out to be. The thematic committees and restructuring commission in the CA had more or less finalised a roadmap for federalization. The lack of an agreement on finalising the constitution had much to do with both politics as also with a last ditch effort by status quoists to prevent a deal.

Keeping this in mind, there is very much the possibility that the status quoists will seek to overturn a number of features of the deliberations in CA-1 in the second iteration of the CA. The draft constitution being worked had envisaged a number of progressive features—seeking a robust regime of rights and a governance system that sought to combine recognition and redistribution. But these were sought to be done by using a state structure that had not necessarily changed from the days monarchy ruled Nepal. With the Nepal Army, police, bureaucracy (and even the judiciary) as intact as it was from those days, the CA's decrees were not necessarily going to reform Nepal substantively.

The deep state therefore has successfully resisted "comprehensive change" in Nepal. Meanwhile, the people seem to have tired of the machinations worked by the so called agents of progressive change and have returned the section that was least resistant to the status quoists back to power in elections to the second CA. Seen in this way, the developments do not augur too well for a resolution of issues in the second CA.

The other deal breaker in the CA was structural and related to the patronage system of politics practised in Nepal. The constant jostling for power among the parties was because being in power in government as opposed to sharing one in a national consensus government was a prerequisite as "patronage" was an important form of attaining support and legitimacy. Constant machinations to hold on to power or seeking to overthrow various iterations of government were a consequence of Nepal's standing as a poor underdeveloped country which had a weak state and which has been dependent heavily on external aid by both non-government as well as state sources.

The Maoists in particular did not delineate themselves from the NC and UML which had already had an image of "patronage dispensing" machine parties during the 1990s. The Maoists had also disbanded their alternate structures of governance in the areas of their influence and had also abandoned radical measures such as land reforms in order to complete the peace process. The Maoists ended up being subject to a split within themselves as they were unable to take along a radical section that was committed to building socialism and also because the "establishment" faction among them ended up making a number of concessions on issues such as "land reforms", integration of their armed cadre in the Nepali Army among others. The split significantly weakened the Maoists as the UCPN(Maoist) finished third in the second CA elections.

Conclusions: The CA Process in Sum

The CA process has been a unique experiment in Asia to create a Constitution through universal adult franchise and a popular elected Constituent Assembly. While this was indeed laudable and a practicable maneuver in a largely divided and unequal society with historical baggage of deep inequities, the political actors were over-ambitious.

They tried to combine a peace process that followed a decade long civil war with a CA writing process and set a difficult deadline of two years, only to postpone it twice by a year each. Combined with the fact that getting to positions of power was seen as imperative in a patronage system, the CA process was inevitably held hostage by unrelated political issues.

The mechanisms evolved by the Nepali polity in order to resolve political differences were through the involvement of the leaders of the four main political outfits. The lack of involvement of these leaders in Constitution-making and instead in constant power play led to a process over and above the CA process and resulting in the inability to reach a consensus.

What does the CA process and its successes and failures mean for the Left project in Nepal? Dogmatic opinion among "classical Maoists" especially the Indian Maoists has been that their Nepali "counterparts" were mistaken to embark upon the CA process. Contrary to that opinion, the Maoists were able to break through with pockets of support beyond their strongholds in remote parts of Nepal.

Despite its identitarian basis and not having a "pure" class orientation, the "state restructuring" issue coincided with a social upsurge against centralisation in Nepal. If the Maoists had not engaged with it, it could have led to fissiparous tendencies in the country, which has not happened.

Like in Latin America, the experience of engaging in a Constitutional process has only strengthened the leftist forces. The Maoists have avowed to take up as their new weapons of creating a socialist Nepal—as the "street", the "sanvidan" (Constitution) and the state, as opposed to the classical weapons of the PLA, the United Front and the party. If the Maoists resisted succumbing to the patronage system and retain emphasis on rebuilding their alternate structures that altered power relations in rural areas, emphasized manual labour, built model communes and alternate education centres, they would have possibly retained their popular support.

Would a left populist constitution pave the way for a socialist Nepal? The argument in favour would be that a strong welfare state that emphasizes redistribution, expanded role of the state and egalitarianism will work against the logic of capital —expressed in the Nepali context as aid dependency, unplanned and skewed development and a hitherto weakened state.

That said, the Nepali Left should be well aware that it cannot succumb itself to "liberalism" and "statism". The retention of their alternate structures of power that took on entrenched casteism, semi-feudalism and emphasized voluntary labour, cooperativisation and even communes is a must. This should have been possible if the split had not happened and there was more unity with other leftist forces in Nepal. Perhaps there is still the possibility as the second CA is in session to finish writing the Constitution in "Naya Nepal" as this article goes to press.

NOTES AND REFERENCES

1. Interviews with Embassy officials in Kathmandu, September 2011.
2. Shyam Shrestha (2014), "Maoist Defeat in Nepal", *Economic and Political Weekly*, January 25.

Notes on Contributors

Aijaz Ahmad has taught in universities in the US, India and Canada. In New Delhi, where he resides, he has been a Professorial Fellow at the Nehru Memorial Museum and Library. He has also held the Rajiv Gandhi Chair at Jawaharlal Nehru University (JNU) and the Khan Abdul Ghaffar Khan Chair at Jamia Millia. Currently, he is on the editorial board of the Delhi-based publishing house, LeftWord, and Senior Editorial Consultant for newsmagazine **Frontline** where his political essays appear frequently. His analytic and theoretical work appears in a range of journals such as *Socialist Register*, *New Left Review*, *Race & Class*, *Social Scientist*, etc. Some of his books in English are: *Ghazals of Ghalib* (New York, 1971; New Delhi, 1994), *In Theory: Classes, Nations, Literatures* (London, 1992; New Delhi, 1995) and *Lineages of the Present* (New Delhi, 1996; London, 2000.

Anindya Sekhar Purakayastha, is a professor in the Department of English, SKB University, Purulia, West Bengal. Formerly Assistant Professor in Central University of Orissa, he has contributed to journals like, *Parallax* (Routledge), Postcolonial *Studies* (Routledge), *South Asia Review* (Pittsburgh),*Contemporary South Asia* (Routledge), *Journal of Postcolonial Writing* (Routledge), *Historical Materialsim, International Journal of Zizek Studies, Journal of Post-colonial Cultures & Societies, History and Sociology of South Asia* (Sage), *Journal of Indian Council of Philosophical Research*, etc. His chapter in the book, *Media and Utopia: Imagination, History, Technology* (Routledge) is forthcoming.

Badruddin Umar, doyen among Left Intellectuals of Bangladesh, has written many books on the politics of East Bengal, Left politics in East Pakistan, and the evolution of the society since the birth of Bangladesh. He received his honours degree from Oxford University and was a teacher of Philosophy and Political Science at Dhaka and Rajshahi Universities. He was for many years the President of the Bangladesh Lekhok Shibir (Writers Association).

Dhritiman Chakraborty, a PhD Research Scholar in Center for Studies in Social Sciences, Calcutta, teaches in the Department of English, Pakuahat Degree College in Malda, West Bengal. His PhD thesis focuses on dilemmas of postcolonial development and the emergent modes of the politics in India. Earlier, he completed a UGC funded, jointly-researched project on the Folk Political form of *Gambhira*. He has published works on the postcolonial political, rematerialising postcolonial theory in different journals. His jointly edited volume on *Post-9/11 American Identity and Third World Pedagogy* is forthcoming from Author Press, New Delhi.

Gorky Chakraborty received his PhD from Dibrugarh University. The subject of his research was the river islands (*char*s) of the river Brahmaputra. His other research area includes issues related to development in the Northeast India. He has published *Assam's Hinterland: Society and Economy in the Char Areas* (2009) and co-authored *The Look East Policy and Northeast India* (2014). At present, he is an Associate Professor at the Institute of Development Studies Kolkata (IDSK), where he is engaged in research and teaching.

Maidul Islam studied Political Science at Presidency College, Kolkata and Jawaharlal Nehru University (JNU), New Delhi. As a Clarendon-Hector Pilling-Senior Hulme scholar at Brasenose College, Oxford, he studied politics for DPhil. In July 2012, he was awarded the doctoral degree from the University of Oxford. From August 2012 to February 2013, he was Assistant Professor at the Tata Institute of Social Sciences (Tuljapur Campus). From March 2013 to December 2013, he was a Fellow at the Indian Institute of Advanced Study, Shimla. At present, he is an Assistant Professor in Political Science at Presidency University, Kolkata. His research interests include political theory, identity politics, and cinema. Recently, he has signed a book contract with Cambridge University Press to publish his doctoral thesis—*Limits of Islamism: Jamaat-e-Islami in Contemporary India and Bangladesh*.

Mathew Joseph C. is an Associate Professor at the Academy of International Studies (AIS), Jamia Millia Islamia, New Delhi, India. He obtained his MPhil and PhD Degrees from the School of International Studies (SIS), Jawaharlal Nehru University (JNU), New Delhi, India. Before joining Jamia Millia Islamia he was with the Department of Strategic and Regional Studies (DSRS), University of Jammu, Jammu and Kashmir, India. Currently, he specializes in studies related to Pakistan, Bhutan, South Asia, and international relations. His major publications include *Ethnic Conflict in Bhutan* (New Delhi: Nirala Publications, 1999) and *Pakistan in a Changing Strategic Context* (New Delhi: Knowledge World, 2004), a co-edited volume.

Meghna Guhathakurta is Executive Director of Research Initiatives, Bangladesh (RIB), a non-profit organisation that specializes in participatory action research with marginalised communities. She has a PhD in Politics from the University of York, UK and has taught international relations at the University of Dhaka from 1982 to 2004. Her research interests are gender, marginalisation, migration and political economy. Her recent publication includes *The Bangladesh Reader: History, Culture, Politics*, which she has co-edited with Willem Van Schendel. She is currently coordinating an action research project on 'Strengthening Human Rights Institutionalisation through Vulnerable Groups' Empowerment' with seven communities in Bangladesh. Her organisation, RIB, is also conducting a research project on 'Fostering Agrarian Strategies for Overcoming Small Farmers' Challenges in Bangladesh', which is being sponsored by the Rosa Luxemburg Foundation, South Asia.

Prabhat Patnaik has taught at the University of Cambridge and at the Centre for Economic Studies and Planning (CESP) of the Jawaharlal Nehru University (JNU), New Delhi, where he held the Sukhamoy Chakravarty Chair in Planning and Development at the time of his retirement and is currently Professor Emeritus. He has written a number of books and articles, including *Time, Inflation and Growth* (1988), *Economics and Egalitarianism* (1990), *Whatever Happened to Imperialism and Other Essays* (1995), *Accumulation and Stability Under Capitalism* (1997), *The Retreat to Unfreedom* (2003), *The Value of Money* (2008) and *Re-envisioning Socialism* (2011). He is the editor of the journal, *The Social Scientist*.

Prasenjit Bose works as a Senior Research Associate in a ICSSR sponsored research project on 'Financial Globalisation and India'. He received his PhD in economics from Centre for Economic Studies and Planning, Jawaharlal Nehru University (JNU). He is a political activist on the Left.

Ravi Kumar teaches at the Department of Sociology, South Asian University. His works include *Education, State and Market: Anatomy of Neoliberal Impact* (Delhi: Aakar Books, 2014); *Social Movements: Transformative Shifts and Turning Points* (Delhi: Routledge, 2014);

Education and the Reproduction of Capital: Neoliberal Knowledge and Counterstrategies (New York: Palgrave Macmillan, 2012); *Global Neoliberalism and Education and its Consequences* (New York & London: Routledge, 2009); *The Crisis of Elementary Education in India* (New Delhi: Sage Publications, 2006). He is co-editor of a book series on *Social Movements, Dissent and Transformative Action* (Delhi:Routledge).

Ritwika Biswas is an Associate Professor in the Department of History, University of Calcutta. She has authored a book titled *The Radical Face of Democratic Liberalism: A Study of Communist Politics in West Bengal 1947-1977.*

Sobhanlal Dattagupta had his education at Presidency College, Calcutta and Calcutta University between 1963 and 1968. During his long career of teaching and research he was associated with Presidency College, Burdwan University, Centre for Studies in Social Sciences, Calcutta and Calcutta University till his retirement from the University of Calcutta in 2008 as Surendra Nath Banerjee Professor of Political Science. His published works include the co-authored *The State of Political Theory: Some Marxist Essays* (1977), *Justice and the Political Order in India* (1978), *Comintern and the Destiny of Communism in India: 1919-1943; Dialectics of Real and a Possible History* (2006; revised and enlarged edition, 2011).

Srimanti Sarkar is a Research Assistant at Maulana Abul Kalam Azad Institute of Asian Studies (MAKAIAS), Kolkata. Her research interests are 'Democracy and Democratization in South Asia' with particular focus on Bangladesh and Pakistan. At present, she is working on a project entitled 'Rethinking the Concept of Democracy in Bangladesh' at MAKAIAS. She has also completed her MPhil dissertation on 'Democracy and Democratization--a Factor of Neighbourhood Policy: A Study of Indo-Bangladesh Relations' from Department of Political Science, University of Calcutta.

Srinivasan Ramani is the senior assistant editor of the prestigious journal, *Economic & Political Weekly*. He is the recipient of the Appan Menon Fellowship for the year 2011–12 for his work on Indo-Nepal relations and his writings on the political processes in republican Nepal. He is completing his doctoral research on a theoretical study of Indo-Nepal relations from 1990 to 2009.

Subhanil Chowdhury is an economist who works in the areas of macroeconomics, development economics, and political economy.

He is currently engaged in researching the contexts and contours of imperialism in the current era and issues related to labour in the Indian economy. He has a PhD in Economics from Jawaharlal Nehru University (JNU) and is currently employed at IDSK as an Assistant Professor. Apart from economics, he is interested in politics, literature, and movies.

Subhoranjan Dasgupta, editor of this publication, is a Professor of Human Sciences at the Institute of Development Studies Kolkata (IDSK). He received his PhD from the University of Heidelberg. His special areas of interest are Marxian politics and aesthetics, the partition of Bengal (1947) and post-war German literature and creativity. Author and editor of several books, his notable publications are *The Trauma and the Triumph: Gender and Partition in Eastern India* (co-edited with Jashodhara Bagchi, in two volumes); *Elegy and Dream: The Creative Commitment of Akhtaruzamman Elias; The Tin Drummer's Odyssey: An Evaluation of Gunter Grass's Creativity and Politics.*

Taimur Rahman is an Assistant Professor of Political Science at the Lahore University of Management Sciences (LUMS) in Lahore, Pakistan. He is also the spokesperson for the popular Leftwing band called Laal (red). And he is a nationally respected grassroots activist of the progressive and labour movement in Pakistan.